# GO SEE THE BEAUTIFUL

*(Inspirational
stories from an
old man running
26.2 miles)*

# R. L. Johnson

ISBN: 978-1-09837-046-6

Library of Congress Registration Number: TXu-2-235-935

Scripture references used within this book are from the New American Standard Bible (NASB). Any references to historical events, real people, or real places are used fictitiously. Names, characters, and places are products of the author's imagination.

Front cover photo by Brian Erickson (@brianericksonco) on Unsplash, edited by Andrew Myers, and used with permission. https://unsplash.com/license

Book design and formatting by BookBaby Publishing.

Printed by BookBaby Publishing, in the United States of America.

First printing edition 2021.

For more information on the author, visit his website at: goseethebeautiful.com

*This book is dedicated by my wife and me to our three daughters, the absolute joy of our lives; to their husbands, excellent men all; to our nine grandchildren, wonderful and full of promise; and to all those in our lineage who shall come after them. We give you this solemn mission . . . finish your race!*

# CONTENTS

# Pre-Race Warm-up

A note of orientation concerning the style of this book: Chapters are referred to as "miles." When you run a mile, you first complete the distance of a quarter mile, then a half, then three quarters, before reaching the mile marker. Similarly, there are subsections in each chapter of this book. While reading chapter 2, you may see subsections of 1.2, 1.5, or 1.7 before finishing that chapter. Hopefully, it makes sense as you get used to the theme.

The writing of this book was birthed on the eve of my first marathon. As I sat in an Oklahoma City hotel room, looking out the window at a stretch of the racecourse, I was suddenly struck with how my journey to get to that moment was an example of the life we lead.

There had been the vision to accomplish something big. I had faced many obstacles. There were times of discouragement, almost defeat.

But I also had moments of fierce determination and renewed hope. I experienced minor victories and major accomplishments. And always, always, there was training.

I saw amazing sunrises and ran through sudden rainstorms. I faced attack birds, crazy cows, and early morning skunks. But I also ran by waterfalls, ocean waves, and mountain peaks. There was everything wonderful and many things monotonous. It was life and it was good.

As I considered it all, I felt compelled to write to my family about this amazing life race that we are all given as a gift from God. I wrote about our purpose and attempted to convey the message that, in this race, we must never quit. We must cross our finish line having completed the purpose with which we were entrusted.

As the writing of a book unfolded in my mind concerning four big themes of life, the challenge to complete four marathons settled into my spirit.

Train and write. For almost three years, that was my task and one of my time-consuming aims. Amazingly, the lessons kept coming as I often arose before the sun and watched the Creator begin to paint His beauty across the sky.

There were moments in the writing of this book that I felt I was being "given" key portions. When that happened, I realized that the words were of a quality and importance that I could not dream up or convey from my own ability. One such moment came at the end of "mile 16" as I wrote about the death of a son on a battlefield in Vietnam.

I hope there are stories herein that will cause you, the reader, to stop and reflect and receive something that is spoken directly into your own heart. I hope you will be challenged to consider new things, new ideas, and new ways of looking at age-old problems. I hope you will find new strength that will help you in your own challenging endeavors, whether that includes running a marathon, climbing a mountain, or making it through the next day in one piece.

If you are inspired with renewed hope and uplifted with new vision, then my years of writing will have been worth the effort. The race may be long, but there is so much beauty along the way.

*"Record the vision and make it plain, that the one who reads it may run."*

*MILE 1*

# The Race . . .
# Where Less Than 1 Percent Go

A triumphant smile broke out of my heart and onto my face. It was April 29, 2018. I was standing among almost 25,000 anxious and excited people, thinking back over the last 5 months- the last 5 years really- that had led to this moment. And I realized I was smiling, a loud smile. If the other 25,000 people had not been there, if someone had seen me standing in the middle of the street with the big goofy grin spread across my face, there would surely have been concern. I couldn't help it. I had to smile.

The journey to arrive at this moment had been long in many ways, and the most physically challenging of my 54 years. The will to accomplish what just one-half of 1 percent of people accomplish had been there, along with the dedication to train, to plan, to learn, to endure. But it was hard, very hard.

An injury had occurred when the runs grew long. I'd taken a short time for recovery and had determined to start again—too soon. The pain became intense. So much so that, for the first time in all the months of training, I was not accomplishing my goals. I discovered that "will" cannot always overcome injury. And one gray morning after I'd made one last deadline with the determination that this would be the "go, no-go" moment, I failed yet again. I called a son-in-law to pick me up on the dirt road a few miles from my home and tried to hide my defeat and my deep discouragement after yet another failed attempt. And in that moment, I almost . . . *quit.*

But then, with a few passing days, a new hope and new plan arose—and a thought that, maybe, if I just do "this idea," it will all work out.

Three weeks from the big day, I set one last deadline. And I went. Painfully, I went.

Early miles went by and pain set in. I kept going. More miles went by; deeper pain set in. I kept going. With each passing mile, the pain increased. And I paused to consider it all. "Why?" I asked myself, but then I started again. *The pain would not leave. It was just as determined as I.* But for the first time in many weeks, I completed my goal. With every step during those last hours I told myself to remember this pain, which was informing me that I should *not* try to go through with this crazy plan. "You *are* old after all!"

But a few days passed, determination arose once more, and then, out of the blue, unexpected help came. For two weeks, I rested and healed. Just before the day to depart, I went out to run and behold—no pain! I couldn't believe it. But the real test had not come. It had just been a short try. Still, there had been no pain! That's a good sign! A firm decision now had to be made. The day was here. And so, I went. I had not quit!

The night before the big event, inspiration set in. Among the jitters and excitement, it all hit me—the "why?" and I said to myself once and for all . . . "I am going to run and come what may I will—*I will* cross that finish line. Come on, you 1 percent, this is our ground, and *this* is our day."

So there I stood on hallowed ground, where men had died, where women had died, where innocent children had breathed their last; here, where mankind decided that they would fight on in the face of all adversity and against every evil plan. Here I stood, ready for this physical challenge that in no way compares to what those had once faced; I was determined . . . inspired . . . ready . . . once and for all. And a big smile was on my face.

"Run a marathon? Are you crazy?"

# .5

Vision. I would hazard the opinion that great conquests of man almost never occur absent the declared purpose by an often-charismatic leader, a leader who is painting a vivid picture of a preferable future. Cross the ocean, fly around the world, be the first to climb Everest.

What possessed John F. Kennedy to lay down the gauntlet and challenge America to land a craft on a moon that flies in orbit 239,000 miles from the earth? It is vision that causes a man to literally "reach for the stars" at a time when society is being rocked with the chaos of awakened inequality, propelling man to still dream big dreams at the very moment when it seems that all is close to falling apart.

But vision is not confined to great leaders on a world stage. Vision can explode within the hearts and minds of individuals in homes across the world. It can be very personal and can direct the choices of our everyday lives.

It is vision that causes great men and women—charismatic or not—to commit to love and devote themselves to one person for a lifetime; to raise children whose hearts are turned toward their parents in love even as the world throws at them so many "better" offers for their devotion and their time.

It is vision that causes a very bright young lady to decide to raise her children at home rather than bowing to the pressures of this world that tell her that she is less intelligent and will be less fulfilled should she not return to the working world rather than staying home in a cocoon of dirty diapers, with constant babbling as her only communication. And it is not one day. No. It is day after day, for weeks, months, years. It is the marathon of a woman whose children will arise one day and will bless her, will emulate her, and will seek her out when they raise their own.

It is vision that causes a single mother or father to get up early each morning to get their kids off to school or to grandma's house, to then work a full day in a dog-eat-dog world, return home to feed, bathe, pray over, and love on their children before dropping into bed from exhaustion, determined to awake early the next morning and do it all again. It is the marathon of a parent whose children will one day be strong when others are weak, and who will return to honor the one who planted these reservoirs of strength into their young souls.

It is vision that causes a worn-out man who has just returned from a long day at work to greet his wife and children with joy, to keep the television and every electronic device that would entertain his tired soul turned off, and to instead spend the evening hours playing with those little impressionable souls who cannot wait for his return each day, who run shrieking to the door with shouts of, "Daddy's home!" It is vision that finds him helping his wife, creating new games for his brood, tucking them in with a prayer and a song. It is the marathon of a man whose child will one day be asked, "Who is your hero?" and without pause will say, "My Dad. I love him. I want to be just like him."

We are all in a race. But where are we running and what is our aim?

I heard a wise man one day who was sitting on a witness stand in a court of law. Twelve of his peers were listening to him speak about the depths of anguish as he watched his wife battle with cancer and come as close to death as you can come before the evil beast began to be beaten back. He spoke that day of the equality of all mankind. He told about walking into an elevator, with his wife attached to tubes of all kinds, when he saw a man of another nationality, and likely of another worldview and religion, standing next to his own wife with an equal number of protruding tubes. The two men looked at each other and their eyes were caught. In that moment, there was nothing between them. They were two men, loving two women who were fighting for their lives. All that was required was a nod of the head to each other, and they were one.

And as he neared the end of his story, he said, "When we are in our twenties, we all wonder if we will be successful. Later, many of us wonder if we are respected by our peers. At some point, though, I think we find ourselves wondering if the things we have done with our lives have really made a difference."

Vision is what drives some humans to "really make a difference" rather than just passing through until their time is done.

It is not a short race, this. It is a marathon of marathons. It is full of every challenge, every emotion, every kind of resistance, every kind of joy; of surprises both wonderful and difficult—sometimes the difficult are so hard that it seems they cannot be borne. It is a race with hills and valleys, with wind, heat, cold, and rain, where wave upon wave will sometimes come with incessant regularity, battering our souls like they would batter a boat stuck in the sand, surely to break with the next monstrous wave; only then to see the most beautiful sun break through the clouds and the sea become glass, gently washing the pain.

Where will we go in this crazy life race? Vision declares it! Through every storm and on every wave, vision says "On! We will not cave!"

# 1.0

So here I stood, me with my smile. Here on this very ground where 168 of my fellow citizens had died in a senseless and tragic moment of American history when on April 19, 1995, the Alfred P. Murrah Federal Building in Oklahoma City, suddenly and without warning, exploded.

Each year tens of thousands of runners from all over the world gather at this site in honor of those who died on this hallowed ground. Each person begins an arduous journey of 13.1 miles or 26.2 miles, declaring to themselves and to the world that they will not stop, and they will never quit. In the face of whatever life throws their way, they will run on.

Troubles may come, conditions may be harsh, but we will endure. By God's grace, we will run.

# *Training for the OKC Memorial Marathon (Running... and Family Life)*

*"I do not regard myself as having laid hold of it yet; but one thing I do: forgetting what lies behind and reaching forward to what lies ahead, I press on toward the goal."*

# *Vison and Total Commitment*

Most people don't wake up one day and decide that they are going to run a marathon. My own journey started with an "ambitious" goal: stop being a couch potato and run a 5K. I didn't really care about the goal of reaching the 5K distance. But the program my brother-in-law told me about was called "couch potato to 5K," so 5K became the goal. I discovered that accomplishing big goals is often the result of accomplishing hundreds of tiny, seemingly insignificant, goals . . . and then moving the goalpost even further away until one day you say to yourself, "I can reach this huge goal I'm now shooting for!" And wonder of wonders, you get there! You accomplish a goal you never would have dreamed possible at the beginning.

I remember beginning my 5K quest. My wife had purchased a Garmin Forerunner 15 watch for me so I could track my progress with GPS accuracy. It is still the watch I use today, many years later.

The 5K training plan was easy to begin with. Walk 5 minutes, jog 1 minute, walk some more, jog a bit more. Nine weeks are allowed for you to build up the endurance required to run without stopping for

3.1 miles. The goal includes being able to get to that distance in about thirty to thirty-five minutes. Easy, right?

On my first day out, after about 1/10 of one mile, I was gasping for air. What?! I have to go 30 times this far?! That will *never* happen. It's surely impossible, I thought.

So it began. Set small goals, accomplish them, move on to the next day. I could "will" myself to keep jogging for 60 seconds and turn my mind off to the outrageous thought that I would someday have to keep that up for 30-35 times that length of time to accomplish the 5K goal. All I have to do today is jog 60 seconds without stopping. And day by day, each challenging goal was accomplished. Small victories. Then one day a jump came, requiring not just 10 minutes of constant running, but 20 minutes! And . . . it was accomplished! Wow!

If I had allowed myself to think early on about the impossibility of running without stopping for 30 minutes, if I had dwelt there, I very likely would not be running today. In the back of my mind, I knew the goal seemed daunting. But also, there was the very exciting fact that the old goals that had once seemed impossible were now easy, and the pain necessary to reach them was a distant memory.

I have come to realize over the months and years of increasing bodily challenges that these bodies that God has given us are quite amazing. When trained to certain conditions, they adapt. Put a human in Siberia and the body adapts. Put a human in the most sweltering hot and humid place on the planet and the body adapts. Train a human to run great distances—and the body will adapt. Slowly? Yes. Painfully? Absolutely. Sometimes screaming in resistance? Without a doubt. But adapt, it will.

So the quest to run the Oklahoma City Memorial Marathon of 2018 began because of a determination to accomplish a seemingly difficult goal of getting my lazy self off the couch and developing the endurance to be able to run 3.1 miles (5K) and live to tell the story! Although those accomplishments are now well in the past, I still remember the joy of crossing my first pumpkin run and turkey trot finish lines victoriously.

The motivation to run comes in all kinds of ways. Some do it for health, some for companionship, some because they love the challenge. But when one sets a daunting goal, there must be something deeper than just a whimsical motivation. There must be commitment.

Commitment is to look at the task and understand the cost and still decide to do it no matter how hard it may become.

For a runner, part of the cost includes early morning runs, runs in the cold, runs in the heat, in the wind, and in the rain. It means weekends ruined by 4-hour training runs and special events with family interrupted or not joined because of exhaustion from the day's run. It will require regular stretching, muscle building, blister care, and enduring sore body parts. It includes dealing with excited animals placing themselves into your running experience (stories you will hear in later miles). And you will occasionally encounter the odd person hooting at you to "Run, Forest, run!"

All of this and so much more is in store if you determine to do this thing. Knowing all of that, will you do it?

There must be something inside that says, "I can do this; I can rise to this challenge. Not only can I . . . I will."

## 1.3

Occasionally, when I'm feeling particularly tired of the training, of the humdrum everyday activity of getting up early to run, or running after work in the heat, or delaying a fun event on a weekend because of a long run that takes precedence, or when I'm wondering why in the heck I am doing all this . . . during those times I occasionally glance online at the finish line portrayals of an upcoming race. Most races have awesome footage of races past as a seed to plant in the mind of potential future participants. I see beautiful scenery in amazing cities or in gorgeous mountains. I see moments of triumph. I see men and women struggling and overcoming the odds. And I get renewed inspiration and determination. Vision of the finish line spurs me on. I want that moment, that feeling of overcoming all obstacles to cross the line of victory.

Vision creates commitment. It answers the "why" questions. It responds to the doubt, the fear, the pain, the turmoil. Vision moves your legs out from under the warm blankets on cold mornings. It drives you forward when the mind says to pause and relax a while. Vision separates those who will from those who think about it or those who dream only. Vison establishes the prize and the upward call so worth obtaining that, at times, a person will go after it even at the cost of his very life.

Sound dramatic? Stop and think about the cost of the freedom Americans hold so dear.

For hundreds of years we have enjoyed it, so much so that it has become expected and the ignorant (most of us) have no clue what the cost was for those men and women who forged past insurmountable odds to win the day. While the lines of our nation's anthem can bring goosebumps, most of us cannot grasp what those brave men and women sacrificed to make freedom a reality.

If you took the time to research the signers of the Declaration of Independence, you'd discover that 56 men put their names (and their lives) on the line that led to hundreds of July 4 celebrations in our country. But before the celebrations were ever conceived, those men committed their families to unbelievable sacrifices. While most have heard of declaration signer Benjamin Franklin and a few of his exploits, I would hazard a guess that fewer than one-half of 1 percent have heard about Carter Braxton.

Carter Braxton, of Virginia, was a wealthy planter and trader who signed the Declaration and subsequently saw his ships swept from the seas by the British Navy. He sold his home and properties to pay his debts and died in rags.

Oh, you may know a bit about Thomas Jefferson, a Declaration signer who served as the third President of these United States, but what about Thomas McKean, who was so hounded by the British that he was forced to move his family almost constantly? He served in the Congress without pay (imagine that today), and his family was kept in hiding. His possessions were taken from him and poverty was his reward.

Thomas Nelson, Jr., added his name to the freedom declaration. Later, at the battle of Yorktown, he noted that British General Cornwallis had taken over the Nelson home for his headquarters. The home was destroyed, and Nelson died bankrupt.

John Hart penned his name to the hallowed document and later was driven from his wife's bedside as she was dying. Their children fled for their lives. Hart's fields and his gristmill were laid to waste. For more than a year he lived in forests and caves, returning home to find his wife dead and his children vanished. A few weeks later, he died from exhaustion and a broken heart.

Heroes? Yes. How many of you would like to sign up to be heroes? Me neither. And yet, these men (and many others) weren't thinking of themselves as heroes, nor were they signing to make a name for themselves. Rather, they were common men, businessmen, landowners, quiet family men who were proclaiming that they were committed together to a cause that was worth the ultimate sacrifice.

Join me in honoring the words of Patrick Henry, from a speech he made to the Second Virginia Convention on March 23, 1775, at St. John's Church in Richmond, Virginia.

*"It is in vain, sir, to extenuate the matter. Gentlemen may cry, Peace, Peace but there is no peace. The war is actually begun! The next gale that sweeps from the north will bring to our ears the clash of resounding arms! Our brethren are already in the field! Why stand we here idle? What is it that gentlemen wish? What would they have? Is life so dear, or peace so sweet, as to be purchased at the price of chains and slavery? Forbid it, Almighty God! I know not what course others may take; but as for me, give me liberty or give me death."*

(Note: Henry is credited with having swung the balance in convincing the convention to pass a resolution delivering Virginian troops for the Revolutionary War. Among the delegates to the convention were future U.S. Presidents Thomas Jefferson and George Washington.)

Why would they do it? What causes a man to declare words such as "I know not what course others may take"? Why would they leave their families and follow leaders who could not promise them either food or warmth or safety, who could only assure a kinship and a brotherhood of trials and suffering, often of great loss. Why? Surely it was because of a vision for a better future for sons, for daughters. Vision propels us on in the face of unbelievable adversity—convinced of a brighter day—tomorrow. And with that vision deeply imbedded in our hearts, we commit ourselves to trials, tribulations, peril, sword;

to persevere through whatever may come that would dare try to keep us from that vision for the future.

# 1.6

I had a moment of such vision strike my life. It was at the funeral of my grandmother and at the words of her son, my father. It was unexpected. It was unplanned. I had no clue it was coming.

My grandmother was a saint of a woman. She would sacrifice her last piece of bread for her family if need be. She was quiet yet strong. She was also rigid; some would say judgmental. And yet her love toward even those who might be critical was undying and abounding, and everyone knew it. She was determined to fight for and believe for what was right in a world gone very morally wrong. She would stand her ground come what may. That same determination was passed to my father.

Then it happened: Standing that day beside his mother's grave my dad suddenly lifted his voice and spoke toward the heavens, "Mom! I've got the baton!"

I don't recall what else he said. But those five words hit me with force. He was declaring to the heavens, to the earth, to all that stood nearby, to forces seen and unseen, that the God whom his mother served so passionately was his God. That her life had mattered. That she had passed to him something of such great value that it had not only directed his past, it would also direct the remainder of his days on this earth. Everything in his life that mattered (his family, his friends, those he personally counseled in life) would be impacted by the driving vision of a great race in which he saw himself wherein the purpose of his mom's life was admitted—no, declared—as having been passed from her . . . to him.

It is vision and a commitment to that vision that guide decisions made; that determine which road is taken at the crossroads of life. That same commitment to vision has now become mine. A baton is still passing, even while my father yet (thankfully) lives.

What does it mean, this holding of a baton of vision? And how does it translate to my own three precious girls and to my nine grandchildren? How has it changed my life and the life of my wife? Where has it led us? Where will it lead us still?

## 2.0

The overriding purpose of this book is to compare the challenges, the joy, the pain, and the triumphs I have discovered in running with various areas of life.

In section one, I will look at a key building block of society, the family. Section two will examine the driving forces of the inner man (both good and bad) and will include some reflection on how we treat one another. Section three may be a bit emotional as we dig into some of the most difficult challenges that life throws at us. Finally, section four will evaluate the bigger picture of life's purpose and the underlying forces at work in it all.

I hope to discover vision in each area and find the commitment that, come what may, we will run on through every test and trial.

We will not stop . . . because the finish line is so amazing that it is beyond our comprehension. It is worth every drop of blood, sweat, tears, and suffering that life may bring our way. It is the race of all races.

My hope is not only that you find some inspiration from the following stories of running, but also from the stories of life. And that a deposit of vision will be made into your heart whereby you too will say, "I'm going after an imperishable prize. I will press on. I've got the baton. And I will run."

*"Survey the path for your feet, and all your ways will be sure."*

## MILE 3

# This Race Is Not Like Most

The effects of an EF5 tornado, the most powerful classification in tornados, are amazing and terrifying to behold. Powerful winds of up to and over 200 miles per hour can bring trees, telephone poles, houses, even hospitals into complete submission. During a 70-year period, from 1950-2019, only 59 officially rated EF5 tornados occurred in the United States, per Wikipedia. And that is what struck Joplin, Missouri, on May 22, 2011, claiming the lives of 161 of Joplin's citizens, making it one of the deadliest storms in decades.

Here are the 7 deadliest tornadoes to touch down in the United States, according to figures from NOAA (National Oceanic and Atmospheric Administration):

1. The Tri-State Tornado killed 695 people and injured 2,027. It traveled more than 300 miles through Missouri, Illinois, and Indiana on March 18, 1925.

2. The Natchez Tornado killed 317 people and injured 109 on May 6, 1840, along the Mississippi River in Louisiana and Mississippi.

3. The St. Louis Tornado killed 255 people and injured 1,000 on May 27, 1896, in Missouri and Illinois.

4. The Tupelo Tornado killed 216 people and injured 700 on April 5, 1936, in the northeastern Mississippi city.

5. The Gainesville Tornado was a pair of storms that converged on April 6, 1936, in Gainesville, Georgia, killing 203 people and injuring 1,600.

6. The Woodward Tornado wreaked havoc across parts of Texas, Oklahoma, and Kansas on April 9, 1947. The storm, which killed 181 people and injured 970.

7. The tornado that struck Joplin, Missouri, on May 22, 2011, killed 161 people and injured more than a thousand. The storm packed winds in excess of 200 mph and was on the ground for more than 22 miles. More than 550 businesses were destroyed and 7,500 residential dwellings were damaged by the storm; of those, well over half were completely destroyed, causing some 9,200 people to be displaced.

*It had been more than 60 years since a tornado as devastating as the Joplin tornado had hit the United States. Indeed, this storm was not like most.*

## 2.2

The storm hit on a Sunday evening. It was later described as having been "rain-wrapped," making it difficult for local weather stations to discern. Warning was very limited despite the fact that we can often predict storms with uncanny accuracy.

My own home, sitting near the Oklahoma State Line Road, about 10 miles south of Joplin, provided enough distance cushion that I had no clue what was occurring in real time in the city where we work, shop, and recreate. My perception of the storm as it was coming through our area was that it was just another thunderstorm, something I'm very accustomed to, having lived in the northeast corner of Oklahoma my entire life. But the aftermath was unlike anything I've ever seen.

By Monday morning I was aware that a major tornado had occurred, but I drove to work that day without any expectation of seeing what I saw or hearing what I heard. Streets that cross my usual route were closed. In some areas there was a complete absence of any identifying mark, no utility poles, street signs, or traffic lights.

The feeling of the city was eerie, almost as if a bomb had been dropped. For hours on end, sirens were heard throughout the city as emergency vehicles moved in response to the tragedy. One would begin and slowly fade into the distance. But before the sound was gone, a new one started. Over and over, the odd sound of still another alarm repeated. Emergency crews from many states responded as lives were being lost, heroic search and rescue missions were being conducted, and remnants of homes and businesses were being searched and searched again, looking for survivors.

For me to be at work felt disrespectful. By noon, the few people who had made it in to work that day had been sent home. This was not a day to work as if nothing had happened. This was a day to help others and pray.

What we are always struck with in times of national devastation is not just the loss but also heroism in action—the bravery of men and women (and children) who pull together to help those in need. This was absolutely one of those times. Aid came from everywhere as a wave of workers descended on the scene of destruction.

Within days, my son-in-law, who was a medical student at the time, arrived in town from his home 4 hours away. He wanted to help. That was the way of the time. "How can we help?" was the creed. So we pulled together a crew of our own, brought a 16-foot flatbed trailer into town and slowly began driving through areas where the giant had struck. The scope of destruction was stunning. Vehicles were piled onto each other like blocks, homes completely gone, huge trees obliterated. I clearly recall driving down streets and thinking, *I have no idea where I am,* in a town that only days ago carried the familiarity of a lifetime of living.

Each place we looked, the devastation was met and matched by that wave of people working with grim determination on their faces. After our little group had worked for hours and decided it was time to head home, the thought crept in that we hadn't even made a dent. The task was monumental.

A silly old saying came to mind: How do you eat an elephant? Answer: One bite at a time. And that is what Joplin did, aided by thousands of volunteers.

As the years following the tornado progressed, things were rebuilt, and the city overcame the catastrophe. Yet there was a loss that could not be measured by brick-and-mortar repairs. It was the shock of loved ones lost in a moment of time.

In part two of my account of the Joplin Memorial Run (at mile 17) I will tell the story of two co-workers and friends of mine who experienced the event in a very personal and moving way. But I did not personally lose a friend or family member that day. So I will not here disrespect the great loss some endured by acting as if I understand or by attempting to write something that would try to quantify or explain the loss. I am sure it is immeasurable. What I will do instead is focus on the spirit of people to overcome what seemingly could not be borne.

The "Joplin Memorial Run" is one small way that the people of Joplin have chosen to remember what happened to change a city, possibly unlike anything in this city's history. The run incorporates an extension of the great spirit that exists here. It also happens to be the first "long" run in which I participated.

# 2.5

The yearly Joplin Memorial Run is not like most.

Individual flags were constructed that bear the name of each life lost in the 2011 tornado. Those flags line the way for the first blocks of the run and later serve as the finish line reminder for why we ran. I have seen individuals stop short of the finish line to find the flag of a loved one, stand beside it or touch it for a moment with tears in their eyes, and then finish their race.

Again, I will not taint what those loved ones do by trying to dramatize it further for my story. I will not infer that their pain is comprehensible by those who didn't experience it themselves. I will say that watching the runner stop beside the flag of a departed loved one cannot leave the onlooker unmoved. It touches our hearts as we realize the fragile nature of this life.

I remember gathering here for my first opportunity to test my running endurance in May of 2017. I'd been building up from my occasional 5K runs and my one very ambitious five-mile pumpkin run the October prior. I found a nice plan that had me build up to ten miles a couple of weeks out from the half marathon. It was tough, but it was also fun to try. My almost 53-year-old body was holding up to the challenge. I thought I was ready to go.

I stood with possibly a couple thousand runners. I recall the excitement of it all. *Could I do it? Would I crash in the end? Would my body really hold up and keep going for 13 miles?*

*What in the world am I doing here?*

My unofficial running coach, who is also one of my bosses at work (I'll call him Joe), is an excellent runner. He has completed more than 26 marathons and has run in places like Rome, New York City, the California coast, and many more. He freely offers help and instruction to anyone who asks. He was running on that day as a pacer for marathon runners. Another friend of his, who was at a similar place in his training as I, was also in the race.

I'd heard that Joe's friend could run a 10-minute per mile average. I wondered if I could somehow keep that same pace. I'll pause now for all good runners to roll their eyes at my slow pace. But truthfully, I've discovered that runners are an excellent group of people who are positively upbeat and encouraging of anyone who has the audacity to get out and run. I think the heaviest people on the racecourse get the most encouragement and garner more praise than the sleek, the fast, the very fit. Because they (maybe I should say "we") have been brave enough not to care what we may look like or how slowly we may traverse the course. We are going anyway.

I heard the race announcer say, "Could you have asked for any nicer weather to run in?" as the racers began doing the anxious dance in place, waiting for the last few prerace moments to end.

And then it comes . . . no, not the gun to begin . . . instead, 161 seconds of silence in honor of those lives who are not here today because of that awful storm.

Thousands of excited participants gradually grow silent as the realization spreads through the crowd of what is occurring. And then there is nothing but quiet thoughts. A netting of 161 balloons is released into the gray morning sky. The hushed crowd watches. Heads turn as the balloons slowly become tiny points in the distance.

I reflect on how long 161 seconds takes when we stop and really do nothing for that entire time. Strange how that is—161 seconds can in one instance seem long, but 161 days go by fast as time seems to go careening at breakneck speed.

Reflection is over. Someone is counting down the seconds now. A gun goes off and the announcer shouts over the tromp of thousands of suddenly moving feet. The electronic beeps of watches occur all around as most of the runners hit "start" on their GPS watches that will guide their pace. And we are off. My first long race has begun.

I'm amazed at some things. Within a tenth of a mile, my breath was already becoming a bit labored. It almost always does this, even after running for many years and having, by this point, completed multiple marathons. But no matter the training buildup, it seems that my body wants to respond with "What are you doing?!" every time I begin running. But soon it settles in for the task. The breathing and heartbeat slow as the pace gradually becomes normal. What a wonderful thing God has made for us to use in these amazing bodies.

Another amazing thing: People talk during long runs. I'm just trying to breathe. Other people are yacking like they have just seen a long-lost friend and they are both lying back on their yacht sipping a diet cola. Yack, yack, yack. Sometimes I get embarrassed. Do I really need to hear about your romantic escapades? No, please. And what is wrong with the elders from that church? Oh, the conversations are rich. It's like eavesdropping on dozens of people as you trot by them or as they trot by you. Really though, I enjoy it. I enjoy the chatter all around. It is part of the atmosphere of camaraderie.

I discovered during my training for my second marathon, for which my buddy and brother-in-law joined me, that I too could summon the wind to chat even while I was trying to survive a long run, and it became one of the more enjoyable parts of the entire running experience, companionship.

My first half marathon was great. At about mile 3, I saw my boss's friend just ahead. I determined then and there to do my very best to stay with him. And mile after mile I did just that, trekking ever so slightly behind him without him ever knowing. He had a friend running with him and like the rest of the runners who ran as pairs, they chatted merrily for miles. I was running alone—breathing, enduring, soaking it all in.

A spot on our course featured a turnaround cone where you stopped heading south and began to go back north. A place like this on the course is enjoyable because you get to briefly see people ahead of you and behind you, face on.

I saw my boss, who could have set a blistering pace for the full marathon. But instead, he was serving as a pacer and encourager for a slower group. He was truly "trotting" even though, for me, his was still a decent pace. But because of his service as a pacer, he was slightly behind me, enough so that at the turnaround cone, we saw each other. He'd been aware that this was my first attempt at a long run but really wasn't aware of how much work I'd put into it. He saw me, saw that I was barely behind his other friend, his eyes widened, and being ever the encourager, he shouted "Rusty, stay with him!" as he pointed at his friend. I think he was surprised I had kept that lofty pace of under 10 minutes per mile for what was now approaching 8 or 9 miles. Indeed.

Staying with him (I'll call him "Jon") was exactly what I intended to do. And I did, almost.

At about mile 10, Jon slowed at the water stop, as did I. But he took a bit longer than I desired. I hesitated, but then ran ahead. Maybe it was a mistake, I don't know. But I had the Garmin watch that my wife had purchased for me and I thought I could possibly maintain the pace even though I was about to cross into new territory—beyond 10 miles.

Then the hills came.

Ugh. The 26th Street hills. They aren't horrible hills. But to me that day, they were. Determined to keep my pace, I plowed on and made it past, but they took a toll on me I wasn't ready for. As the ground flattened again, so did my energy and my determination, and for a moment so did my pace. Around mile 11.5 or 12, I saw Jon and his buddy come trotting by me. They looked almost fresh, as if there was still a bounce in their step. I summoned, but could not bring up, the will to give chase to keep up with them. Somewhere inside my being, a pronouncement was made that I've made on many of my long runs: "*Never again* will I do this. Why am I doing it in the first place?" Still, I lumbered on.

Mile 12 passed, and the final mile began. The street that leads to the finish line is very long and straight. You can probably see almost three-quarters of a mile down the street to make out the finish line banners and the huge flags representing those who we were here to honor. A bit of energy renewed inside me and I picked up the pace again. As the line drew near, my speed increased more and more. And then I was very close, attempting to pass a last person or two . . .

. . . *and there she was*: my gorgeous and supportive wife with whom I've shared every triumph and every defeat over the last three-plus decades of my life. Standing beside her was my first grandson, who'd lived almost all his 7 years just over the hill from us. He was there to cheer along with my wife as I "sped" across my first half marathon finish line. It was wonderful! In a moment of good fortune, a finish line photographer pushed a button on her camera from the opposite side of the street, catching me racing across and showing my wife and grandson in the background. I crossed with a last burst of energy, slowed, and immediately thought that I might just throw up on the spot, right in front of everyone. But aside from that one awful sensation, it was a feeling of jubilation, completion, and victory. And having my wife and grandson there to witness it gave it so much more meaning for reasons that can be explained only in the depths of true loving companionship.

Here I was at my first finish line. And my adored and adoring bride of 34 years (at that time) was there to see it. She was my first, my only . . . for everything; she always has been. She always will be.

## 2.7

"You have touched a place deep inside my heart; a place that was reserved for only one."

These are the beginning lines of a song I wrote to the girl who would soon be my wife. I was standing there, guitar in hand, beside a babbling brook of water, singing to her in front of "these witnesses" on a beautiful late spring day in 1983. As I write this now almost 36 "light speed" years later, I am more deeply enthralled with my lady than I was when I first sang those words to her. How can such a thing be possible? It almost blows the mind.

Someone once said something to the effect that real men, real lovers are those who can make one woman fulfilled and happy for her entire lifetime and that the Hollywood idea of great lovers being those who go from one hot woman to the next is completely ridiculous because any dog can do the same. I wholeheartedly applaud and agree with the sentiment.

But one man and one woman for a lifetime? This idea that used to seem so normal has now become a fading wonder in our world.

## 2.8

*"The two shall become one flesh. What, therefore, that God has joined together, let no one put asunder."*

Hah! What a crazy old, outdated idea . . . two people being one.

"Well, nobody is going to stop me from being me! As long as we go good together and make each other happy, great! But as soon as it becomes a strain or less fun or demanding or requiring too much, or as soon as either one of us gets unhappy, then forget it! Why should we live our short lives being unhappy, right? And the kids? Well, they will be *much* better off with happy, separate parents rather than with arguing, fighting, angry parents." Right?

There is surely complexity behind the breaking of a vow that goes deeper than those few sarcastic words I just typed. But I believe the root behind the actual reasons for breakup or divorce is often utter selfishness and rampant immaturity in a relationship that calls for the opposite of those attributes. At its core, there is a failure to understand the meaning of the word *vow* or *covenant*. Or that this joining of two people for a lifetime is going to include good times, great memories, unbelievable joys, bad times, hard times, and excruciating sorrows. Oh, we say those kinds of things in the vows ("in sickness and in health," etc.) but we don't truly "get it" until the rubber meets the road and the two souls (minds, wills, emotions, thoughts, plans, expectations) collide.

This "mile" is about the early years of this covenant, the early years of this incredible part of life that is unlike anything else.

Entering into marriage, I had some rough ideas of how things would go. I'd had a good mom and dad as my example. I thought I'd take care of my wife. I thought that man gets woman, man takes care of woman, woman is forever happy being taken care of and is so smitten with man that her every desire is focused on him and being with him . . .or something like that.

My expectations as an immature husband were that everything would go smoothly, I loved my young bride so much that I'd sacrifice for her, and there would never be a real reason for a disagreement, an argument, or a fight. I voiced something like this at a gathering once and an experienced husband was unable to choke back a loud guffaw. I was a bit insulted by his laugh and probably felt sorry for him that he didn't understand what I so clearly already had a handle on. And then the marriage happened.

On our glorious trip to Estes Park in Colorado for a week-long honeymoon, my bride discovered for the first time what I might be like about 5 seconds after leaving the wedding.

You see, I have only one brother, and I trust him. And I had one best friend from high school whom I trusted. Only these two knew where I was hiding our getaway car. I had it all planned. I had a destination in mind, and I wanted to get there. Nobody could know where my car was so that nobody could mess it up so that I wouldn't have to waste time cleaning it

. . . nobody, that is, except my trusted brother and best school friend . . . one of whom became an absolute traitor.

As I saw my car arrive, I looked on in total shock. It was a beautiful *mess!* And so it happened that five seconds into my bride and me being alone, she discovered that I was a big baby and didn't like my plans being messed up. I was mad. Yes, her knight in shining armor was mad about five seconds into our first moments alone. At least I wasn't mad at her, right?

After the car was adequately cleaned and as the miles passed and the conversation flowed, all in the world became well again. We were together, forever, on our way to the trip I'd been waiting on for years. Nothing else could go wrong. All would be bliss from this point forward. (Where is the loud guffaw when I need it?)

Maybe it was day 2, maybe day 3, I can't remember precisely. But there we were in our mountain cabin with the rushing mountain stream outside our door. Beauty and peace surrounded us. I suggested we go outside for a bit and sit beside the water; that's what I wanted to do. My wife of two or three days had a different idea. She thought she'd stay inside and read a book while I went on a walk by myself. *By myself!* You mean, she doesn't want to be with me *all* the time?

So I went and sat by the stream and . . . pouted. I came back in, still pouting. Or maybe there was a mixture of anger in my mood. Our first encounter with different expectations had occurred. She thought she could enjoy being with me and also enjoy being by herself. I thought she would only enjoy being with me all the time. How could I have possibly gone so far wrong in my thinking?

Things were patched over soon. We had a great time in Colorado getting to know each other better. We laughed a lot. In fact, today, we still talk about that period with great fondness.

Days later, we pulled into the driveway of our first rental home just as we'd begun a conversation about something that surprised me.

Our first argument in our new house began about 1 second inside the door of the home. Was I a great find or what?! (I can only imagine any females reading this right now are thinking "What a jerk!" And they'd be about right. I was young, immature in my thinking, and without a true understanding of what the union of two souls meant or would entail. Still, they'd be right. I was a big ole baby.)

I distinctly recall that the first two to three months of our married life were filled with lots of fun and lots of my shocking immaturity, which tended to include me being upset for some astounding failure of my wife (i.e., failing to be home one day when I got home from work because she lost track of time. Shocking!).

Gradually, I grew up. I still adored my wife. She adored me right back and put up with a lot of my immaturity in a very loving way. And slowly we began to learn about life with one another. I found out she wasn't perfect. She found out I was far from it. I found out she was independent. She found out I was needy.

And then children came.

About 16 months into our married life, my heart was absolutely transfixed at the sight of our baby girl. Suddenly, a seriousness came into our young married life.

If we had not understood the selfless aspect of life that is needed in a truly rich marriage union, the introduction of an utterly dependent baby will bring the message home quickly. It wasn't as if she was a demand on us. It was the desire of our hearts to sacrifice for this precious child God had given us.

But the childbearing years had begun. The meaning of this to us will be explained in the next two "miles" of this book. But suffice it to say that these gifts from God helped us grow up into the family we were supposed to be.

Together, my wife and I took on the challenges. We learned to allow each other to be who we are. We also learned that parts of each of us needed to be changed and shaped so that we could be, each to the other (and to our kids) what we needed to be.

Somewhere in the child-rearing years some couples grow quite distant. The needs of the children can replace everything, and couples forget that their union is the chief relationship in this family. With all the demands that must be met—babies fed, diapers changed, baths given, multiple middle-of-the-night cries, worrying sicknesses, clothes vomited on, shower-less days for mamas at times, demanding late nights at work for dads—all of this and more can collide with the unmet emotional needs of young husbands and wives and can create a breeding ground for discontent, for fantasies not met, and for new fantasies (of escape to a better and easier and more fulfilling life) to begin.

And then the attack is sprung. In the middle of a man coming home to a harried, exhausted wife and a baby who won't seem to stop crying, a cute and very attentive young lady enters the picture. The scene may be at a cubicle next to you. It may be while you are working your new pizza business in the back end of a small convenience store and the only employee of the store is a cute young girl who is bored and enjoys leaning on your pizza counter, chatting about anything and nothing, standing there looking attractive and being attentive to your every word . . . laughing on cue.

Or it may be the neighbor boy about 18 years old and ripped from his constant workouts that are geared to impress the girls. And your husband is out working late yet again, the baby is napping, and you are planting flowers. You've not talked—really talked with your equally exhausted husband about how you're doing for months, it seems. And here is the impressive young man from next door, fresh from mowing his yard, sweat on his brow, looking fine; making you

laugh, making you feel pretty and important . . . paying special attention to your every word.

The attack can come in countless ways upon the unsuspecting.
And for reasons as varied as the pizzas you can create or the flowers
you can plant, an unexpected stirring starts inside you, a stirring of
desire for someone other than the one to whom you, not that long ago,
pledged your life.

*Avoid the path that leads to that door!* Because walking through
that tempting door may cost you your life.

Yes, your life is challenging. Yes, these days are hard. No, everything didn't happen just like you expected. No, your "needs" aren't
always met just like you'd like. This is life. It is the true way of things.
But you made a vow . . . didn't you?

Somewhere along the line, vows seem to have lost their meaning.
Depending on the sources you read, you are likely to discover that 25
to 50 percent of marriages end in divorce. Which means that, for so
many people, the vow means "unless I change my mind later."

I would like to introduce an odd concept. Love doesn't support
the vow. How you *feel* about your spouse at any given moment isn't
what props up the covenant. Feelings change. They ebb and flow. What
should be true instead is that "the vow (or covenant) supports love."
Let me explain.

I was the man in the pizza store. I had a wonderful and devoted
wife of three years and I had two small children. (Daughter #2 came
along one year after daughter #1. Double the fun!) And one day I discovered that in the craziness of trying to keep my business afloat, working days and nights six days out of seven, my wife being that tired and
harried young lady who was trying to keep up with 24/7 demands of
two young daughters... in the midst of all this, the feelings we'd enjoyed

at first seemed to wane for a very brief time. And the attentiveness of the cute young lady from the convenience store caused a warm and fuzzy feeling somewhere in the pit of my stomach.

And so, having a depth of love and commitment to my wife, this feeling alarmed me. I wisely (occasionally, I did something wise) talked to a trusted elderly gentleman one day.

Without telling him about the young lady at the convenience store, I was able to discuss the changes in the feelings I'd originally had with my wife. He said to me, "*You are now beginning to understand what it means to love your wife.*"

He explained how feelings can change with the events of the days, and he seemed to insightfully understand the temptations that can follow. Without any foreknowledge, he told me that I must be on guard against any temptation during this period of time and cut such things off immediately. He explained that we cannot be guided by our feelings. He said that we are guided by our covenant and that the covenant will create a true and deep love. And that's exactly what I did and exactly what happened.

From that moment on, if the girl came to chat, I acted too busy to talk . . . almost to the point of rudeness. With ruthlessness, I choked out any way and any manner in which the creation of that warm and fuzzy feeling could begin to germinate. And I began to bring my attention to any way that I could serve and fulfill my wife—beginning to understand for the first time that true love is selfless, it is service of another, it is not in asking for my own self and my own needs to be fulfilled. *My job is to serve . . . not be served. Revelation!*

And from that moment on, things changed. I can honestly say that I have never once— in all these years—thought of being without my wife. I've never wanted to have a day without her. I've never wanted to experience life with any other woman. I can look back to those moments from three decades ago and I can see the path where a crossroads could have been created, a crossroads that many people come to without the value of a wise counselor; and a fork in a road that, if the fork of entertaining unfaithfulness is taken, will create a depth of hurt and loss that is utterly excruciating. I've seen it in others I love. It starts with the fuzzy feelings and the whispers of a liar right at the point of our weakness and our need. Thank God, I never came close to that road.

My wife and I traversed the early years with some ups and downs; but mostly they were ups, mostly they were wonderful and blessed. I've told my lovely lady many times that there has never been a day I wasn't excited to enter our home and hear her voice.

The early years of this union had challenges. But they were mostly wonderful years. One wonders, have we crossed the halfway mark of our time together on earth? Only God knows. But a place deep inside my heart—a place that was only to be touched by one—has indeed been touched.

And a miracle happened. The two started to become one. And the two will not be parted; at least, not on this side of heaven. Therefore, in all that life brings, this is our road, this is our race, and we will run it together . . . till death do us part.

## 3.0

(In the midst of my sarcastic comments about the fickle nature of many people's weak level of commitment these days, I want to acknowledge something that is very important. There are situations of real physical and emotional abuse—historically, I think, attributed to the behavior of men toward women. It disgusts me. And I would tell any person in a relationship of that nature that they should not put up with it—at all. Where there is abuse, there can be no loving relationship.)

*"You were running a good race. Who stopped you?"*

## MILE 4

# *Picking Your Pain*

People like to say that the certainties of life are death and taxes. There are others, of course.

How about pain?

I've read books about the problem of pain, with people smarter than I attempting to explain the purpose in it. Without delving into purpose here, I will simply focus on the fact that pain is an absolute certainty in life. Physical or emotional, it can be excruciating and debilitating. It can be temporary or long-term. It is often unexpected and random, not a respecter of persons, rank, or title.

And then, there is a different category . . . it can be self-inflicted. In other words, some pain can be avoided. Or a lesser pain can be chosen in the place of a greater pain. Let me explain.

People near my age will remember the old "Pay me now or pay me later" commercial that was based on getting a bit of routine mainte-nance for your car in order to avoid an awful death of the engine later. Pay $4.00 now for that special oil filter or pay several hundred dollars later, when your engine breaks down.

This is true in life and in running.

My first real encounter with (almost certainly avoidable) injury-based pain occurred as I was running my second Half Marathon, the Williams Route 66 race in Tulsa, Oklahoma.

I was fairly new to long-distance running and had not sufficiently educated myself concerning the best training methods. I was about to learn some of those training lessons the hard way.

November 19, 2017, dawned as a crisp morning in Tulsa. The wind was almost non- existent. The temp sat squarely at 40 degrees. As I got off the bus that delivered many of us from area hotels to the starting stalls, I was greeted by the chilly morning air, but I still had my sweatshirt and sweatpants on over my shorts and T-shirt. I headed for the heated tent for which I had paid the extra $40 and joined the gathering runners. Probably 30 minutes before the gun, I had the sweats off and was surprised to find the air invigorating as my insides began to churn in anticipation of my second long race.

I gained two pieces of advice from my boss and running expert, Joe. First, he educated me about the proper clothing for a chilly morning. Forty degrees with little wind, he said, would be perfect weather for a long-distance run. He suggested I take some gloves and something to cover my ears for the first mile or two, but he thought I'd ditch both shortly into the run. He said shorts and a T-shirt would be great. I had my doubts. In my mind, 40 degrees meant only 8 degrees above freezing. But I scored a small victory. I followed his advice. I soon discovered he was absolutely right.

As the race began, I was practically giddy with how great I felt. The training in September and October had prepared me adequately, I thought. I felt fantastic. And it seemed that my legs carried me almost effortlessly over the first few miles. My restraint was exhibited only in that I decided not to pass the two-hour pacer (a pace of 9 minutes, 9 seconds per mile). I just kept him about 10 to 20 paces ahead. This was going to be a wonderful race. In those first few miles, I felt certain that I'd make my 2- hour half marathon goal and improve on my first Half Marathon time by ten to eleven minutes overall.

Joe's second piece of advice was to shoot for the 2-hour marathon by starting slow and finishing strong. He said many inexperienced runners go out too fast because they feel great at the start and they soon run out of juice because of that fast start. He said I should start a tad over my desired pace, gain speed in the later miles, and turn it on at the end. It is what I should have done. But alas, I discarded the advice of the experienced one. It wouldn't be the last time I'd make that foolish mistake. So on I "sped" at my personal breakneck pace. Miles 5, 6, 7 went by and I was holding my ground, slightly amazed and feeling strong.

Beside these good feelings, the run through downtown Tulsa was enjoyable. It included the art district and some very nice residential neighborhoods. Cheering crowds lined the streets in various places. We were pumped up by singers and musicians. I remember coming down one street and being greeted by several pounding drums, rhythmically beating out the steps for my feet. Tulsa does a great job of supporting its signature race.

Looking back now at my splits (races are usually divided into sections so you can see what your pace was at the beginning, the middle, and the end), I see that I logged the first 6.2 miles in 57 minutes, 26 seconds, for a 9:16 pace. The two-hour pacer was still in my sight. I ran on for at least two more miles, possibly three, feeling reasonably strong and with the pacer very nearby.

Then it hit me—my first "wall" experience in long-distance running. After my vast number of prior races (equaling *one*

Half-Marathon), I thought I could keep running like this the entire way. I had run the entire race in Joplin. I was doing great here. I was about to make my goal. I couldn't imagine what would prevent it.

But if someone had placed an actual wall in front of me, it would not have been much different from what happened to me that bright, brisk morning. I believe it occurred at around mile 9. Almost suddenly, my energy was gone, simply gone. I could not will myself forward at this pace any longer. I am sure I slowed markedly.

I now understand the lessons of nutrition and hydration, both leading up to a long race and during a long race. I now know the importance of whole-body strength training in order to avoid the pitfalls of a repetitive injury. I now know about monitoring the age of shoes and using the correct shoes in the first place. I now know these things and much more. The details and depth of the importance of some of these lessons are explained in later miles.

But at that time, I really didn't understand the importance of any of it. My "wall" came with full force, and injury was about to follow.

By mile ten or so, the unthinkable happened. I began walking. And somewhere over the course of the next 3 miles, my slow jog mixed with times of walking, I noticed that my right knee was hurting—badly. My gait included a definite limp. Ugh. What was happening here? I was confused and disappointed. The two-hour pacesetter was nowhere in sight. I looked ahead and saw a long and steep incline. As I approached it, my will again evaporated, and my jog turned to a walk. I literally hobbled up the long incline. I think this came at around mile 12 so, thankfully, my misery was close to the end, with thoughts of "never again" seeping into my mind.

As I approached the finish line, I did my best to put on some kind of pathetic, hobbled burst of effort. Maybe onlookers would be fooled into thinking I was running the entire race. Coming through the finish line gates, I grabbed my medal with an odd mixture of despondence and a trickle of satisfaction of another race finished. I looked for my wife as I always do at the end of a race; found her, and hobbled over in pain. I could hardly walk. This was bizarre. I had never hurt like this before in my brief running career. The only thing I could think was that I needed to make it back to the hotel before the pain got any worse.

My finish time was 2:09:59, or 9:55 per mile. In those last 4 miles I was so slow that I lost about ten minutes of my hoped-for finish time. Overall, my second race ended with an improvement of about one minute over my first half marathon time. Progress? I guess. But it didn't feel like it.

Discouraged and experiencing an injury for the first time, I faced a choice at this early juncture in my running experiment: Would I quit running because of pain from the injury or would I begin a process that would take months of education, training, and discipline—a different kind of pain—that could lead to health? Using my earlier example, would I take a path of paying the price of the early oil filter in order to avoid the cost of an overhaul? Or was it too late? Had I already caused enough engine trouble that an overhaul was unavoidable?

A full marathon had not yet entered my mind, but my choice would be to continue. Giving up is not in me. We must go on! As later "miles" of this book will explain, the task wasn't easy and it would come with periods of great internal questioning, pain that grew worse before it got better, and a slow (painful) course to a much better race.

# 3.3

Once, there was a king. He would one day be the greatest of kings but, on this day, he was in a very humble position . . . especially for a king. Although a small portion of the people viewed him as the actual king, the great majority did not. In fact, the majority still swore allegiance to the king our hero was supposed to replace. Oh, he'd been anointed king in the usual ceremony, but the old king was still around and not yet ready to give up his throne. In fact, the old king decided to do what kings often do—kill any challengers to his reign.

And so the future king went away into hiding. He attracted some ruffians to his side—some strong, rough and tumble, discontented warriors. These became his troop. It was a ragtag gang, hiding in caves and hills, making their way here and there, always looking behind them for the coming expected onslaught of the old king.

And on this specific day, after having been in a little-known realm for a while, he came to a shepherd's house and asked for an insignificant thing. He noted that his band of men had treated the shepherd fairly while they were in the area. They had not attacked the shepherd's hired hands or taken any sheep as their own. In fact, quite the opposite—they'd been an unexpected, un-hired, unpaid shield for the shepherd. If any potential attackers came into the area thinking to take from the shepherd by force, they encountered a fierce band of men who stood as a wall of protection, guarding the area.

So on this day, the young and humble king sent a few of his men to make mention of this benefit they had provided to the shepherd and see if he'd like to offer some food to them in exchange. It was an equitable trade. It was even generous, perhaps.

Alas, the shepherd was a proud man. He refused the humble king's men and did so with insulting words. It was not a wise move, for the king's men were ferocious if the need arose.

Upon hearing of the refusal and the arrogant words of the shepherd, the young king, for once, began to walk toward establishing his own rights and his own might. And who could blame him? Wouldn't you do the same? He arose before his men, saw the light of battle in their eyes, and proclaimed that the sun would not set before the shepherd and his men were annihilated, wiped from the face of the earth.

But a wild card was about to be played, for the idiot shepherd was the husband of a wise woman. When the shepherd's men saw what their master had done, they reported it to his wife, who immediately prepared everything the humble (but now angry) king had asked for, and more. And rather than the king and his men encountering the shepherd that day, their path was intercepted by the woman. Her words were few, but they were wise.

She fell on her face, bowing before him (the respect a king should receive, by the way) and declared with humility that all the blame for her husband's actions should be on her alone. She owned her husband's sin.

And then came the words that won the day . . . "*Please do not let my lord pay attention to this worthless man . . . since the Lord has restrained you from shedding blood, and from avenging yourself by your own hand . . . let this gift be given to the young men who accompany you . . . and please forgive our transgression.*"

She spoke a few words further about the certainty that the young king soon would be king of all the land, and that this moment where he had almost taken vengeance into his own hand would not trouble him in later days . . . if he would only be so kind to restrain his hand from killing her worthless husband and all his men.

As you may have guessed, the young king was moved by the humility and wisdom of the woman and did restrain his hand. And he soon was king of all the land. And the foolish shepherd died, without the king's involvement. And the lady? She was most beautiful (I almost forgot to mention that part). She became the wife of David, the greatest king of the nation of Israel who ever lived.

# 3.6

The young king almost did what most of us would do. He almost asserted his own rights, focusing on himself. Don't we do that every day?

I declare that this is a ME generation. We are obsessed with ourselves. And who could blame us? Every media outlet informs us that we deserve everything we can get our hands on in the pursuit of personal happiness.

A favorite comedian of mine had a bit that applies here. He said, *"If I'm going to be working out, I want to look at myself. I want to look at myself while I work on myself."* He went on to describe listening to himself while he worked on himself while he looked at himself, including looking at Facebook so he could look at photos of himself while he looked at what he's written about himself. Humorously stated, it is very indicative of what our society has become . . . self-focused.

Here's my point. It's all a lie. The promises of fulfillment through self-focus and through demanding our rights—in short, our claim to our right to *ourselves*, is all a lie.

Fulfillment comes in loving and serving others, not in serving ourselves. My point is that self- focus leads to injury, sometimes to a debilitating level. Others-focus is painful at first because it is often very sacrificial in nature. *But* that is the path that leads to true and deep fulfillment. It leads to life.

*Death to self leads to life.*

If I tend to always focus on and serve myself, the result is temporary and fleeting satisfaction and long-term pain.

If I tend to focus more on others and serving them instead of myself, the result is temporary discomfort and long-term depths of satisfaction.

So which pain do you do you choose? Which reward do you want?

# 4.0

A portion of the next two miles will be dedicated to the proof of my assertion that death to self leads to life. I'd ask that those of you who are questioning the concept give me some time to explain in greater detail. Possibly you can do what I sometimes do with the "running" counsel I receive—doubt it a bit but try it out to see if it might be true.

In the meantime, let me say this: Over the course of my life, I have had the great privilege of working with or for my older brother. This first occurred when we were young and reoccurred during the last eighteen years.

Many could not stand to be in such a position. Brothers fight, right? Well, not this set of brothers. The key is in him. It is not in me. It is because he is humble of heart. He seeks to establish what benefits others. If an error is made, he does the opposite of what most of us do.

He doesn't find the culprit or scold the one who is to blame. He takes the blame on himself, sometimes very creatively so, even when it is obvious that I was the one who messed up. At the odd time when there is simply no way he can shield the blame or bounce it to himself, he simply says "No worries, we'll figure it out." And then he'll find a reason to boost my ego back up.

What is this example? It is others-centered. It is the opposite of self-serving. And what has the result been? For this, and other many reasons, he is quite successful. He is viewed with respect by his peers. But his success reaches deeper than monetary accomplishments. It is displayed in the depth of loyalty from his staff. He cares about them and they know it. He builds pathways for them to succeed. He does not walk on them so *he* can succeed . . . as is so often seen in our ME-centered world today.

My brother has learned the lesson that is key for leaders: *Leadership is a place from which to serve; it is not a place from which to rule.* This is true for business leaders and CEOs, for presidents, kings, and pastors or elders of churches. It is also true for parents. These whom I'm leading are not my underlings. They are human beings and my equals. I am not here to get them to do what I say. I am here to help them succeed. Service, not rulership. Such leaders have followers who love them rather than fear and/or hate them. This "service" mentality is the key. And while serving can be "painful" at times, there is no greater reward.

The greatest leader of all time, Jesus, said, "I came to serve, not to be served, and to give my life as a ransom."

I think that many of those ultra-successful, corporate ladder-climbing people are the saddest and loneliest people in the world, up on their mountain of success. Not long ago, one of those billionaires committed suicide in his jail cell after being accused of preying sexually on young children. Ugh. What a miserable life for a self-absorbed and sick person. What a waste of time on this earth. One can only imagine the depth of pain such people must be in.

And so, I say, death to self and our selfish ways may be difficult. It may not come naturally to us at all. It may be painful in very practical ways. But it leads to an abundant life and it avoids the depths of pain that come when ME is all I really care about.

So which pain do you choose?

*"At the time, all discipline seems a cause not for joy but for pain, yet later it brings the peaceful fruit of righteousness to those who are trained by it."*

## MILE 5

# Consistent Training and the Heart

Athletes, perhaps more than people in any other walk of life, are often asked about heart. Do they have what it takes to battle through all the challenges facing them? Do they have the heart to put in the time and effort to accomplish great things?

I imagine most people have heard of Michael Jordan, the best basketball player the world has ever seen. Many of us who watched him play in his heyday would say that what made him the greatest was his heart. He exhibited unbelievable drive to be the best. Many people have had similarly amazing athletic ability, but few had that little bit extra, the warrior heart.

Possibly the most famous example of Jordan's heart was game 5 of the 1997 NBA championship series when he scored 38 points, leading his team to a tense 90-88 victory in the pivotal game of the series. I still have the image in my mind of how he hung onto his teammate, Scottie Pippen, who practically carried him off the court at the conclusion of the game. Michael was the picture of utter exhaustion. The performance was astounding because he had the flu! Most of us won't get out of bed when we have the flu. But Jordan simply refused to miss this important game.

So what is the heart? The simplest way for me to describe it is to say it is a combination of the mind, the will, and the emotions. The heart, in a way, is that which binds these three together. Some may refer to it as your innermost being. It is what makes you, you.

Some days my emotions say they don't want to get out of bed. It is cold out, the covers are warm, my wife is beside me, and I'm still tired. But my mind says that the bills won't get paid if I am not a dependable employee. My will takes a cue from my mind; it informs the emotions that we aren't listening to them right now; and the mind directs my hand to pull the covers back, then directs my feet to swing out and onto the floor.

On another day, I might notice that my wife has a need of some kind. My emotions engage without my bidding and they begin to instruct me on what is needed and what to do. My mind might bring up everything I was supposed to get done that day, but one look at my wife causes my emotions to tell my mind to shut up and go help my wife because nothing else matters right now.

I'm sure you get the picture without more examples. The point is that the heart is a combination of the things that direct the course of our decision-making and our lives. The emotions being in complete control is a problem waiting to happen. Emotions are up and they are down (see mile 21). But neither do we want the mind totally in control, with our emotions shut down as we become intellectuals only and stoic regarding the happenings of the world. No, we need each part of our makeup connected and directed with purpose.

Similarly, for any true commitment to running long distances, the heart must be involved. On any given day, the mind or the emotions may attempt to direct the will away from the task of training. But what causes things to be accomplished if the emotions, some days, seem stronger than normal? It is vision, which has been burned into the heart, causing us to overcome every challenge, pressing toward the high goal.

My "vision" early on was only to get off the couch and get in better shape. Calling it vision at that stage is not even accurate. It was more of a decision based on a realization that age was catching up to me and my mid-section was growing. Then I had a whimsical curiosity about whether I could train my body to run a half marathon. Sometime later, I looked at the full marathon distance as an amazing challenge and wondered if I could, at the grand old age of 53, actually accomplish a thing I'd only gazed at in wonder during the Olympics. It took my mind by storm. But even at that stage, I had no vision of the *why* of it all. I just liked the thought of the challenge.

It was not until the evening before my first marathon that vision set in. But because that part of the story is personal and pertains to my family, I will not share it in detail here. I will only say that something grabbed ahold of my heart at that time—a vision—and a purpose beyond merely running 26.2 miles just to say I could do it. I decided to do three marathons, each with a specific purpose.

And then something unexpected happened. I began writing. In the beginning, I was writing to or for my family. But with my wife's encouragement that the words I was writing might be an encouragement to others, my vision expanded to running . . . and applying lessons learned from running to life. Then this book began to take shape in my mind, with four separate sections concerning four separate themes of life.

And so, the possibility of completing a fourth marathon appeared on the horizon in my vision; possibly a capstone attempt to run the New York City Marathon in 2020. At times over the years, I have become a bit tired of running. But vision pushes me on. My heart says it will comply. The training must proceed.

## 4.2

If you set out to run 26.2 miles, simply having the "heart" to do it or the "vision" to do it is not enough. Not by a long shot. At least for me, with five decades of life behind me and no running background whatsoever . . . for this *"old man running"* there is no way in the world I'd accomplish the feat simply with heart or desire alone. Consistent training would be paramount. It would be mandatory.

Five weeks after my third marathon (see mile 21), I went out for an "easy" 5-mile weekend run. Let me set the stage for you.

After the marathon, my wife and I had enjoyed a week of relaxation in Washington. We ate out when we wanted. We lounged most days while looking at the ocean. We totally chilled out.

I took the week off from running as a reward for completing another marathon, and purposed to focus time on my wife, who sacrificed regularly to accommodate my long weekend runs.

After the relaxing week in the mountains, we landed back home in Oklahoma, and an annoying cough set in that soon turned into a three-day fever. The cough hung on for four weeks. I didn't feel great for running, and I was a tad burned out after the last 6-7 months of dedicated training as I had prepared for the marathon.

So on the morning of this particular five-mile run, I'd taken the previous month off from running. The morning was a good, cool morning for a 5-mile jog, but I soon discovered that my level of conditioning had waned greatly. By my turnaround point at 2.5 miles, my emotions said it was time to stop running. My mind and will chimed in, telling me to ignore my emotions. I recalled just how recently it had been that I was doing long training runs of 18, 19, 20 miles and that the in-between weeks of running 12 miles were referred to as being "only" 12 miles. I recalled how great it felt to run 12 miles after having run 20 the week before. Twelve was easy!

But today, just 5 weeks after from my third marathon, I was struggling after 2.5 miles. Wow! I did complete the task of running the entire 5 miles that day because I'm used to encountering this issue after years of running and occasions of taking a few weeks off or of slowing down for a few weeks. The truth is that the body trains up to amazing capacities with consistent training and then the body trains back down to somewhere near your old conditioning level if you go "cold turkey" into no training for a few weeks. Still, it is amazing to me how fast you can lose it.

So while there is no doubt that running a marathon requires vision and heart, there is an equally important requirement of consistent training if we want lofty goals to become reality.

Put another way, consistent training is the practical application that makes one able to accomplish the ambitions of the heart. Train, train, train, day after day after monotonous/glorious day.

And of course, consistent training born out of visions of the heart is the same principle at work if we want to accomplish other lofty goals.

# 4.3

In October 1985, our first daughter was born. I will call her Denee. With her dark hair and beautiful dark eyes, she is determined and loyal. She didn't need help tying her shoes at a young age because "Daddy, I can do it myself." She mirrors the beauty and many of the attributes that I love in her mother. She will always be my girl. She is the delight of my life.

In October 1986, our second daughter was born. I will call her Lynn. She has blond hair and beautiful blue eyes, and her happy smile brightens my day. She is by nature a peacemaker. Unexpected and hilarious things come out of her mouth. She is the definition of sweetness, gentleness, and genuine kindness. She is my blond-haired, blue-eyed, smiling girl. She is the delight of my life.

In October 1989, (what was going on in January?) our "baby" daughter was born. I will call her Camille. With sandy brown hair and beautiful blue eyes, she is sensitive and intuitive. She thinks deeply and enjoys real conversation about important things. I still remember her as a small child scrambling up into our bed early in the mornings. I recall the feel of her tiny hands on my face as she lay beside me. She is the delight of my life.

These three are the joy, the blessing, and the driving purpose of life for my wife and me, guiding them, supporting them, loving them, and watching them become who they were meant to be. The moment I laid eyes on them, my heart was captured and connected to them. And a vision was dropped into my heart for their futures, even more—for their eternities. Vision, love, dedication, what more could be needed? The answer: Consistent training, which would quite often call for the death of my own selfish desires.

If ever there is a place that vision is needed, it is in the arena of raising children. I fear that great losses have occurred in this area and I wish to address it in this and the next mile.

# 4.5

Call me crazy, but this dad believes that a dad and a mom are *the* anointed instruments of God to love and direct their children. It is not the job of their friends (although surely a 15- year-old friend with such enormous life experience has more wisdom than a person's parents in navigating the emotional minefield of life. Yes, this is heavy sarcasm).

It is not the job of teachers. It is not the task of "a village" although I know, at times, kids do need rescuing from awful parenting situations. And it is not the job of pastors, priests, youth leaders, or counselors .. .although I know these too are often called upon to help the desperate children of today.

But I declare, if things are functioning in the order that God intended, it is the job of parents to love and direct their children's lives into becoming all that God means for them to be.

As I looked at my girls, it was as if a burning coal of purpose had been deposited into my heart for them. Although it may sound kooky to some, I believe my wife and I had received "revelation" in this area from a wise older gentleman about the relationship that could exist between parents and their children. It changed my life and set my heart on fire with vision.

Did I do things perfectly? Oh boy, no. How I wish I could go back for a redo on some things. But I think I can safely say that there has never been a day that my three lovely ladies didn't love their mom and dad and want to be around us. It is a blessing that is worth every moment of sacrifice and every bit of effort expended. How can it become a reality for others? Read on to get one big key.

# 4.6

I am a St. Louis Cardinals baseball fan. I have been a fan ever since I was a little boy and my dad took my brother and me to Busch Stadium. One day many years ago, I was sitting at home reading an article from the *Sports Illustrated* magazine that I received each week.

Although I was armed with the burning desire to have a loving relationship with my children, and although I tried hard to foster that relationship with regular attention to my girls, on this day, as I was reading my sports article, my darling Denee came walking up to me and said to me quite innocently and without forcefulness or anger, "Daddy, you're always reading the sports magazine." *Boom!* She was about 7 years old at the time, but her words packed the wallop of a heavyweight champion.

Let me point this out: I believe it is absolutely fine for a man to have interests other than his family . . . interests, but not idols that he cannot seem to get through the day without. As a dad, I can enjoy a ball game, but I cannot eat, drink, and sleep Cardinals baseball, or my family will suffer. Here, the key word from my daughter was *always* which, although exaggerated, was indicative of how often she viewed my free time being spent with the sports magazine instead of her.

But what came out of my daughter's mouth that day showed me that I had a blind spot and that my blind spot was causing me to fail in meeting my daughter's needs. I looked at the value of my devotion to sports and how much my time with it added real value to life. I compared that to the value of my daughters and how much my time with them added value to my life, to theirs, and to the world as a result. I guess you could say that I felt "conviction" that it was time to release my Sports Illustrated subscription so that this devotion to sports could diminish, allowing my devotion to my girls to increase. Practical decisions.

I came to realize that building a loving relationship with a child that will stand the test of time is a function that requires daily consistent training of myself, of controlling my selfish desires so that I can impart into these impressionable young lives the things that will mold them into people who are not just obedient but are also loving, caring, responsible, honest, hard- working, creative, genuine . . . you get the idea—everything most of us want to see in our children. It takes work every day to give my time to them when, many times, I want to rest and/or keep my time to myself. Denying my selfish desires is a function of turning my heart to my children. It is not a sprint. It is a marathon, a long-distance run. And *thinking about doing it* is not doing it. *Doing it* is doing it.

If you, like me, can look back and say "Boy, I blew this aspect . . . or that aspect," now is the time to start curing that, at least as much as your child is interested in allowing you to do so at this point. In other words, if a person starts with this as a foundation when the child is an infant, the connection is easy, and the connection grows ever stronger. If a person takes on this understanding when the child is older, especially if he or she is approaching age 10, 11, 12, one can endeavor to repent of old selfish behaviors and, going forward, determine to make himself available. But at that point it would likely be unwise to force the relationship. Still, the power of loving attention may yet win the day and the bond may become much stronger than it has been before.

I believe children are born with an innate devotion to mom and dad. They crave their attention, their adulation, their approval.

It seems that this phenomenon continues no matter how old we are. My wife still finds a degree of comfort and security when her dad is around, especially if life is a bit challenging. It is not a threat to me. Her devotion to her dad doesn't subtract from her devotion to me. It only makes her stronger as a person to have two such men in her life, who can always be counted upon. So her heart can be given to me and still be turned to her dad.

How tragic it is when this is not the case. When a child is raised in a home where they seek the attention and praise of their father and instead find selfishness, disinterest, criticism, and hatefulness, the result is often deep feelings of rejection, which lead to great insecurity, low self-esteem, and all manner of self-destructive behavior.

Therefore, building a deep and loving relationship with one's children is a most important building block for the family unit, and thus one of the most important (drastically absent) building blocks of society. Building this relationship begins with turning the hearts of the fathers *to* their children and *away* from their very natural selfish desires.

Pay me now or pay me later.

## 4.7

A dad goes to work and comes home to his family. He then has a choice of self-focus or family focus. His emotions may say he needs some down time, some "me" time, some rest time. His mind might say he's done his fair share for the family today because, after all, the emotions and mind are typically self-driven, self-preserving, and "me" centric.

But when that same heart is on fire with vision for a different result, then a dad can use his will and reject the tendency of the selfish thoughts and emotions. Thus, a short-term bit of "the pain of selfless-ness" for a dad can yield an abundant crop of blessing ahead, children whose hearts are wholly devoted and dedicated in love to their parents.

The choices are so practical, so simple. Do I sit on the couch and watch television each night? Do I play video games and attend to hours of online entertainment at night (while the kids tend to themselves)? Do I commit to constant phone interactions, texting with count-less "friends" or group chats? Do I stroll through hours of mindless Facebook postings, while the kids say "Dad, Dad, Dad, look at this" with nothing more than a mumble in response?

Or do I plop my tired behind on the floor most nights, interacting on a toddler's level?

Am I up for playing make-believe with dolls or building Lincoln-log cabins and army men wars? Or how about playing "Ring Around the Rosy" 17 times straight just to see how many times those little faces will squeal with joy and say, "Do it again." So practical. And when your heart is given to them—*so fun!*

It is a thousand nights of interaction at their level, building rela-tionships and listening to them talk. It is playing a game at the speed of sludge because in between each move they want to talk about 15 things other than the game. Tip: Game playing is not to win or lose or to say that you dutifully spent time with them. No. It is *to be.* Simply to be with them and listen to the amazing things coming out of their mouths as those creative minds form and explore. And in so doing, you earn the right to direct the exploration of their minds toward uplifting things and away from death and destruction.

Being with them is countless evenings playing games in the yard, pushing them in wagons, catching fireflies. It is making mud pies on a rainy Saturday afternoon. It is building snowmen in the freezing cold. It is defending the charge of Santa Anna against your make-believe Alamo.

It is devoting a family day just to the family and not allowing the surrounding distractions to interfere. It is daddy/daughter date nights as they grow, allowing them to choose where to eat, listening to them chatter gaily about whatever floats through their minds. (So enjoyable!)

It is refusing the constant bombardment of things that could tempt you away from those nightly moments: the softball league, the night out with the guys, or the late nights at work so you can convince your boss that you deserve more authority, more responsibility, more pay.

(The offerings for pleasure and power will come without fail. And if you choose them often, it is you who will fail where it matters most.)

It is tucking them in at night with a song and a prayer. It is running your fingers gently through their hair as they chatter on about their day and you hear them gradually grow quiet as eyes finally droop closed.

And in your weariness, you thank God for this beautiful treasure who screams "Daddy's home" when you walk through the door, one who loves you with the purist devotion. *Oh, God, how can I be so blessed? This sweet child has overtaken my heart.*

*Time* is the greatest commodity and gift that can be given. Children don't want our money. They don't want things, not really, even though they may scream for them. What they really want, what they crave, is you.

And before you know it—in a flash, in a moment of time, the years have passed. Along the way you discover that time with them is no longer a sacrifice of playing with dolls. It is a joy to be with them and it increases with each year your heart is turned toward them as their hearts stay turned toward you, even as they encounter times of life that bring strain and emotions.

Amazingly, *you* become their fortress and the rock on which they depend. It is *you* because their hearts are knit together with yours.

Obviously, a tortured day is coming when a dad must release those hearts to explore new things. But that will only come after they have come to an age where they can face those things and succeed. And even though you will free them, the most amazing thing occurs: They still (as my wife does with her father) find security in your presence and in your guiding words. Because their hearts—once secured—will never leave you . . . even when their hearts become wholly devoted to a new love of their life, in marriage.

## 4.8

If time is the *commodity* that must be provided, then gentleness, tenderness, and kindness describe the manner in which time is spent. Time with a grouch is no fun at all. Time with the stressed, and those who are griping about their day and their boss, does not lend itself to joyful gatherings. Time spent with harsh words being poured out, or hard looks, or stern tones, is time that tears down what you are otherwise trying to build. The manner of a dad must be gentle. It must speak peace during turmoil. And even when correction of an action is needed, the manner must always be gentle or the correction is harmful rather than constructive.

I doubt anyone has lived without witnessing the screeching of frustrated adults as their kids do something unacceptable. I cringe when I hear adults shame their children, screaming about their bad behavior, and in public, no less! Is it any wonder that those children grow up hating or distrusting their parents?

No, correcting the behavior of a child must be done privately or it is abusive to the tender heart of a child. The enforcement of any boundary must be done from love and gentleness, even when firmness is required. Because in every situation I am after my child's heart, and a heart is not won with anger or humiliation. It is won with love.

Therefore, all of this that I've described must be built upon the foundation of relationship. *It is all about relationship. It is not about rules.* Relationship gives life. Rules lead to death. Even boundaries, when combined with a loving relationship, yield an abundant fruit that is about the best-tasting thing a parent can ever hope for. You just might hear your child say one day, "My dad is my hero." And after you catch your breath, with tears in your eyes, you will whisper to God, "Thank You for this divine revelation: that our Father *is* love, and what He imparts to His children is not rules—it is relationship that has been built upon sacrificial love.

# 5.0

Once I had three consecutive 5-mile runs that were miserable. The reason was clear.

My training had been almost nonexistent during the weeks leading up to them. My nutrition had not been good, and my hydration had been low (things I'll focus on in coming miles). And the result was misery.

I think many parents wonder why raising children seems so hard. Here is a big part of the answer. While you may devote a bit of time to them here and there, you are not meeting their emotional (relational) needs because most of your focus is still on yourself. It is similar to training for a marathon one day a week and expecting a good result. It won't happen. Many may think they are spending quality time with their kids, when they really aren't, at least not enough to meet the needs of a given child.

Doing it for a day or a week or a month is not enough. Doing yard work together may be nice and may teach them the lessons of hard work, but even that is not the quality time I'm driving at. Watching TV or a ballgame together is not it. Instead, it is being with them when nothing else is distracting you from talking, playing, and interacting with them on a very personal level. And doing that day after day, for weeks, months, years. *That* is what builds a quality loving relationship that will withstand the storms of life.

My wife and I did some of this well while raising our girls. Still, I wish I could do it over again and get it better. I see it so clearly now. And I call out to you who are reading . . . fathers, turn your hearts to your children. There might be some momentary pain as you learn to deny yourself and serve your children. But the reward! The glorious reward! You might gain your child's heart and undying devotion, and you will see them walk in truth as strong and secure adults in a precarious world. There is no greater joy than this. The question is, *Will you do it?*

I wonder what moms add to this selfless daily cause. Read on.

*"I run in the path of your commands, for*
*you have set my heart free."*

## MILE 6

# *Core Strength*

(This mile is dedicated to the women in
my life, ladies of strength, all.)

*"A house divided against itself cannot stand. I believe this government*
*cannot endure, permanently half slave and half free. I do not expect the*
*Union to be dissolved—I do not expect the house to fall—but I do expect*
*it will cease to be divided. It will become all one thing, or all the other.*
*Either the opponents of slavery will arrest the further spread of it . . . or*
*its advocates will push it forward, till it shall become alike lawful in all*
*the states, old as well as new—North as well as South."*

On June 16, 1858, a candidate by the name of Abraham Lincoln
spoke these words as he accepted the Republican nomination
to run against incumbent Stephen A. Douglas for the U.S. Senate and
delivered his famous "House Divided Speech" in the Illinois state
house. With that speech, the Lincoln-Douglas debates commenced.

In November, Lincoln lost that senate race to Douglas, but he
later wrote: *"I am glad that I made the last race. It gave me a hearing*

*on the great and durable question of the age, which I could have had in no other way; and though I now sink out of view, and shall be forgotten, I believe I have made some marks which will tell for the cause of liberty long after I am gone."*

Of course, Lincoln did not take that defeat and "sink out of view" but instead he allowed the temporary defeat to push him forward, not down, soon becoming a candidate for the Presidency of the United States; a position to which he would be inaugurated in 1861. He will forever be known as the 16th President of this great nation and a champion of freedom. For barely a year after his inauguration, one of the darkest and yet most important periods of our nation's history began, as Americans began to fire upon one another over the right to make their own decisions, including the right to own slaves; over the cause of human freedom, and over the issues at the very heart of Lincoln's speeches on "the great and durable question of the age."

What causes some men and women to crumble at adversity and defeat, but others use those same circumstances as fuel to drive them toward even greater goals? What made that famous man able to resist political foes, weather resounding defeats on the battlefield, endure impertinence from the very generals he was trusting to prosecute a civil war, and yet push on through every obstacle?

Present in individuals such as this is surely deep conviction and strength of character such that almost nothing can change their course, once assured of what is right . . . and what is not right, no matter what other voices or equally determined forces say in opposition and, importantly, no matter what personal cost that position may require. It is core strength, defined as that which is underlying, fundamental, essential.

Some leaders, some politicians (although seemingly fewer these days), some moms and dads, and some of you reading these words have core strength like that of President Lincoln.

Although you may never run for public office or run a business or lead a movement, you still provide those around you with rock solid steadiness through every storm of life. Even as you read these words, a special person in your life may come to mind, one who has endured almost more than you can imagine, and yet continues on.

They are people who hear dreaded words from a doctor and instead of collapsing in despair, they provide words of comfort to their family; people who endure tragic loss with incomprehensible grace; people with something in the core of their being that refuses to quit when all odds are against them. If you have anyone such as this in your life, you are blessed indeed.

I have benefited greatly from several key women with the same kind of tenacious excellent character, women who shaped and still affect my life, women who exhibit core strength when it matters most. They are: one mother, one wife, one mother-in-law, and three daughters.

Six great ladies I am blessed to have as part of the core strength of my life.

## 5.2

Schlump, schlump, schlump. It is the sound of my feet on the underwater treadmill as I "run" at a speed so slow it likely could not be quantified. The effort for my legs is normal but the result is not. Schlump, schlump. I glance at the camera showing my legs pumping up and down. It is an odd sight to behold. I've never seen my legs as they run.

And the running motion is not quite normal. My legs splay out a bit as though they are octopus tentacles reaching out in one direction and curling down in another. Or maybe that is just a trick played by the underwater camera.

The aquatic rehab pool had not been in the training plan for my first assault on marathon distance. And yet, here I was. Tromping, sloshing, pushing my legs forward against the water's resistance.

The knee issues that arose with the running of my second half marathon had occurred in late November of 2017. After allowing a month for healing from my iliotibial (IT) injury, (a repetitive friction injury of the IT band rubbing against the leg bone, often caused by running in the wrong kind of shoes or by weak surrounding muscles) I seemed to be walking normally again. The idea for running a marathon formed in my mind and the plans began to be laid to give it a shot in Oklahoma City in late April of 2018. I felt fine. My knee felt good. And so, with an industry leading "Hal Higdon novice 1 marathon training plan" laid out, with daily runs detailed on monthly calendars, I began.

The miles grew. I was sore but excited. Soreness, I was told, was to be expected. I had strategy built into my long weekend runs and I was hitting my goals! Saturday after Saturday, the miles increased, and I was happy to come trudging painfully in. I completed an 18-mile trek one Saturday and hobbled into my designated finish line, which is the office where I work. It was my longest run to date. Thinking back to my couch potato days, I couldn't believe I had actually just kept my legs pumping—without stopping except to refill the bottles on my water belt—for well over three hours. It was simply amazing.

I remember seeing a cleaning crew in the office after completing my run. I must have looked like a haggard old fool. I could barely walk up the stairs to my desk to rest. I commented to them that I was preparing for a marathon, hoping that would explain my appearance, or maybe pridefully hoping they'd be impressed. I think they probably raised an unimpressed eyebrow and mumbled "oh" in a manner that conveyed the thought . . . "You not too bright, old man." (I apply my Chinese accent to their thoughts.)

As hard as these runs were, I was surprised that my body was adjusting, or seemed to be doing do so. Eighteen miles! Wow!

And then it happened. The normal soreness of legs and knees gave way to an abiding pain in my right knee. It was almost uncanny how it "normally" went. Saturday long run—hobble in with very sore legs. Sunday morning—can hardly get out of bed or walk. Monday at work—walk up and down the stairs at the office by putting one foot down one step, then the next foot down to the same step, slowly, gingerly, gaining support from the handrail . . . co-workers looking on with a mix of concern and amusement.

And then by about Tuesday, the soreness began to wear away, my gait got closer to normal, and my sore legs began to adjust and recover as they prepared for shorter midweek runs and the next Saturday's assault of even greater distances.

Until eighteen miles. After that run, the pain in the side of my right knee didn't go away. It increased. I began to get mildly concerned. After talking to my running mentor, I went to see a local nurse practitioner, described the issues, and was diagnosed with iliotibial band syndrome. He prescribed what runners refer to as Mobic, an anti-inflammatory that is supposed to do wonders for this issue. But it didn't work any wonders for me.

I had rested from one long run at the NP's request. But I was impatient. I had goals set, man! I had to reach them. I went out for a Saturday run of twelve miles and wham! By around mile 6 the pain hit. Big pain! By mile 8, I was barely doing what anyone would call a jog. It was hardly a forward shuffle. By mile 9, despair set in. I knew I couldn't do it . . . but I had to, so I kept going. By mile 10, I stopped. I began walking toward my car. I was finished. The thought of not getting to my first marathon began to creep into my mind. *Old man, what did you expect? It was stupid to think you could.*

At this point I became somewhat desperate and tried anything and everything to overcome the pain, which soon became bilateral knee pain because I was obviously putting too much reliance on the good knee as I was favoring the bad knee.

I tried every kind of supportive tape and knee brace on the market. I watched videos. I read all the information I could find. The problem was that rest was needed and I didn't have time to rest.

With each new plan and each new attempt, failure came. I could get my short weekday runs in without too much problem. But by the time I hit 5, 6, 7 miles, the pain became too great.

And so it was that I discovered a local gym that had an aquatic rehab pool. As I explained my problem to the guy behind the desk, a big smile spread across his face. "I have just what you need. My rehab pool is what Adrian Peterson (famous running back from the Oklahoma University Sooners and Minnesota Vikings, at the time) used to rehab his knee."

I guess it helped. I could only use it for 30 minutes at a time (a short run, for sure) and my knee didn't hurt at all on that underwater treadmill. But the marathon was just a few weeks away now and I still couldn't gain the strength to successfully accomplish those long training runs that were by now supposed to be hitting a peak of 20 miles.

With each new run attempted, I had another failure to add to my psyche. "I can't do it; I can't use my will to overcome this pain," was my testimony following my long run attempts. But with each new Monday morning, I came up with another idea to try . . . an idea that would fail, fail, fail.

And just as I had about given up, I attempted one last long run, a run of 15 miles. To be sure, I had not finished the Higdon program. I never reached 20 miles, never climbed to 19. But I thought if I could just get 15 miles in, maybe I could summon the adrenaline to do the full marathon when that April morning came.

Out of the blue a good doctor friend called me and said he'd been thinking about my dilemma. He offered to prescribe me a topical gel and a steroid pill that just might give me enough relief to get through the race. I imagine I would be banished from the National Football League for taking it, but I wasn't competing against anyone but myself . . . not really.

By this time, I had little hope of anything working, but I seized on that lifeline and tried it. Amazingly, the pain subsided. I was now just days away. I went out for a very short run and felt great. Great! I didn't attempt any long miles. I decided to save it for the race and test it there. So my wife and I went to Oklahoma City, checked into the race area hotel, and prepared. And race my first marathon, I did, the story of which will be told in the next mile.

After it was all said and done, accomplished, and overcome; after the medal had gone around my neck and the "finisher" shirt provided, I sat back and reflected on the problems.

I learned things I'd never considered before: that to take on a goal such as running a marathon, more than just lung, heart, and leg conditioning is needed if you want to do it successfully and have a better chance of being injury-free . . . especially if you're an *old man running* it for the first time. I learned that my core needed to be strengthened, that there are exercises that do just that, that a totally new area of commitment was required, and that, just as in life, so it is in running . . . if great challenges are ahead, you must have a solid core as part of the foundation for the long and arduous journey. You must have a degree of core strength if you're going to be an old man running 26.2 miles . . .

. . . or a person starting a new business or career,

. . . or hearing a cancer diagnosis or facing a tragic loss,

. . . or starting a family and raising children in these days,

. . . or, oddly enough, being a woman who has chosen to be a "stay-at-home mom" rather than entering or reentering the workforce after bringing new life into this world.

And here is where the path of mile 6 is leading. For a change has occurred in this nation since the days that my mother raised me. And there is a rising tide such that if you make this choice to be at home each hour of each day raising those gifts that God has given you, then you must have strength of conviction, strength of character. You mut have *core strength* to stand and face the criticism and the wave of a rising tide that says blatantly (or through disdainful or sorrowful looks from others), that you are less intelligent, less ambitious, and less of a woman for so choosing; that says freedom is outside your home; that says value is found in your peers; that says only when you "discover yourself" can you really be a good mother.

Oh yes, you must have amazing core strength to take on everything that will face you in the high calling of being a wife and stay-at-home mom in this age. You'd better start working out those internal abs right now.

# 5.4

I feel it is necessary to add two points of clarification.

First, what I am about to portray is how six women have impacted the world around them and my life. In so doing, it may seem that I am simultaneously judging strong women who have done things differently from the women with whom I've been surrounded. That is *not* my intention. I've had the benefit of working around hundreds of female professionals in my life and I work with several excellent ladies now. These are professional women in the workplace who also care deeply for their children and serve those children each day. I've been impressed by the tenacity and drive some of these ladies have exhibited in accomplishing big goals, doing excellent work, and still maintaining a loving relationship with their cherished children. I am not here desiring or intending to criticize or judge any of them. Instead, I intend to explain what "my" ladies have done and what they have accomplished with their lives. They are my focus, not others.

Second, in the age in which I write these words, our nation has become a hotbed of hostility among people of differing opinions. Our legislative process seems poisoned by the inability to listen to any thought other than one's own thought. It is regrettable.

I respectfully ask that anyone who doesn't agree with what I'm saying to simply consider it as an opinion that is different from theirs and not take offense by it. And if you are feeling really generous, possibly calm yourself and actually give consideration to a different point of view, to see if there could be anything of value to glean from a thought that isn't directly in line with your own worldview.

And with that, I will proceed . . . and will tread as carefully as I can where angels to tread.

I believe that men and women are equal but very different. Are we okay so far?

I think the thing inside most little girls that makes them love to mother their dolls is different from the thing inside most little boys that makes them want to pull the doll's head off and see how the stuffing inside fills out the legs, the stomach, and the arms. It is why boys love driving any toy in the yard through a mud puddle while girls intelligently walk around those same puddles.

I know this is a generalization. But my life experience has shown me that it is true the great majority of the time.

I also think these differences are shown in how parents interact with their children, as mothers are most often the ones with an innate nurturing instinct.

## 5.5

Vivid memories. Lying in my bed at night before central air was a modern convenience for every home, a fan stuck in my window blowing the muggy summer air through my room, possibly cooling it down a degree or two. My mother is sitting on my bedside, running her fingers through my hair. This didn't happen every night. It only happened when I called to her. Most nights I think I went to bed and easily went to sleep. But on the occasional night that something wasn't quite right inside my little soul, one call to my mother changed the night. She would come without complaint and comfort would fill the room. Maybe a soft word or two would be spoken. What I primarily recall is her fingers brushing soothingly, slowly, through my hair. In minutes, I was adrift into peaceful sleep.

Having gone through the challenges of parenthood and providing for the daily needs of the home, I now know what I didn't know then, that she may actually have had something else to do when I called. I didn't even consider it then. She never made mention of being busy or of finally getting a moment to rest. She was simply available, bringing comfort and peace.

I now watch my own girls come to an exhausted end of a day and I see how parents almost seem to live for that one hour of solitude, of quiet conversation between husband and wife. It is a moment to recharge the battery. Surely my mom needed that too. Surely my brother and I weren't so perfect that she would glide through the day without a care or effort expended. No, each day was full of work for her, tending to the needs of her family. And yet, she did not once bring to my consciousness that anything was more important to her than my momentary nighttime need.

(With that impartation, I developed my own love of the precious moments lying in bed beside my three daughters, talking quietly about the day or about the plans for the next, or running my fingers through their hair.)

My mother was there. That is the memory. During my school years, she occasionally took a daytime job to help with the finances. But when I was home, she was home. Supper was always on the table through her diligence. Clothes were always clean when they were needed.

A healthy breakfast always started the day, and my lunch was always packed (I never ate cafeteria food. That would not have been healthy enough for my mother's sons). She was there. She was present. She daily planted her values into my life.

I did nothing to earn this care. I was not special, although she made me feel as if I was. I know many others of my schoolmates had nothing nearly as wonderful as this. My father provided safety and strength. My mother provided comfort and a gentle touch. Both possessed an abundance of wisdom. I will forever be thankful for the blessing of my mother and the core strength she provided for my life.

# 5.6

Vivid memories: The beautiful girl who had changed my life and rocked my world was walking back and forth in the cool air, trying to get labor going. Hours later, hearing the determined strain of her voice as her eyes focused with fiercely determined intensity at a spot on the wall, as if, by the force of her will, she could bore a hole right through the painted hospital wall blocks. Soon, hearing her joyous and muted sobs as she held our first child, fresh from the womb. A determined face had so quickly turned into one with a heavenly glow, the glow of exultant motherhood.

For 25 glorious years the voices of our three daughters added life and pleasure to our home—25 light speed years.

While I used to say that my mother was the greatest woman I've ever known, now one has surpassed her. My wife has served me and our girls (and now our 3 sons-in-law and our 9 grandchildren) with unabashed pleasure.

Every smart man tells others how much smarter than himself his wife is. But my wife is a voracious learner. Where my enjoyment comes from relaxing with a good ballgame or a movie, she seems to prefer to read and learn something in her relaxation time. And the motivation for her learning is almost always in order to somehow serve her family.

This herb will heal this ailment; this exercise will aid pelvic floor health for young mothers; this way of planting your garden will yield a better crop; and don't even get her started on the art of having babies.

In her learning endeavors, she became a DONA (Doulas of North America) certified birth Doula. Helping young mamas have babies has become an empty nest passion. She still cries with each birth ... sometimes doing so when watching births on YouTube, while I'm plugging my ears to escape the sounds.

But she never gave a thought to working outside the home. Her work was her home and her daughters her mission ... schooling them through graduation and continuing to impart to them even today as they are raising their own. A sacrifice? Never. It was a calling to her, the highest calling there was. Those three girls were shot like arrows toward their own high callings.

I will be forever thankful for the core strength she provided not only to my own life but to the lives of the three gifts—three daughters— God gave us to guide and direct. When they need help with almost anything, she is their first call. "What would Mom do, what would Mom say, what would Mom think?"

Her children will rise up and bless her; her husband also, and he praises her saying, "*Many daughters have done nobly, but you have excelled them all*" (Proverbs 31:29). That is my wife and that is exactly what I believe.

## 5.7

My mother-in-law is a unique lady. And there is an aspect about her that provides strength to all those around. She prays, really prays. . Everyone has events that occur in this life where worry is a temptation.

An unexpected crisis hits. A physical ailment or possibly a threat to a long and healthy life occurs. An emotional event arises, a crossroads in life appears on the horizon. Or maybe a major decision must be made—should we buy this house, should we start this business?

One of the greatest strengths I've ever felt has come from the knowledge that in all of these things, my mother-in-law is praying. Not only that, but she has been praying well in advance and, at times, has had an uncanny knack of knowing things before anyone should have known. It is almost like she has an inside track to One who sees everything and knows everything before it happens. And I think she does.

Not everyone is like this; I think they may actually be few. But at times I come across people whose children or grandchildren are going through the crisis of a lifetime and I see that a praying mother or a praying grandmother is undergirding the entire event with a base of support that keeps the world from falling out from beneath the participants on the grand stage of life.

This is my mother-in-law . . . a loving and caring and wise soul. I will forever be thankful for the core of strength that she's added to our lives.

## 5.8

My three girls . . . how can I describe the beauty they have added to my world? Rather than embarrass them here by displaying a dad's love for his daughters, a love they are aware of already, I will stay on point.

These three have taken up the baton passed to them by their mother, by their grandmothers, and in some degree by me. Every day of every week of every month and every year, they pour themselves out for the benefit of their children. They are each smart and vibrant.

They could take the world by the horns and endeavor to make a name for themselves. They could act. They could run businesses. They could entertain and make people laugh. One could sing in front of thousands, I believe. They could do numerous things. Or . . . or they could be moms to their own precious gifts from God, daily dealing out to them justice, righteousness, and strength.

Oh sure, day care is available for all of them. But the thought is laughable. Why would they entrust their beloved children into the hands of someone who cannot possibly love them in the same way, cannot possibly care to direct them in the way they should go? No way!

So they will forego the strokes and fame of mankind or "success" as the world measures it. They will not attempt to make a name for themselves in the annals of history. They will not seek the "fulfillment" of accomplishment of rank or title or power. They won't strive to establish their own "identities" as something separate from their children. No indeed.

Here are the title and fame and identity they have chosen . . . wife, mother, and servant of the Lord.

They will choose to hear "Mom, hey Mom" a hundred times a day. They will choose to play make believe with their toddlers, to change thousands of diapers, to see first steps, to hear first words spoken, to laugh at amazing comments that erupt in the minds of those young miracles. Yes, this is the course they have chosen. And I praise them with the highest praise.

While the world ridicules them, looks down on them, shakes heads at them, says, "What do you do for a living? . . . oh, I could never do that," they will go right on, whether through difficulty one day or pure pleasure the next, they will go on and lead these impressionable minds and lives on a path that nobody in this world is better equipped than they to lead. Why? Because they are mothers; they are wives; they are women of God; in their heart of hearts, that is who they are. *That is their identity.*

I will forever be thankful for the core strength they provide for the lives of my grandchildren and the lives of their husbands . . . and, in these days, my wife and me as well. My beloved girls. There is joy unspeakable that is full of glory ahead for you. You are heroes.

# 6.0

This has been our way. It used to be the norm in our country. When I was being raised, women were usually workers at home, tending first and foremost to their families. Where it changed, I am not sure. Possibly due to the mistreatment and arrogance of men who took them for granted and caused them to feel like second-class citizens while the men were "important" decision-makers of the world. But whatever the cause, it has changed and now women who do not work outside the home are looked down upon as if something is wrong with them. We have felt it. But there is nothing wrong with my girls. There is something very right about what they are doing.

And let me tread more dangerously now, although I truly do not wish to offend anyone. I believe that what they are doing is the intention and plan of God for them.

Many years ago, one of those hard-working women with whom I worked had a daughter. She took a couple of months off work to recover and then one day she returned to work. She had goals that were quite high. She would reach those goals someday. And yet, on this first day back to work, I witnessed her in the back room, crying. I ventured back to see if she was okay.

She intimated that she would be. It was just hard to leave her daughter. Why is this?

I also worked with a lady who had a child later in life. She informed me she would *not* be returning to her job after having her baby. She and her husband decided they would raise their children rather than allowing a day-care or someone less devoted than the child's own parents to do a big part of the daily caring and imparting of values to their child. I was ecstatic for them. This was not a "Christian" decision for them. I don't believe that is a part of their lives. It was simply a choice of what would be best for their child.

Please give me the grace to tread, briefly, a bit more dangerously as I put forth some questions and thoughts that may seem out of touch these days.

Is it possible that there are unique paths that will set our hearts free while the world's usual paths will put our hearts and lives in chains, with those chains being disguised as the promise of freedom?

Is it possible that the core strength of the home has departed and is now in the working world and the children of this age are without a rudder, wandering aimlessly into fields of poison and death?

Is it possible that fathers and mothers no longer performing what they are called to do is part of the reason that the world is so full of anger, hatred, and malice; of shootings, bombings, and suicide? Is it possible that fathers being disconnected from the hearts of their children, and mothers not being the constantly available guiding hand for their children's hearts has yielded a generation in this country that is plummeting into despair? Is there any chance that going after the "redneck's guns" is not the answer, and that going more perfectly and diligently after the hearts of our own children is?

In everything there is balance. I know many ladies are working today and providing loving guidance for their children. I know that is true. My question, then, is whether it is the best for children even if it is attainable. And whether some discover that they simply cannot do it all and indeed something (or someone) must suffer because of the exhausting grind that has been undertaken by the great women of this age.

My wife will tell you that her mother is a go-to core of strength for her life. My daughters will undoubtedly say the same about their mother. It is a glorious reward for my wife; one of the best rewards there is. It is better than silver or gold or fame or position or anything this world may offer in exchange.

*"Your path sets my heart free . . ."*

And against every force of this age, on this path my six ladies have run, unto the glory of the One who made them.

*"Do you not know that in a race all the runners run, but only one gets the prize? Run in such a way as to get the prize."*

## MILE 7

# *"Finish the Darn Race"*

My first recollection of watching a marathon was during the Olympics in the 1970s and early eighties. The great sports announcer, Bob Costas, was just beginning his long tenure at the helm of NBC's coverage.

I remember watching Flo Jo (Florence Griffith Joyner) set world records in the 100-meter dash with flair, grace, and joy. I remember Sugar Ray Leonard's lightning-quick boxing speed as he dodged the death blows of a bigger and stronger opponent to win the gold medal.

The summer Olympics became an anticipated event for our family every four years, with its signature theme song reverberating in our house countless times each night over the course of two weeks.

There is a final, capstone, event to every summer Olympic Games. Here at the end of sixteen days of medals, tears, and national anthems was one more moment of desire over weakness, of triumph over pain—the running of the marathon, 26.2 nonstop miles of grit and determination.

Frank Shorter is the first marathoner I recall. I guess it was at the 1976 Olympics that his effort is burned into my memory. He had won the gold in the 1972 Games (Games I do not recall from my age of 8 years old) and he was expected to do so again in 1976. I recall an East German athlete shocking Shorter and the American viewers by taking the gold. There was Shorter, running the last miles with what appeared to be a strained gait. The announcers noted it as well. The East German had passed him and seemed to be running with perfect ease. (The winner's name was later associated with performance enhancing drugs. Possibly the true winner that day was Frank Shorter after all.) Regardless, the lasting image was of the East German runner keeping his pace and proper form all the way into the stadium and through the finish line while the second place America hero, Frank Shorter, exhibited broken form and great anguish as he willed himself across the finish line for the silver medal.

Personal interest stories seemed to be just breaking onto the scene in those days. I remember footage of Frank Shorter doing his training runs in the foothills of mountains, making it look like such a pleasure, just a jaunt in the hills. But a marathon is not just an easy jaunt. It is a race that challenges the mind, the will, and the body in ways you'd never imagine. It can bring you to great highs emotionally. It can cause equally intense discouragement.

A line from a favorite movie of mine comes to mind. *"If it wasn't hard, everyone would do it. It's the hard that makes it great."* At the time of my first marathon, I am here to tell you, it was hard. But it was also great. And it was unlike anything I'd done before or possibly will ever do again from the perspective of a bodily challenge. Twenty-six amazing . . . long . . . excruciating . . . yet somehow wonderful miles.

## **6.2**

Saturday, April 28, 2018. It is 5:00 a.m., about 25 hours before I will leave my room and take the short walk to the starting line of my first marathon. I should be sleeping now, collecting all the rest and energy I can possibly muster before the greatest test of physical endurance of my life will begin. In that odd state between sleep and consciousness, a thought hit my brain: *I'm going to dedicate this race to my kids and grandkids.*

Many times during my injury-plagued training, I'd asked myself why. And I hadn't really had an answer other than, "Because I started and must finish, that's why." My running mentor had made a comment about the race before I left for OKC. He said, "If you do decide to run it, finish the darn race!" This same mentality had hit me during training. I'd started so I needed to finish. But I'd never really had a good reason for the why of it all other than the enjoyment of a big challenge that most people don't attempt.

But all that changed, 25 hours before the race. I decided to leave a message to my kids and grandkids that life might be brutally hard at times, enough so that you feel like you can't go on. Don't quit. Finish your race. Inspiration hit me, and I got out of bed and composed a 7-page letter to all of them. Little did I know that years later the contents of that letter would form most of the basis for the "miles" of this book. The letter is personal and will not be shared with others, but a flavor of what was in it can be gleaned as a reader glances at the title of each mile.

I remember looking out over the dawning skyline of downtown Oklahoma City as I wrote. I saw runners begin to appear in the distance, doing their shake-out run, preparing for the morrow. Juices began to flow inside me, and I declared to myself that this was going to be great.

## 6.3

Sunday, April 29, 2018. I am up at 4:00 a.m. taking in my morning carbs and a bit of water, but not too much. All my garb had been carefully laid out the night before. Trying not to wake my wife, I begin the morning prep.

Within a couple of hours, I take the short walk to the starting gate. By myself for a block, I notice movement of other people in the grey dawn of the morning. A block or two later and I join an ever-increasing throng, with chatter all around. Nervous people, excited people, all ages, all shapes, all sizes. People with knee braces (I'm intimately aware of their pain), supportive tape, and running shoes of all colors and design. The morning is warm, a bit too warm for April 29 in Oklahoma. Bummer.

A young man is confused about where we should be. I add my two cents and that is about what my advice is worth. I too am trying to find my way. There are stalls beginning at each new block, separating the elite runners from the good runners, good runners from the average runners, and average runners from the slow runners who don't mind walking as much or more than they run. They just want to be here to participate, some to honor and remember those who lost their lives in that horrible bombing more than two decades ago. I considered myself to be somewhere between those last two groups, but my actual placement was in the third stall, the average group of runners, hoping to finish in 5 hours or less.

And then I am there. At the starting gate among 25,000 people, with that smile on my face. With an explosion, we are off, very slowly at first because it takes a moment for a throng of people to begin to move 50,000 arms and 50,000 legs and find enough space on the packed streets so that we don't become a 25,000-person pile-up.

My original goal had been to run a 5-hour marathon, or 11:27 per mile for 26.2 miles.

But really, after the training and injury issues, my true goal was simply to finish. Could I do it? Could this old man run a marathon?

I planned to start slow, but not too slow. I became concerned in the first half mile because there were so many people crammed together that my pace was slower than desired. I expended energy to zig and zag among the mass of humanity. My wife was positioned on our race path in front of our downtown hotel, at about 2 miles in. She'd be filming as I went by.

I saw her before she saw me. She was standing among 50 people, but I was running along with 25,000. I zagged again, working my way through the throng, weaving toward my lady.

"Lisa," I yelled, uncaring what my running mates thought. She didn't hear. Too much tromping, too much gabbing by the still excited and not yet tired enough runners. "Lisa!" I shouted again, as I drew closer. I gained her attention. She is the girl this boy is still trying to impress. I couldn't stop, of course. A high five as I passed, and we parted. I'd see her again at the finish line, I hoped, maybe 5 hours later.

Through the downtown miles of Oklahoma City we ran. The running crowd began to thin by miles four and five as some ran ahead and some fell behind. The euphoria of starting among them all began to fade as the miles gradually ticked by. My pace was right on schedule. I had no pain in my knee. No pain at all! After all those weeks of misery, this both astounded and excited me. I wondered if it could possibly last.

By miles 6 and 7, the euphoria had fully dissipated and the realization had set in that this was going to be work, lots of hard work.

I don't recall much of the next several miles. They went by and I managed them. I do remember the last mile or 2 of the first half of the race. As my energy began to wane, my will kicked in. I had stayed on track for my five-hour marathon up to now and by golly I was determined to get to the halfway mark in 2.5 hours. But a toll was requesting payment now, a toll of having not been able to complete my marathon training plan because of the injury, of having done no runs longer than fifteen miles over the last six or seven weeks. My will was paying the difference, while my body was beginning to go in the red.

If a half marathon in two and a half hours had been my ultimate goal, then I won. I made it! I willed myself to it, crossed the 13.1 mile timing mat, and immediately knew my mind was done paying the extra fees. It now obeyed the calls of my tiring body and I slowed appreciably. For the next two miles, I jogged on, no longer caring how fast I was running. Somewhere in these miles my right knee began to ache, but it was not bad at all, really. And in fact, it never did become a debilitating issue for the entire race.

By mile 15, I made a turnaround at a beautiful lake area and then found myself heading back toward the finish line *into* the wind. The wind. I'd heard about the wind that is often a factor in this late April Oklahoma race. And boy oh boy, was it today. The wind was blowing in the 20-25 mph range. Nice running out with it at your back; torture running into its teeth almost the entire way home.

During the last 11 miles home, my race became a walk/run race. Whatever my time was no longer mattered. Finishing mattered.

That was it. I walked probably a half mile or so into that fierce wind and watched as runners continuously ran past me. I cared little. My poor training now coming fully to bear, my tank was empty. Walk, jog, somehow slowly get there. It was when a fellow who looked to be about 80 years old came by me that some reserve of pride awoke and said "Say what? Are you gonna let that old dude run by you?"

So I groaned and obeyed my pride and began jogging again, slowly. But not for long. He stopped. I stopped. He started (groan), I started. Pride said, "You must keep up with this 80-year-old guy, you must!" I obeyed.

Somewhere in the next few miles, I summoned enormous unseen reserves of will and passed the old guy. He impressed me then and impresses me still. Age is a number. The will can move you on. Since that day, I've been passed many times by people I thought should be weaker than I am.

As I reentered the downtown area, I was met by two opposing sounds. Drums. There was the beat of drums as a group of encouragers provided the marching orders for our worn limbs and feet. I tried running to the cadence. It helped. Then sirens. I heard the call of an ambulance more than once coming down the barricaded streets, surely coming to rescue a runner with an ailment either minor or serious. I've heard of people dying at marathons. Yikes!

The medical tents came more often in the waning miles. I saw men and women, younger than I, in tears and in obvious pain. Ripped guys, muscles oozing from every inch of their bodies, lay in torment on the ground beside a tent as health care professionals tried to ease their pain.

At about mile 22, the wind seemed to have reached a crescendo and it was battering us. It would take a person's will simply to walk upright in that gale. I saw a lady about my age stop and crouch in the middle of the street. I stopped to see if she was okay. I was only jogging at the speed of a snail anyway, so the stop wouldn't hurt my time. She looked up at me with a face twisted in agony and said, "This wind!" She wasn't hurt, just worn. She rose and began to push herself forward again. I did as well and very gradually left her behind.

Now I'm closing in on the final goal. The distance between runners now might be 20 yards, 40 yards, or more. Occasionally one goes by and occasionally I pass someone. The 25,000 have gone. There is no more crowd. For the most part, I'm alone on my island. It is me, my determination, and my now exhausted body, moving slowly on.

Encouragement must come from within. I will finish this race.

And then the finish line, my first marathon finish line, is approaching. I'm a half mile away. I can hear the crowds. I begin to envision the sight of my wife and of enjoying a moment of completion, a unique event in our lives. I'm flashing back to all the months of training, the injury, the decisions to keep on. And now there is no doubt that I will finish the race!

Minutes later, I see the finish area down the street just a few hundred yards away. To my right is a fence that separates participants and spectators. Lisa is there and, to my great surprise, there also stand my oldest daughter, my son-in-law, and two of my grandsons! They drove four hours to get here!

I cut toward the fence and lift my hand to them in greeting, seeing their smiles (is it amazement that I'm alive?) and hearing their cheers of encouragement. What a cool surprise! I'd later be joined at our hotel by others of our children and grandchildren. Those to whom I'd dedicated my race.

On I went toward my finish line. Raising my arms, I crossed, 5:33:58 from start to finish, so my second half had taken just over 3 hours. Overall, I'd averaged 12 minutes, 45 seconds, per mile.

A bottle of water, a "finisher" medal, a shirt that says OKC Memorial Marathon 26.2 *"finisher."* The shirt hangs by itself, unworn to this day. I will never wear it. It is to me a memento of achievement of something unique, and of completion of a dedication to my family.

*Finish the darn race? Yes, sir. Oklahoma City Memorial Marathon - Done!*

## 6.5

My wife and I stayed overnight at our downtown hotel to allow recuperation. The next morning, we walked back down to the scene of the starting line. I thought for a moment about what had occurred twenty-four hours earlier and then my thoughts turned to what had occurred twenty-three years prior. We walked around the monument where the building once stood, saw the pool shimmering in the morning sun and the stones erected to honor those who needlessly died that day.

What matters has a way of sinking into our innermost being during moments like these. Thankfulness for what we have—no, not what . . . who. Gratefulness for the years with this lady beside me, the one I'm pledged to for our life's great race and the one who has pledged herself to me. Grateful for today, for this hour. Thankful for life and breath and the beauty that surrounds us. Ever aware that evil is still around the corner, that sorrow and despair can be but a moment away too. There is a choice: Walk in thankfulness and recognition of the blessing we have, or walk in bitterness, fear, and despair.

I hope that the running of the yearly marathon is not merely a way for a racing company to make more money or for athletes to brag about their newest accomplishment. I hope it does in some small way honor those things that we hold dearest, that is, love for one another, kindness to strangers, help for the weak and the poor, and a determination that we will persevere over every evil and every dark wind that comes our way.

Walking hand in hand with my wife, I enjoyed day one after my first marathon. And I'm grateful for every day with her since.

## 6.7

As I conclude section one of this book, I've related the joys and challenges of preparing for a first marathon and I've applied some of the lessons learned to the joys and challenges of family life—being a spouse, a dad, or a mom. Here at the conclusion of this section, let me return to where I began, with the concept of one man and one woman, staying together for a lifetime.

My wife and I have been blessed with very immediate examples of how this can work.

My mother and father were married for 47 years before an incredibly cruel disease took my mother at the very early age of 65. During those hard final years of her life, we watched a man love a woman with the most amazing and tender love imaginable, as my dad honored his vows to the utmost and cared for my mom in every facet of her life. She did not spend a day in the care of a home. My dad was her hero.

I realize as I write this that not every couple can do what my father did for a wide variety of reasons. I do not mean to judge that in the least. I am only speaking of what my father was able to do because of his season of life, his physical capability, his financial independence—all coming together to make possible the opportunity for his pure love and devotion to her to be manifested in daily sacrificial care.

This has been one of my examples. But there is another. My wife's parents have been married for 55 years and are still going strong. They are, in a sense, a rock of strength that their children and grandchildren look to during their own trying times of life.

Going back to the words of a man I referenced in mile 1, that at a certain time in our lives we wonder if the things we've done with our lives have made a difference. These two sets of examples for my wife and me (and for our children and grandchildren), have made that difference with the 7 decades of their existence. They have imparted a truth, that this marriage vow really can be until death do us part. It really can be in sickness and in health. It really can be whether rich or poor. It can last and get better right up to the end.

## 7.0

Lisa and I married young. For 25 years, the focus of our goals and our efforts was primarily geared toward our children. And then suddenly it all changed. Our kids flew the coop, each one married and began a life of her own, soon to raise children of her own. And suddenly, we were alone like we'd only been for barely a year way back when everything for us was brand new. One year together, 25 years with children, and now the rest of the journey with just the two of us. And so, we returned full circle to that original commitment, the original vow.

Every day, I come home and she is there. I still can't wait to see her and hear her voice. My love for her seems to be only increasing. My appreciation for her grows. I find myself wanting to be a better husband than I've been before, to continue to grow and change and become the kind of man I should have been years ago, loving my wife the way she deserves.

Every night, I lay down to sleep and she is there. It is the comfort and reward from the commitment we made those 36 years ago. Her presence in the room is all I need. Her assurance on decisions, her adjustments when I'm wrong. It is all vital to my life and I see it now more than ever before.

We are growing older together. And it is good.

I don't know what the years to come will hold. Great pleasures, fantastic memories?

Probably so. Storms, difficulties, illnesses, weakness? Most likely they will come. Five more years, or forty-five? Somewhere in between? There is no way to know. I only know that this race is going to be finished together, and nothing this life can throw will change that fact.

One day, one of us will go from this earth and the other will remain . . . for some time, whether long or brief. Until that day, I will love every moment of being Lisa's husband. She is my joy and the love of my life.

I hear that in heaven we are like angels, not married and not given in marriage. I'm holding out hope for something special. I know the scriptures that indicate otherwise. And I also know the heart of our Creator who created the theme of two becoming one, and what He has put together should not be separated. If this is in a heavenly Father's heart, then maybe we'll be pleasantly surprised with some special relationship He has planned for the union, the glorious union of a man and a woman, who ran their race together . . . to the end.

# Training for the Bass Pro Marathon (The Inner Man)

*"Let your eyes look straight ahead; fix
your gaze directly before you."*

## MILE 8

# *Setting Big Goals*

A brain cancer survivor passed me at about mile 20 of the marathon, her shirt declaring to all who followed her that she had taken on brain cancer and was still going, so this little challenge of running 26.2 miles was nothing.

When she passed, I was in a low spell of my race and didn't care much about others leaving me behind. It has happened so often—old, young, women, men, ladies pushing babies in strollers . . . all trotting right on by this worn-out *old man running*. But as I jogged slowly on, the message of her shirt drove into my weakened body. It became additional motivation for me to fight back against the weariness I was feeling.

I looked at her in the distance, now probably 50 yards in front of me, and picked up my pace again (slightly), hoping to gradually catch up to her and ask about her battle. Unfortunately, I never caught her, whether as a result of her superior training or her superior determination, I do not know. I didn't find her after the race either, but I've thought about her from time to time during tough spells in my race or in my world.

People so often face seemingly insurmountable odds. Some take the challenge and inspire us all with their strength of will and internal resolve.

I recall eating lunch with my uncle shortly after he had been diagnosed with cancer. This was a man who took a giant bite out of life and brought humor to every family gathering. His stories were legendary, always leaving everyone slightly amazed that he had survived his teenage years. He was a snow-skiing grandpa. He was a person who started businesses and took on any challenge with gusto. He was also a person who would come to your aid at the hint of any need.

In front of us, at least, he took the news of the cancer that would end up killing him a few years later with the same approach he'd had his entire life—that he was going to live life on purpose, that he would fight cancer every step of the way, and he'd do so with a personal goal to enjoy every day he had left.

"Just like this day," he added, commenting on how much he was enjoying getting to have lunch with my brother and me.

When we get to the end of this life, and all of us will get there eventually, what will be written and said about us by those who are left behind? Closer to the point, while we are living now, what can we say about the life we have lived so far and what do we intend to do with the remaining days and/or years we have left?

I've often said to my wife that I want to live life with a purpose so that we don't get to the end and say, "Well, I sure am glad the Cardinals won the World Series again in 2011." Although I may enjoy Cardinals baseball, that is not my aim or my purpose. Hopefully, my purpose has much more value for these few short years that remain for me.

# 7.3

After finishing my first marathon, my thought was, *What's next? All those weeks and months with daily goals and the big goal had been accomplished. So now what?*

A goal-driven person can almost feel adrift after an event for which they've trained if there is not a new goal on the near horizon. At least, it was that way for me with the completion of my first marathon. Within weeks of the event, my "break" from the daily grind and discipline of running had gradually bled into a new thought, *I should try that again, and this time see if I can keep the training up the entire time and possibly run the entire way.* A new goal formed quickly. All I needed was the object of my goal. Which race?

I guess I took most of the month of May as my lazy month after running the OKC marathon in late April of 2018. By June, I was planning my next attempt. But this time, I needed to add something I was missing during all those long training runs. I needed a running mate. A 3-mile midweek run alone is no problem at all. It is a good way to start a morning or end a stressful workday. But a 2-hour Saturday run gets long, 3 hours really long, and 4 hours downright boring. You can only think, daydream, pray, or plan for so long.

My brother-in-law, the one who got me started running in the first place, became the mate I was looking for as we set about accomplishing the goal of running the Bass Pro Marathon in Springfield, Missouri. Christopher and I live about 30 minutes apart so we decided our midweek runs would still be solo, but our long runs would be done together.

I recall setting out on our first Saturday 5-mile run. It occurred at a place called Wildcat Glades, emphasis on the *wild* part. The path is decently tended. It is part pavement, part gravel, and part dirt/grass trail. The entire area is quite beautiful and includes what some refer to as "the falls" where a rushing stream drops over big rocks as it continues on its merry way.

Our long Saturday runs were almost always the early morning variety, mostly because July in the Midwest United States means intense heat and humidity. Thus, the plan was to start near the relatively cooler creek area at sunrise. Sounds great, right? One problem: A path running through thick trees in early morning hours means spider webs, and lots of them! One or the other of us would take the lead through the narrowest portion of the trails, talking as we ran. Inevitably, there would be sudden interruptions with one or the other shouting "Ack!" You knew the other person had just run face first into another thick web. It was not a fun experience, yet I couldn't help but smile (or laugh) every time it happened to him. Why do guys enjoy other guys' misadventures so much?

The final goal was an early November marathon in downtown Springfield, Missouri. Our training would include a lot of runs in heat, many long runs while the city slept as we ran in the darkness at 4:00 a.m., some long runs that included steep hills, and one final 20-mile training run in a driving, cool October rain. We experienced the gamut. And there were two surprising and welcome changes for me.

First, the old iliotibial (IT) band injury did not return during the entire period. I'd learned some things about stretching and strengthening between the two runs that appeared to help. Second, I experienced the great enjoyment of companionship on long runs that somehow included almost nonstop discussions. I didn't know that you could run twenty miles and talk the entire time. I do now.

We discussed everything imaginable, including the taboo topics of the day. Equality, politics, religion, and family relationships. Nothing was off limits. We agreed early on that we would talk and possibly disagree, but we would do so agreeably. What a noble idea in this day and age, huh?

And we accomplished it. Not only that, but it also seemed good that we should do so. The goal had been to run a marathon together. What occurred was relating on a deeper level than we'd ever done before, and we enjoyed it, a lot. I think both of us would later say that this aspect of our training was the most important accomplishment of all.

## 7.7

As I write this section, I am on the last day of a vacation to a resort in Jamaica. Each day, my wife and I have had breakfast, gone to the beach for the morning to read and relax, had lunch, gone back to the beach to read and relax, had supper, taken a walk around the beautiful property, and gone to bed. Five days of complete relaxation and freedom from responsibility.

It is not real life. It is an excursion away from life, from a wonderful life, in fact.

But in other places, life was being lived in the most painful of ways. That week, a person we were familiar with succumbed to cancer that had reached into almost every part of her body and what had originated almost 2 years prior with the diagnosis of terminal brain cancer, finally ended. We were sitting on our beach, enjoying the surf, our dedicated time together, and the 80-degree warm air (while it was 30 degrees back home). They were bidding their loved one goodbye.

In fact, she had been a runner before cancer struck. The Facebook post of the family that day declared that she had finished her race. A photo was included of her crossing a finish line with flair, in what looked like a dancing jump to her step, and with a huge smile on her face. Her finish line had come. And what a life she had lived.

I will call her Norma. I do not have the family's permission to use her name, nor would I request it as they deal with this crushing loss. But if I asked, I bet they would grant it because after her diagnosis, she became a champion to beat all champions. I noticed there were thousands of followers of her daily posts of encouragement, and there were thousands of responses to the news that she had passed from this temporary engagement we call life.

The truth is, I don't really know much about her, pre-cancer. But I've heard the stories about her *after* the awful beast raised its head. She purposed to live. She purposed to thrive and enjoy every minute and every breath, but to do so while inspiring others. She touched thousands of people *after* the diagnosis. She spoke in numerous places around the country as stories of her determined and joyous outlook spread. She worked at the local high school until the last week of her life and was known as an infectious encourager on the campus. She lived by the hashtag #always be kind and it was included in her uplifting daily posts. She exhibited the same spirit as that brain cancer survivor who passed me on the long race that day, not many months prior to Norma's passing. She just kept on running.

She was a schoolteacher and a few days before her death, she called in to the school principal to say she was having some problems and had to go to the hospital. Three or four days later, she was gone. She literally worked and continued encouraging people up to the days of her death, all the while fighting the daily struggles of a person with cancer ravaging her body.

In one sense, I guess we must say that cancer won the battle . . . but only in one sense. We are all born, we blossom, we grow old or weak, and we die. But did cancer really win? No way, not with Norma. She punched the demon in the mouth, refused self-pity, and instead launched a campaign of triumph and joy that carried her to places she might never have been if the disease had not entered her body.

Because of how she lived her last two years, even though I had never spoken to her, the news of her passing struck me personally because I, too, cared about this one who had so graciously and tenaciously lived her last two years of life.

I ask this question: Why is it that some of us live, but some of us seem to *really* live? Is the question too abstract? You can look around and see healthy people who are seemingly wasting their lives. You can also see people who are terminally ill, as Norma was, who are living life with a vengeance and impacting everyone in their wake. Is it sickness that leads to really living? I don't think so. Because some get the cancer curse and simply give up. (I do not judge those who give up. I'm not sure how I would respond. We should not judge where we have not walked. And even if we have walked, judgment should likely be discarded anyway. What is its value?)

But aside from sickness or health, what else really matters? Our race or religion, our social status? What about our level of wealth or poverty? Do any of those things really matter?

If you say *Yes*, I won't raise a vigorous argument against you. I do believe those things can "affect" our choices. I believe poverty can, indeed, beget a poverty mentality. But I also don't believe it has to do so. I have been to Honduras, Panama, and Venezuela. I've seen poverty. I have seen where people use tin huts as a home and dirt as a living room floor. And I've seen in some of those a quality of life that I don't always see in those who have financial wealth. I've seen those who seem to have the means to affect beneficial change for the masses do almost nothing. And I have seen those who seem to have nothing (in regard to this world's wealth) effect positive change on almost everyone with whom they come in contact.

I propose that the choice is ours, no matter our nationality, sex, or station of life. It is not a question of what life will do to us. Not really. It is a question of what *we* will do with life.

# 8.0

What will we do with this precious life we've been given? That is the question my brother has often posed to people. What are we going to do with it? Waste it . . . or treasure it and make use of it?

The rubber meets the road when people of character determine to live the days, weeks, months, and years of their lives with purpose. The rubber really meets the road as we deal with greed versus generosity, pride versus humility, uncontrolled lust versus respect for others, hate versus love, or #kindness versus #rudeness.

Who will we be as we interact with others? What will be the purpose of our lives and how will we set about to attain it? These are the some of the things I intend to delve into in section two of this book as we apply running lessons to the inner man in each of us.

Will we . . . release unnecessary baggage, wear the right clothing, use proper nutrition and hydration? And how will we deal with injury?

Will we simply take up our time and space on this earth or will we be like Norma in her too-short life and really live it? Will we live our life, whether short or long, in a way that matters? Will people look back at us and say, "That was a life well lived!"

*"So, strengthen your drooping hands and your weak knees. Make straight paths for your feet, that what is lame may not be dislocated but healed."*

## MILE 9

# *Wearing the Right Clothing*

It was all laid out with meticulous care. Asics shoes, Feetures socks, sweat wicking shirt with the race bib already pinned, perfect running shorts, Garmin watch, sunglasses, and food for the run. It was 4:00 a.m. on the morning of my second marathon!

The quiet of early morning race prep has an odd feel. It is like the distant memory of Christmas mornings, waking up as a small child, finding presents so carefully placed around an evergreen tree whose twinkling lights are bringing dim yet colorful illumination to your normally bright living room as the clouds of sleep escape your young mind. It is dreamlike but real, and the memory will never completely fade.

Similar is the dead quiet of your room as you carefully make your way through your preparations, allowing the cobwebs to clear from your mind, feeling the slight uptick of adrenaline as each fiber of your being prepares for the physical assault that is about to be encountered, taking in some calories and a bit of hydration—soon to put each piece of clothing to the test, hoping you made the correct decisions in each selection.

How important are the socks and shoes? If you plan to take somewhere between 55,000 to 63,000 steps today (a marathon count calculated by the average male and female step length), how important do you think they are? They are vital! A poor choice can mean great pain, injury, a slow or unfinished race, and great disappointment after all those months of devoted training and sacrifice. A good choice can mean secure steps even on fatigued feet and limbs. A good choice can mean attained goals, personal bests, and the exhilaration of achieving something you never thought possible.

# 8.1

One of the fiercest competitors of my generation died in a tragic helicopter crash. His name was Kobe Bryant. He was one of the few sports figures in the world whose presence seemed to transcend the game he played, resulting in his being known all over the world, even among many who are not basketball fans. Just say the name Kobe and almost everyone knows who you are talking about.

As I listened to sports talk shows the day after his death, Kobe's approach to sports (and to life) came sharply into focus. He was inwardly driven to excel. His nickname was "Mamba" after one of the deadliest snakes in the world. If you were his opponent on the court, he would study and work longer and harder than anyone to find your weakness, exploit it, and conquer you.

One story that exemplified his competitive fire was told by a sports fan who attended a game in which Kobe was playing. This man did *not* love Kobe. He was a Boston Celtics fan, the long-time fierce rivals of Kobe's Los Angeles Lakers. But he had a buddy who couldn't attend the game and the buddy *was* a Kobe fanatic. He asked his friend to try to get Kobe to sign his Kobe Bryant shirt. So there stood the man, wearing his Celtics T-shirt, holding out a Kobe shirt while Bryant walked by. Kobe stopped and asked why the man chose to beckon him with contradicting shirts. He explained. Kobe's response was that he would sign the shirt, but he intended to sign it *to* the Celtic's fan, not to his buddy. Kobe had a spectacular night on the court that night and, every time he scored, he looked straight at the fan wearing the Celtics jersey. What was being communicated by those looks? It was nothing more than the competitive fire in Kobe, showing that he was too great to be beaten by the Celtics.

Stories from players, broadcasters, and fans dominated the radio airwaves, all of them with stories such as this, declaring the greatness of Kobe Bryant, until . . .

One caller came on to challenge the glossy stories. He told the radio host that we at least needed to hear the complete story of Kobe Bryant, one that included the payment of millions of dollars to a lady he (allegedly) hooked up with in Colorado one night, thus cheating on his beautiful wife.

"What about that part of his life?" the caller asked.

Whoa! The talk show host, known for his honest evaluation of people and events, seemed uncertain. In the end, he admitted those events had occurred but decided today was not the day to discuss them.

It got me thinking about the heroes of our society. Another legendary basketball player, LeBron James, passed Kobe on the all-time scoring list the night before Kobe's death. Lebron wore shoes honoring Kobe during the game. On his shoes was written "Mamba 4 life." It was an apt place for a message that would convey the respect from the third best scorer in basketball history (LeBron James) to the fourth best scorer in basketball history (Kobe Bryant).

Basketball shoes. It is a multi-billion-dollar industry, supported by the near worship given to people who dribble a basketball with amazing talent, people who may or may not exhibit any kind of character worthy of admiration, let alone worship. In fact, advertisers have come up with the slogan *"It must be the shoes"* to explain the unbelievable greatness of some of our present-day athletes.

Heroes, shoes, and right living . . . that is where our short run is taking us today.

## 8.3

When I first got into running, simply to get myself off the couch, running shoes were not even a thought. My $25 sneakers would work just fine. Boy, was I wrong. Now, several years into my running endeavor, I've tried multiple types of shoes and many different brands, searching for the perfect shoe for a 26.2-mile run. Of the billions of dollars spent each year on running shoes in the United States, I've contributed my share to the market while experimenting with shoes costing over $100 per pair: Asics, Brooks, Mizuna, Hoka, New Balance, and others.

I track mileage on a pair of shoes like I'm tracking the expenses on my credit card, because I now realize that the right shoe can make all the difference and too much mileage on a pair will mean the loss of support and less spring for my steps.

During the hours before one marathon, I had vacillated between two pairs of shoes. The Hoka brand had been the most cushioned during my training runs. The New Balance 860s had seemed the most comfortable for most of my mid-level runs of 10 to 12 miles. However, when I reached the 18- to 20-mile range, I discovered my feet were really hurting in the New Balance pair.

Back and forth I went. What I hadn't realized at the time was that my New Balance 860s had too much mileage for prime support and effectiveness. I was still learning. Three hundred plus miles were on those shoes. So the night before the marathon, I looked at both shoes, amazed that I was at this stage of training and hadn't made a decision on this key issue. I finally made up my mind to go with the New Balance because I had started developing blisters when I wore the Hokas.

But then, on race morning, I suddenly changed my mind again, deciding I wanted the cushioned feel of the Hokas. It turned into a massive mistake as I ran a race with the biggest developing blisters of my life, finishing the marathon in no small amount of torment in that regard.

So . . . what feels good at the moment, or in a shorter race, may not be the best decision for the long run.

Armed with more experience and understanding, I now know that a perfectly broken-in, but not overly worn-out pair of New Balance 860s is my best shoe for race day.

I also know that the way I walk, the way I stride, and the way I run matters. In running, in sports, and in life, what I am clothed with matters.

## 8.6

How can a hugely successful and beloved person fall from his lofty heights and end up being looked upon with angry disdain? How can a man who has become a household name, who has become known as a star on screen and possibly one of the most beloved comedians ever, become the poster for all that has gone wrong in society, a pariah to all who formerly worshipped him?

It happens when the image or the façade is peeled away, and people get a look into the real life of a person. He who in public is funny, talented, and successful, can in private be lecherous, dominating, and wickedly powerful as he (or she) preys on those who are lonely or weak or confused.

I believe this so often occurs when the principle of "If it feels good, do it" is a person's worldview. In fact, what "feels good" is often the absolute worst thing for us. The impulses of human nature can be downright deceptive. I could give an abundance of examples, from food impulses to anger impulses (doesn't an angry response *feel* great to let out, until a few seconds after you've shouted at someone?) to things that are lascivious in nature.

Who we are, really, is shown in how we walk when nobody is watching.

I believe we can wear filthy clothes or we can wear clean clothes. Thus, in life too, what we wear matters. In fact, what we wear in life matters much more than what we wear to the next race. Is my behavior right? Is it good?

I rejoiced one day in the testimony of one presidential candidate. He is a highly respected and innovative surgeon who blazed a trail for the successful separation of conjoined twins. He is calm and he is kind in his manner and his speech. He grew up from humble means and had a childhood that could have set his course down a very bad path. Instead, he chose a different way. Through hard work and determination, he rose higher than his peers.

His testimony that I reference has to do with how he walks, and what kind of shoes he wears. He wears shoes that are white with right living.

The occurrence came when a money-seeking person claimed that this now famous man had fathered a child of hers. She wanted restitution. She wanted money. Her lawyers requested his DNA to prove their case. I found it humorous that this famous physician said there was no way he was going to give them his DNA and allow them to do who knows what with it to assert that it matches. He was confident that he was not the father of the child. How could he be so confident? He concluded his story with this calm assertion—he had only ever been with one woman, and that was his wife. So there was no way it could be true. He called their bluff, and they released the lawsuit.

That is a walk I wish people could emulate. What is right? What is good? What is kind? What is true? Our shoes should walk toward righteousness instead of evil and toward words that build others up rather than tear others down. Run with those shoes on and you will win, no matter how hard the race may become. Your reputation will be unstained. Your legacy will be secure.

## 9.0

I'd just put on my new pair of New Balance 860 running shoes. And then our dog, who'd just tromped through some mud, proceeded to jump on me when I walked outside. Mud smudges were all over my brand-new beautiful shoes! I couldn't believe it. Neither could my wife believe that it bothered me so badly to have a pair of shoes muddied. After all, I was about to be running down our dirt road in them, right?

It is true, our shoes will get dirty. The right shoes may be dirty on the outside but comfortable on the inside, doing the very work I need them to do, oblivious to the mud and dirt through which they may splash.

The same can be of our lives as we walk through this strangely complicated and violent world. We can run securely, safely, righteously, through a world packed with muck and mire. We can run on through the intolerance of this age and be tolerant and respectful. We can splash past the yuck of sexual predators and run to aid those who are wounded, showing them what they are truly longing for: pure acceptance and compassion.

But we must run righteously, or the aid we would give will only be viewed with suspicion, and rightly so.

We can run through a world that is so filthy with the diseases of hate and lust and abusive power that some say they do not want to even consider bringing a child into it. But God forbid that we walk backwards now. Those who walk right *must* walk forward—against the rising tide of filth that pollutes. We must walk a straight path in a crooked world.

We can do like Jesus, who walked through the dirt paths of Jerusalem, calling out the religious hypocrites who weighed down the hurting with their pious hypocrisy; Jesus, who knelt in the dirt beside a lady who'd been caught in the very act of adultery and was about to be stoned, and He said, "Let the one who is without sin cast the first stone," and moments later to the sinner, "Did no one stay to condemn you? Neither do I condemn you. Now go and sin no more." (Walk in a new way and down a new path . . . into life.)

In sports, the shoes make you great, if you believe the advertising. In life, it is the *way* the shoes walk, and where they walk, that matters.

*"Therefore . . . let us also lay aside every encumbrance . . . and let us run with endurance the race that is set before us."*

## MILE 10

# *Losing Weight(s)*

Nobody ever ran a marathon while carrying a twenty-five-pound medicine ball. No, runners shed every weight possible when the race is finally on.

Weight matters in running. Shave a few pounds off your body, and you'll likely run a faster race.

Ever heard of VO2 Max? How fast you can run depends on your body's capacity for using oxygen, which is known as your VO2 max. If you weigh more, your body needs more oxygen to operate. The more you weigh, the more oxygen, or energy, it takes to run at a given speed. By losing weight, you decrease your body's oxygen needs. This will increase your VO2 max, allowing you to run your marathon at a faster pace with less energy.

Have I put you to sleep yet?

If you weigh 200 pounds and you drop 20 pounds of fat, you can expect to increase your speed by about 10 percent. If you run at a pace of 9 minutes per mile, that would knock 54 seconds off every mile. Over a 26.2-mile marathon course, this adds up to about 24 minutes of savings. Wow! Carrying around unnecessary weight can make a huge difference.

Thus, one of my goals as I prepared to run another marathon was to drop 10-15 pounds of unnecessary weight, getting myself back down to a trimmer appearance I had a few years ago, before this old-age, slower metabolism beast kicked in. Losing weight, though, is not an easy endeavor for so many of us. It requires an ability to stick to a plan, determinedly. More appropriately stated, it requires a change of mindset and/or lifestyle. These suggestions are not for the minimally dedicated. But I think we shall find that the benefits are worth the sacrifice in more ways than one.

# 9.1

Here's a weird one: It's winter, 1981. The kid is in 12th grade in a small school. He's a good student, not because he's particularly smart but because he cares about making good grades and tries a little harder than most.

What about playing football? Nah. Not big enough, strong enough, or fast enough.

Baseball? Nope. Although he enjoys watching it on television and is a big St. Louis Cardinals fan, he doesn't have the skills. Basketball? Aha! Now that is his game. Actually, it is the one reason he enjoys going to school every day.

High school basketball. Thirty years later, the kid would still dream about those days. As a freshman hoopster, in the days when freshman was still middle school and the 9th-grade boys had their own games every week, he was a starter on a good team. And although he wasn't particularly excellent at the sport, he was a pretty good shooter from outside, relatively quick with his hands, and made fair decisions as a point guard, while playing as a supporting member to the more talented starters on the freshman team.

As a sophomore and junior, he played only sparingly, as the older, better, stronger, faster boys kept him firmly on the bench. But he knew his time would come during his senior year, so he endured the bench time and cheered his mates on.

Then senior year came. A new coach had entered the school that very year. The kid's old freshman coach, who'd also been the high school coach for as long as anyone could remember, had decided to take the job as principal of the high school and stop coaching. It was an unexpected blow to the team. And yet, the coach they brought in was a well-respected member of the conference, who'd coached for years at a school just down the road.

The day came for the new coach to place his starters in line. The kid expected to win, and did win, that coveted starting position as a guard on the varsity squad.

The days of playing on the junior high teams came back to him as he was about to make one last run for basketball glory, this time at the highest level he would ever play—starting senior on the high school basketball team.

The kid loved all of it. The daily practices, the camaraderie with teammates; by golly, even the conditioning drills were bearable. The daily scrimmages against the "B" team were enjoyable, as plans were laid for the coming opponent.

Memorable were the late evening bus rides to "away" games and then the ride home on a dark bus that was either raucous with sounds of victory or quiet as each young man thought through the reasons the game had been lost. And there was the buzz of his fluttering heart if he happened to sit next to one of the girls whom he wished he could gather the courage to talk to . . . and the dreamlike or nightmarish occurrence when a word did pass back and forth between him and said girl—dreamlike if he didn't sound like an idiot, and nightmarish if he was certain he'd just said about the dumbest thing that had ever been uttered by a male human to a person of the opposite sex. Oh, the stress and the wonder of life as a high school teenager in a more innocent age. (I think TV shows have been made about this kind of thing.)

And then there were the sounds: walking in the gymnasium door, hearing the screech of sneakers on the gym floor and the quiet roar of hundreds of people conversing in the stands before tipoff; the beating of your heart as you headed to the locker room to suit up; the pre-game jitters as each one played out the game plan in their heads; the glances at mates, quiet reassurances spoken, high fives given, pats on backs applied; a pre-game speech from the coach delivered; then hearing the final buzzer of the girls' game and knowing you were only moments away from taking the court! Finally, opening the side doors connecting the locker room to the court and being enveloped by a swell of applause raining down from filled bleachers above as the court was taken and pre-game drills began. Goosebumps ran up and down the spine, adrenaline fully kicking in.

He was in his own high school heaven. This was the reason to enjoy high school. This was fun. This was a memory of a time that would stay with him for decades to come.

Then the unthinkable happened.

The team was not very good that year. The group who had started as freshmen and had been among the best in the conference hadn't "grown" as some of the competition in the area had done over the last three years. Losses began to pile on top of each other. The new coach began looking for answers, as any coach would do.

It just so happened that this year's freshman team was crazy good. They were destroying all their competitors with such ease that the new coach did what was previously unthinkable: he asked a few of his star freshmen to suit up with the varsity squad. He began substituting a couple of them into the starting lineup, shocking the kid during his senior year with a seat on the bench.

What should have been dealt with as a challenge was instead dealt with in a very immature way. He began to toy with the idea that basketball was no longer fun and that his evening job took his energy away. In a shocking display of weak character, he made the decision and brought his gear to his coach, announcing his decision to quit.

The coach expressed his disappointment. He said he hoped the young man would change his mind and show up at practice that evening. But the youngster stuck to his stupid plan and walked away, a numb feeling coursing through him as he walked from the gym back to the classrooms.

Hours later, one of his three good friends from his high school years, also a starter on the team, came walking by. This friend was known for never holding his opinion back and having strong ideas on a lot of topics. It was one of the reasons the kid enjoyed his company so much because it was often humorous to hear him rant on the issues of the day.

It took just one look and the kid knew he'd disrespected the loyalty that was due his friend and the team. "I'm very disappointed in you," was all his friend said as he slowly walked by. No further comment or explanation was needed. And although the friendship didn't end, it changed in some way after that day.

He had blown it. He had shown a horrid lack of character in the face of a bit of adversity in a silly game that boys play in high school. And that feeling stuck with him for years to come.

For you see, the kid wasn't a druggie; he didn't party; he didn't do what a lot of kids did in their young nonsensical years. He was basically steady and reasonable. He followed his parents' instructions, valued them highly, in fact. Most of the high school looked on him as being "the good kid" in the school, rarely unkind to anyone, never using bad language, respectful to the teachers and his peers alike.

In later years, he often said that he had no real regrets in life of any significance from those years. He had no regrets except that one. That he had quit on his coach, on his team, and on his favorite thing about high school days; that he'd shown such a lack of character in that situation that it shamed him.

About 15 years later, his coach came walking into his place of business, which was a pizza restaurant that the kid (now man) owned and operated with his family. The coach walked in the door to eat. And in a flash, it all came flooding back.

The man approached his coach, cleared his throat nervously, and said, "Coach, do you remember me?"

The coach looked up with a kind smile. "Of course. How are you?" was the response. "I'm good!" And then: "I just want you to know, I still dream about high school basketball. I loved it. I've always regretted what I did when I decided to quit playing my senior year. I want to apologize to you. What I did was wrong, and I still can't believe I did that."

Again, the kind smile flashed, followed by kind words: "Oh, don't worry about it," he said, "we all have made decisions we regret and that's how we learn."

And it was done.

The man would still look back from time to time with regret that he had missed his final year of high school basketball and perhaps many more good memories from the basketball court with his buddies. But that is the way with experiences—we learn from them.

The "kid," who now writes these words, is glad that his old coach walked in the door that day so his conscience could be cleared and the shameful feelings from his one comparatively minor regret are now gone after he finally had been able to apologize to the coach he had abandoned.

## 9.5

Let's move past silly basketball regrets and look at real issues of deep regret that haunt some people's lives.

How about unwanted pregnancies, broken hearts, and broken relationships, or time lost with people you love? Or how about things worse than those? What about things that can put such heaviness on the soul of a human that they can almost despair of life? How about taking the life of another person, whether by accident or in anger, and then living with that for the rest of your life?

I was fairly close to a person who fell asleep at the wheel of a car, which is something almost everyone has battled at one point or another in their lives. But when this person dozed, a crash ensued that took the life of an unsuspecting and innocent driver. How does one live with such weight upon their conscience?

Or what about a mistake of a different kind? What about a misunderstanding at a moment when a police officer is armed and makes an instant decision that is found to be wrong, horribly and tragically wrong, leaving grieving, and sometimes violently angry, people in the fallout? How does one live with a weight such as this?

There is an answer so peaceable and pure that it stuns the imagination.

Let me introduce you to the characters of one of the most amazing scenes I've ever witnessed between two people.

If you google "Brandt Jean's hug" you will find the story of a white policewoman who entered what she (mistakenly) thought was her own apartment to find a young black man actually in *his* own apartment; a policewoman who, perceiving the man as a threat, opened fire and killed him. A true tragedy it was, for the young man turned out to be the furthest you can be from a threat. Instead, he appears to have been a genuinely kind and excellent human being.

As the woman was found guilty of murder and was forced to face the victim's family in the courtroom, the deceased man's brother approached the witness stand and calmly sat down. As his thoughts slowly poured from deep inside him, he began to say the impossible. Some of his words were, "I forgive you. I love you just like anyone else. I personally want the best for you. I don't even want you to go to jail. I want the best for you because that is exactly what [his brother] would want, and the best would be to give your life to Christ. That is what he would want you to do. I don't wish anything bad on you."

Suddenly he said, "I don't know if this is possible—" Turning to the judge, he said, "Can I give her a hug, please?" Quiet filled the courtroom as seconds passed. Then he spoke one more word and his voice cracked with the effort as he repeated his appeal, "Please!"

A few more seconds of stillness reigned in the courtroom as the forgiver awaited the instruction of the judge. And then the judge spoke simply, "Yes."

The camera in the courtroom showed the young man immediately get up and walk toward the table where the convicted murderer sat, when suddenly a sob was heard as she flung herself forward into the young man's open arms. For a minute they embraced, she spoke, he nodded his head, they embraced again, she spoke more words, he nodded more, and they embraced again . . . and again.

Amazing love! Oh, what sacrifice!

The camera catches the judge wiping her eyes. Judge Tammy Kemp, an African American woman presiding over a scene of astounding love played out before a courtroom, at a time when America is usually assaulted with stories of hatred and mistrust still occurring day by day between races of people who continue to encounter bigotry and stupidity.

With those words of forgiveness, a convicted killer can now pay her price to society in jail, with the weight of the world lifted off her shoulders by the only one who could lift it, the ones who'd lost the most.

What is forgiveness? Most simply put, it is an injury, a debt resulting from the injury, and the cancellation of the debt.

That is exactly what the young man chose . . . and believe me, it is a choice. He chose to cancel the debt of the lost life and future of his brother. He said basically, "You don't owe *me* even if society says you do, even if 'justice' says you should. I cancel your debt owed to our family."

Forgiveness + acceptance of it = weight released.

"But wait!" I can hear people shouting. "She doesn't deserve to have her weight released! She killed an innocent young man!"

True enough. She does *not* deserve it. And nobody but the one so deeply hurt has the right to do so. If I was on the jury, I would likely have convicted her and sent her away. That is what justice demands. And yet, I wonder about the families of lost loved ones who do see justice served . . . especially when that justice includes the penalty of death for the convicted.

Here again is a hot topic that divides Americans. My belief? I am for the justice in the penalty of "life for life" when there is an absolute certain finding of premeditated and intentional murder. I am also for the healing power of undeserved forgiveness. Is that contradictory? I don't think so.

Look again at the young man who lost his brother. If the cop then lost her life in exchange, would it truly release the anguish of the loss? Would he walk away and say "Okay, now we're even and justice was done"? I don't think so. The loss is still too acute even if there is some minimal help from a feeling of justice being served.

I think that the only way to avoid a "prison" of the bitterness of loss is to forgive the criminal, not to the point of removing the consequence they deserve; no, not that. But to the point of inwardly declaring them released from owing you for the act of taking so much away from you. That act has healing power for both parties that is beyond comprehension.

The young man became famous for his choice. But he desired no fame and appears to have refused almost all requests for interviews. When he was asked what the cop had said to him during the long hugs, he refused to reveal it, saying it was genuine and it was kind and was meant for the two of them alone to share.

# 9.8

There is a weight that sits upon the souls of men and women, the weight of having taken something so precious away from someone. But there is also a weight on a person who has been wronged and cannot forgive. It is the weight of bitterness . . . the weight of being so horribly wronged that you feel you simply cannot forgive what has been done to you. And in that place, people lock themselves away in cages of smoldering hatred, with the final mockery being that the wrong someone has done to them is not just a one-time occurrence but becomes instead a lifelong chain carried around their souls.

This happens surely in times of marital infidelity, in divorce, in seeing your child wronged, in rape or incest, and in countless other despicable acts that human beings inflict on each other. As the non-involved person who sees these things in the news, I want to see some reprobate individuals and perverts stuck away in a cell that never sees the light of day.

But for the person who was attacked in these ways, I wonder how they live and how they can get up in the morning and face each new day. Sometimes, possibly, they cannot, or they walk as if in a stupor, unable to cope with their great loss and the growing bitterness that eats away in them like an insatiable cancer. And to ask a person to forgive someone who has caused such harm to them or their family seems stupid and insensitive.

But what I'm suggesting is that unless they can, over time, come to a place where they can choose to forgive, they will likely stay locked up in a prison for the rest of their days, with the effect that the horrible person who caused the harm keeps causing them harm day after day for as long as they live. The offender may physically be in prison, but the offended one may be in a prison that is possibly worse, with poison consuming their inner person.

I'm suggesting, then, that forgiveness is the way. the only way, to be free from the actions that are sprung upon us. It is the only way to miraculously turn that evil into good. For so powerful is this word *forgiveness* that just as it frees the wrongdoer, it also frees the wronged. It is a sword with dual edges once wielded with the purpose it has been given.

Not long ago a friend spoke to me about a most-loved person in my life. My loved one had been hurt, brokenhearted even, by one she had received lifelong promises from. Most of us know people like this. Vows made but unkept, cruelty ensuing, crushing weights descending.

But my dear loved one had opted *not* to hold the hurt, but instead to embrace life's joys.

Oh, the hurt did not immediately depart, not by a long shot. It was too deep. But day by day, picking up shattered pieces, choosing to put one foot in front of the other and most often choosing a path of joy and peace . . . and of forgiving the person who'd forsaken his vows, gradually, she won her way to freedom. Piece by piece, day by day, the weight diminished, until finally it could be declared almost gone.

The friend spoke to me about seeing my loved one, not knowing her past or her history. She only mentioned her beauty at an event that both had attended. I thanked her and pointed out that my loved one had an even better quality than her outward beauty. I said it was the inner beauty that impressed me most about her. After having endured the storms of life, she had chosen to live instead of bow down to pain.

The reply from my friend was that she hadn't known about storms of my loved one's life, but that she could tell in how she carried herself that she was both strong and kind—something she recognized because of the example she'd seen from her own mother, another lady who had been shocked and heartbroken by a man.

There is a lesson here: *Bitterness and hatred* are the consequences of wallowing in the wrongs that have been done to us. *Strength and kindness* are the results of the weightlessness gained by forgiving others.

# 10.0

Losing weight, they say, is tough. The weight loss industry is indication enough of this truth. American society is possibly its most obese in history as fast food, busy lifestyles of working men and women, and eating out regularly have become the way of life for so many.

The weight loss plans are as plentiful as the leaves that fall from a tree in autumn, with a new surefire offering floating down upon us on a daily basis.

Recently I saw that the weight loss industry is valued at about 70 billion annually. (It is worth more than the sports shoe industry!) We all want to lose it (me included), and it appears that most of us struggle to accomplish it. But every so often you find a conqueror, who by strength of will has made a true lifestyle change.

A couple of years ago, I saw one such man whom I'd not seen in a few years. He'd been rather obese for as long as I'd known him. When I saw him again, I literally did not recognize him. He'd lost an entire person in weight. His face was completely changed. And upon him was the look of quiet peacefulness, of hard goals accepted and challenges met, of life-sapping weight being discarded from his body. So it is possible. Not easy, but possible. And the rewards are great.

If I drop this weight, if I get rid of this baggage that has assaulted my life, if I can run this life-race as a new, light man—how fast might I run then? What injuries might I avoid or overcome?

Lose some weight today. Forgive. Receive forgiveness. And prepare to run a race with a freedom you have never known.

*"They were stoned, they were sawn in two, they were tempted, they were put to death with the sword; they went about in sheepskins, in goatskins, being destitute, afflicted, ill-treated (men of whom the world was not worthy), wandering in deserts and mountains and caves and holes in the ground."*

## MILE 11

# *Learning from Those Who Went Before*

The day of my first real running injury, I ignored advice given just days before the race by someone who had done it many times before. I made my own plan instead of listening, thinking he didn't understand where I was in my training, thinking what I knew about myself trumped what he knew from experience. My plan worked for three-fourths of the race and then I crashed, hit a wall like never before and ended up hobbling across the finish line with an injured knee. He had given me a plan. I ignored it.

During another race, I ignored his advice, went out too fast, and burned out before the finish line was anywhere close. During yet a third race, I ignored his advice, went out too fast, and burned out yet again.

The funny thing was, at the end of each race, I assessed, recognized the error, and determined that "next time" I would do what the experienced one says. And then, on the day before the race, I began salivating for personal bests, decided my training was better this time . . . that his advice wouldn't be as valid this time; and the same result struck again. Learn, you idiot! Follow the advice of those who have done this many more times than you.

I believe in this concept. I believe that people should learn from the experienced in order to avoid their own school of hard knocks. I believed it for raising children, for business endeavors, and for running. Yet with each race, my mind and my emotions got caught up in the event itself. I imagined an unbelievable race and wound up discarding good instruction to my own detriment.

I have determined not to let this happen again. I have made a personal commitment to run my next race(s) with a "follow the advice to the end" mentality.

I may be old, but I can still learn. I can follow. And if I do, he says I'll run the best race I've ever run and will come out feeling much better at the end, rather than having that feeling of utter exhaustion I've become accustomed to at the end of long races.

Marathon training is intense. It is out of my comfort zone. But if I'm going to set this kind of goal—this marathon endeavor—I might as well give myself the best chance of success, by listening and learning rather than ignoring and failing.

## 10.2

The Hebrew with the fire in his eyes would be taken from him today. The protégé knew it as surely as he knew the sun would rise in the eastern sky each morning. Had he, as a student, learned everything he needed to learn? Was it too soon? There were no answers to these urgent questions within him. Instead, there was only the knowledge that time was short. It would happen today.

The older man seemed to know it as well. He urged his disciple to stay behind as he had one more place to go. "No!" had been the response. "I will not leave you." On they walked from town to town, chatting quietly, intimately, as they went. At several points, the elder asked the younger to stay behind and each time was met with the same response. The student would not lose any last moments to learn from the aged one.

And then a miracle happened; they came to the Jordan River and they could not pass at this time of year. But the teacher grabbed his mantle and struck the waters, whereupon the waters immediately parted, allowing the two to pass through on dry ground.

The protégé's mind went back to the story of another student, whose teacher had years ago stretched out his staff while the Red Sea parted as the Egyptian army was approaching?

They were teachers and students. And this student knew that time was short. His determination grew as he whispered to himself yet again, "I will not leave him!"

Suddenly, a miracle of miracles occurred. Chariots and horses of fire appeared from the sky and separated the two of them as the younger called out to his master, "My father, my father, the chariots of Israel and its horsemen!" And then his "father" was gone, swept up in a whirlwind to heaven.

Never had anything like this happened or been told of in the annals of time. But the young man who had refused to leave his teacher's side had witnessed it, felt it, sensed it all occur. The majesty, the awesome power, the supernatural seen by a natural man. Then came sorrow with the knowledge that his teacher was gone. He grabbed his clothes and tore them, in anguish.

But what had dropped to the ground? The protégé looked and reached out to pick up the mantle than had only a short time ago struck the water and caused it to part. He began the trek back along the way they had come and approached the same water, this time alone . . . this time without his teacher.

Suddenly the trained one stepped forward with fire in his eyes and shouted, "Where is the God of *Elijah*?" as he swung the mantle with force into the water's edge. Immediately the water parted, and *Elisha* crossed over on dry ground.

## 10.5

There is an older attorney in the law office where I work. I've known him now for about seven years.

What I have seen him do is quite interesting. He occupies a tiny corner office in a very large building with three levels and a multitude of offices, both small and great. Associates, young attorneys who are building their practice and trying to earn their way, come to him for advice. Partners, older attorneys who have been with the firm for many years, run the tough stuff by him to gain the benefit of his experience. When it comes to nuance of law, everyone feels best if they have had a moment with the most experienced man in the building.

Wonderfully, it is a place of honor, of respect. He is not too old, not seen as past his prime or too far gone. He is seen as a resource of knowledge, of times in the trenches, of battles long since over.

And even more wonderful, it seems to be his joy to impart what he has learned to those who come. He does not begrudge the time even though he is the one who will often be found working on Saturday while none of the younger ones can be found around the office. No, even if he will work more hours himself because of using his regular hours to advise others, he does it gladly. I daresay he finds more of his joy now in the impartation of wisdom and knowledge to others than he does in working on his own cases. He has purpose. His life has meaning as his years advance. He is depositing a part of himself into others, into younger ones wise enough to seek him out . . . and listen.

## 10.7

Where does a little boy learn how to treat a girl? He learns it as he watches his father adorn his mother with kindness and praise. Or he learns to mistreat girls as he watches his father criticize and complain.

Where does a little girl learn how to treat a boy? She learns from watching her mother praise her father, supporting him in his endeavors. Or she learns to talk about him behind his back, as her mother tells other women about the things she does in secret because "what he doesn't know won't hurt him."

Boys and girls learn how to interact by watching how their parents interact. How do they handle a crisis? How do they relate to their neighbors? What do they say about their bosses?

When do they stand up against injustice? Where do they turn when things are at their worst? Is it toward each other for strength and encouragement, or against each other with fingers pointed in blame?

I believe that children learn first and primarily from their parents. They learn kindness or meanness. They learn justice or bias. They learn respect or contempt. They learn integrity or white lies (or blatant ones). They learn decency or lewdness.

I say, first and foremost, it is the parents. But when the parents are absent or defer in their responsibilities (while the children learn those bad traits from them too) they will reach out to others around them, and in the vacuum of good parental influence, they will learn key elements of attitude and action from the worst place they can learn them, their peers.

I know there can be the lucky instances where peers can be from one of those homes of integrity and they can help impart some of those traits to the other. But usually, I think children learn the opposite from their peers.

Where did I learn bad words existed? From my school mates (not my parents). Where did I learn to sample chewing tobacco and cigarettes (and most may add alcohol or drugs, or worse)? It was from third grade schoolmates. Third grade!

It is on the playground where children single out others with a slightly different look and make fun; where words like *retard* are uttered; where cliques are formed, and someone is declared to be left out of the cool crowd. Indeed! Even the idea of the cool crowd, geeks, weirdos, nerds—it all comes from kids learning from kids.

I recall being a 2nd-grade boy and walking outside during recess to see boys several grades older than I gathered around an innocent animal, kicking it for pleasure. I was horrified and helpless and walked silently away.

These are but a few of the "hard knocks" that young minds and hearts must endure if undirected by proper parental guidance. And so I believe that the purest form of discipleship, of impartation from one generation to the next, is in the relationship of parents to children. And while I don't want to retread the ground we've run in previous miles of this book, it bears repeating for this topic of learning from those who went before. The world is shaped in how a mom and a dad impart life and beliefs to their children.

I know men who want to be just like their dads, excellent men, and it is good. I've also known men who speak of hating their dads and want to be nothing like them, but who seemingly unknowingly repeat the same mistakes and show the very same attributes their fathers exhibited. It is interesting and amazingly important. Teaching another person a way of truth must start in the home.

## 10.9

"They're all dead now."

This is a common refrain of mine as my wife and I watch old movies. One of my favorites is *It's a Wonderful Life* with one of the best actors ever, Jimmy Stewart. But I can't get through that wonderful old show without informing my wife that all of them are dead now. My wife endures my regular reminder and sarcastically thanks me for the negative commentary that's she's grown used to.

As I age, it is hard for me to get away from the brevity of life, the flash that it seems to be and the speed at which it roars along. So many movies, so much talent, so many lives, and what did they leave behind?

I am morbidly fascinated by the regular entries on the internet that ask us to take a look at the famous stars of yesteryear with a "then and now" set of photos. Kirk Douglas, young and handsome, now 100 years + and looking oh, so different . . . and just recently departed at the age of 103, I think. Or the bombshell actresses from the 1950s and 60s, looking so young and promising with their lives ahead and now so ancient, wrinkled, old.

Youth, beauty, athleticism, fame, it is all fleeting. It is temporary. It is an illusion of grandeur. What really matters is what we do with the short days we have on this earth. And one of the key questions of all is whether we have imparted something of true value to those who will come after us.

# 11.0

One of the more painful moments in my life has been referenced in an earlier mile and will most likely make its appearance again, as painful moments have a way of resurfacing from time to time. But there was some odd joy in the moment as well.

For I had a wonderful mother and still do have a wonderful dad. They trained—they imparted (I believe) some of the best things life has to offer. They taught my brother and me how to treat other people with respect. They were our original teachers in so many areas.

As my mother was about to pass from her very short time on earth, family gathered around in my childhood home where she lay as the battle was waning. Soon an older couple arrived at the home. They were some of my parents' oldest friends, dating back probably forty-five years. They had been around as long as I could remember even though the closeness wasn't what it once had been. In fact, you could probably say they were my parents' first mentors when my parents were still in the earliest stages of their married life.

The lady of the couple always glowed. Her nickname was Joy. And she spread it wherever she went. And here in this odd moment of a loved one departing this life, she uttered words I will never forget; stating them with a look of understanding and compassion for what we were all experiencing, spoken as words of comfort to all and with a gentle smile crinkling from her wise old eyes: "*We're all going to die soon.*" Coming from her, there was nothing morbid about it, even though it normally would seem so. From her, in that moment, it was a peaceful declaration. In fact, it was one of joy.

Here at the end of my mother's life, her very early mentor was still imparting peace to my mother and to all of those around. There is something better beyond these years and this life. There is hope beyond. There is joy beyond. And without trying to do so, she was teaching us the lesson: We are here for a very short time . . . to do good, to serve others, to love . . . and then to go on to greater joy. My mom is gone now. That same couple who came to be a part of her departure are gone now as well. But they lived well, imparting the life that was in them to more people than they could have ever imagined.

Men and women of whom the world is not worthy live lives such as this. May those fortunate enough to hear and receive from excellent teachers, run . . . and do the same . . . learning from those who went before.

*"No testing has overtaken you that is not common to everyone."*

## MILE 12

# Pebbles in Your Shoe (Dealing with Injury)

I was running one day and felt a pebble in my shoe working its way under my foot. It was on the 20-mile training run (in the rain) that is more fully described in mile 15. I don't recall exactly when it finally stopped me in my tracks, but I endured it for a few miles until it began to feel like a boulder. I had to stop. I sat down on the wet street (which caused no problem to my running shorts that were already completely soaked) and pulled off the shoe with the offending monstrosity inside and turned it upside down. Out fell a piece of gravel about the size of a grain or two of sand. I couldn't believe it. Can such a little thing cause such a large problem? Yes, it can.

It reminded me of the time I got a piece of sawdust in my eye while working at a sawmill as a young man. Sawdust in eyes is the stock in trade in sawmill work. But that time I was unable to clear the debris. As the day wore on, I felt like I was going insane. The staff eventually took me to the ER for an eye flush. It didn't get better. I endured another day or two of going completely mad with the constant irritation before finally going to see an eye specialist who withdrew something so insignificant that it could hardly be seen with the naked eye.

*Proving that the application of even the tiniest pressure in the most vulnerable place can be excruciating and can lead to injury.*

Blisters are another small and seemingly insignificant injury that can be a dilemma for runners. We must get the next training run in, but with each training run, the blister that is trying to heal is rubbed raw again. I've tried Band-Aids, special slip-resistant socks, and unique ways of tying my shoes. I even bought a stinky balm that farmers rub on the udders of their milk cows. It is called bag balm. No kidding. The weird thing was, it helped, as promised.

And yet, during the race that would be my third marathon (mile 21), I had developed a blister over time that never seemed to fully heal. At the hotel in the beautiful mountains of the state of Washington, I pondered the problem. I purchased some huge specialty Band-Aids that entirely covered the blister and sealed onto the skin. Problem solved. Or not.

By mile 6 of that marathon, I was feeling the rub and knew it was about to become a major problem. At the end of the race, as I gingerly pealed back the covering of the Band-Aid, a monstrous blister was revealed. *Proving that a seemingly small problem can become a major one, over time, when not properly tended or allowed to fully heal.*

## 11.1

The running mentor I mention frequently in this book, the one who has run marathons literally all over the world, finished a race one time with a broken femur. He also happens to be a very fine wordsmith and one of my bosses for the last 17 years. I think it is only appropriate that I allow him to relate his story in his own words, with few edits from me. (Used with permission.)

*April 2, 2016*

*Railways are designed to be flat. Kansas is known for being flat. So imagine a race on a trail that used to be a railway in the middle of nowhere Kansas. Now imagine flatter. That's it! One day I was on this trail for a 50-mile race. I wasn't looking to break any records except my own.*

*Great day, good run. At turnaround point, I refueled a little. I was feeling tired and sore, but I was on track for a personal best. This race would be my first sub 8-hour 50 miler.*

*It was getting crazy hot. I was tired and ready to be done and my hip was hurting. I had felt some twinges in it over the last weeks or month but nothing bad. It was kind of like neck pain if you sleep on it funny or a minor hamstring pull that lingers. But now, at about mile 30 or 35, the pain kept creeping up; pain like a 2 or a 4 on the pain scale quickly became a 7 or 8.*

*I noticed I was limping at about mile 39. I've felt pain before. I know that when you push yourself without enough training you pay for it. Train more, suffer less. Well, I'm not very diligent at training. But I'm very good at suffering.*

*I limped on. I was running, hobbling, walking, shuffling, running. Every step hurt. But if it hurts to walk and hurts to run, you may as well run. Oh heck! It hurts lots more to run. My limping jog was the best I could do. I walked some. I just had to finish the last 10 miles. I knew I could. I knew I would. But I was now hot, alone, hurting, and wondering why in the world this hip/leg thing was going on.*

*Fifty miles can be a long way if you are pushing your best time. Pain is to be expected. But this was starting to worry me a little. Maybe I pulled something bad. Maybe a stress fracture. I've read too much to think this kind of pain was okay. Now I'm 4 miles out. I'm gonna make it. How much worse can it get. (Lots!)*

*Still, if you start a race, you need to have a bone literally sticking out to not finish a race, in my world anyway. I managed to shuffle and limp in. I even jogged a bit at the end—people were watching at the end!*

*No sub 8-hour 50 miler. But it was a new personal best for me; 8 hours and 9 minutes.*

*The last hour was terrible!*

*But even after I stopped, the pain didn't. Oh no! Something's wrong. I hobbled and got food and drink. I sat down. I could hardly get up. I was pretty sure I broke something. I limped with every step.*

*Eventually I saw a doctor. I had a stress fracture in the femoral neck. The femur is the biggest bone in the body. The ball at the top goes into the socket of the hip. I say I broke my hip, but I really just cracked the biggest bone just below the ball.*

*I saw an orthopedic surgeon who wanted to have me stay off it. He stressed to me (no pun intended) that if this stress fracture extends, I will break the head (ball) off my femur and then bad things happen; like not walking right ever, possible embolism, or immediate emergency surgery with almost certain hip replacement. He offered many times to put in a plate and screws. But that had potential to cause issues with running. I told him I'd stay off it.*

(Later, after being released to walk…)

*I walked a marathon with my daughter. The marathon was okay. In case you wonder, it takes 7:53 to walk a marathon with a half-broken hip. (I had a cane with me.)*

*Doc threatened to fire me as a patient. He showed me the increased white streaks on imaging that showed I'm closer to hip replacement. He encouraged me to find another doc if I was gonna be stupid. I reminded him he said I could walk. He left the room.*

*I did get crutches and used them for months. I didn't run another race until November.*

(My addition to the story): *proving that a real injury must be tended to and, if it is not, it can become debilitating.*

Determination can only get you so far. At some point, the mind's strength must bow to the body's inability. Get rest. Heal. Then go again.

## 11.4

I enjoyed a recent movie about a young lady who was overweight and dealing with the stigma that many overweight people can be tempted to give in to, as society puts forth the definitions of "beauty" that our young ladies can never seem to satisfy, at least in their own minds.

The lady in the movie determined to change her life and do so in a big way by running the NYC marathon. She began the grueling process of changing her eating habits and sedentary lifestyle and joined a running group, devoting herself to the training that is necessary to run 26.2 miles.

Unfortunately, while dealing with some of the emotional issues in her life, she went out running too often and too hard. Running became her escape. And when life threw too much at her, she retreated into running, with a vengeance.

A repetitive injury began to afflict her. Instead of listening to her body, she "willed" herself forward even faster. The result was a true injury that made it impossible for her to race in the NYC marathon that year, despite all those sacrificial months of training. Her outer injury was, therefore, caused by the inner wounds of her soul, hurts that had never healed and that once laid bare, became a festering ailment that demanded attention.

The story ends happily. The runner found a measure of inner healing that she had needed for years. And she began training again for the marathon, completing it the following year.

Healing leads to health. That makes sense, right? And health can lead to the accomplishment of great goals.

There are running injuries that require healing. But it is the soul injuries that go way beyond the affliction of the body. They are much deeper.

In a way, if seen with the proper vision, one can look out at our world and see people walking around looking normal on the outside but carrying crutches on the inside. There are many broken people who respond to others out of their hurt and brokenness, sometimes making people incapable of maintaining healthy relationships with those who would love them.

People worry about an attack from Russia or North Korea. They are legitimate concerns.

They can make our lives more difficult. They can even end this life. But those things can only steal outer things from us.

There are injuries that are greater than any that a foreign army can inflict. They are the injuries upon the tender souls of children (and sometimes adults) when they are trusting another human and looking to that person for love and care. But when they instead find harsh and hateful treatment from those who should love them, or when they are abused by others because those who should have protected them did not do so, *that* is the hurt that will not heal and can potentially maim a life for the next 70 years, doing much greater damage than a bomb from North Korea could ever inflict.

These deep wounds require the healing power of genuine love, applied day by day over an extended period of time until the injured one can allow the old wound to be opened and the poisonous infection to be cleared out.

It may seem impossible . . . but healed we can be.

## 11.7

Bear with me for a moment as I glance at the darkness.

Charles Manson was a crazy man in my growing-up days. One look at his eyes and you thought "Wacko!" Yet he somehow got a devoted following of young women and dominated them to the extent that they were willing to kill for him in ways that shocked the world at the time.

Later would come names such as Jeffrey Dahmer and Timothy McVeigh, people who brutally killed innocent men, women, and children.

Later still would be the name Osama Bin Laden, who changed the world by commanding his followers to fly airplanes into buildings, a moment in time that my generation will forever remember. As my elders used to say concerning the day JFK was shot or the day Pearl Harbor was bombed, I recall exactly where I was on 9/11 and the horror of watching people jump to their deaths from dozens of stories in the air just before the skyscrapers came crashing to the ground in a heap of metal, glass, and concrete. Also etched in my psyche from those days are the videos of religious Muslims dancing in the streets in their country as they rejoiced over the victory of their spiritual leader, Bin Laden. It is a sign of the most grotesque parts of humanity, and surely doesn't represent what all Muslims stand for.

To equal that kind of horror, one must go back to another crazy man named Hitler, who rounded up millions of people and either starved them to death, shot them, or burned them in his gas chambers . . . all in the name of racial cleansing.

What is wrong with humans! I will tell you my thought on this. It is called the sin nature. And we are born with it. All of us.

Before I get too many rants about how most would never do these atrocities (a fact I completely agree with), don't forget that something only slightly less evil is at work when a man rapes a woman or molests a child, an occurrence that is said to happen over 400,000 times per year in America alone. *Four hundred thousand!*

And what is at work in the 44 people who murder another human being each and every day in our country?

Are you not convinced yet? How about this figure: There are 2.9 million cases of child abuse *reported* in our country each year. The most vulnerable of us all; the most innocent, abused. This sickens me to the core. And it does sicken most of us, I still hope and believe. So are most of us are good despite the 2.9 million? I wonder.

Far down the road from Hitler's and Bin Ladin's abode, a sharp turn at the corner from where rapists and abusers live, down a steep hill from where murderers dwell, lives another section of mankind who may normally be kind to their neighbors and generally love their spouses and children. Yet in a moment of weakness they cheat on that spouse so they can get a thrill, and in so doing they crush hearts and destroy lives. How do we categorize that?

*These "decent" people have now caused fracture-like hurts that may leave people crippled for years to come if not somehow healed.*

What about the times a normally loving person yells at their spouse because their day was bad, or they didn't appreciate the tone with which a response was made?

Step inside the closed doors of many homes and hear children being called stupid or being yelled at harshly for some accidental offense, or for being needy or obnoxious or disobedient.

*These "loving" people have begun to cause blister-like wounds that, if repeated long enough and without healing attention, will begin to build infection and cause lives that "limp."*

Turn down a street that may be even closer to yours and you will find hardworking people who do what the boss says, come home every night to enjoy their family, but quickly become angry when an elderly gentleman pulls out in front of them and then express that anger with gestures and a contorted face to a possibly gentle old soul. Am I hitting too close to home?

Step onto school grounds and hear what kids say to one another, commenting on their peers' deficiency of looks, or ability, or intelligence, or even the way he or she talks, if it is just a bit different from others.

*Here we find repetitive wounds like the grinding of a tiny piece of sand in our shoes—or death by a hundred cuts—affecting self-image and every step that will be taken as an adult.*

I could go on with endless examples in this glimpse of darkness where people hurt people every day, even hurting those they love the most, sometimes surprised at themselves after doing it. I am included in their number.

And I hate to break this last bit of news. Time does not heal all these kinds of wounds. That is a nice thing we like to say, but it isn't true. Time covers them over, sort of like a scab. And when least expected, the infection will come bursting out and the pain comes rushing back as if the experience happened yesterday.

Can there be true healing? Can we step away from this dark place? Yes. There is a way and there is a place.

# 12.0

The very root of healing power is love. Time doesn't heal wounds. Love does. Gentle and tender care does. Acceptance does. And there used to be a place that dispensed this kind of healing balm as part of its core purpose for existence.

Alas, I fear that place is now seldom found to be what it was intended to be. Instead of being a place of love and healing, it has too often become a place of judgment and self- righteousness. Where it is supposed to be a place of truth, it has often become a place of whatever is thought to sell best and bring the biggest crowd. It has become a mockery. It is full of hypocrisy and dead men's bones.

But that is no surprise really. And neither is it something new. Jesus, the One sent by God to be the representation of God's love on earth, ran into the same mess when He encountered the religious leaders of His day about 2,000 years ago. He called those leaders blind guides who loved the praise of men but wouldn't lift a finger to help others. In fact, while He was an example of love to outcasts of society, He was probably the biggest critic of the so-called "church" of His day.

That church ridiculed Him and called Him a "friend of sinners." He got the name because he hung out with the "undesirables" with the sole purpose of helping them, healing them, and loving them into a new life.

That church called for this gentle and loving man's crucifixion, beating Him as He was led to His death.

There He hung, His blood pouring down from the nails and the beating. And every sin ever conceived of in man's evil heart, every action of the Hitlers, the Dahmers, the Mansons, the Bin Ladens, and every one of us, every evil thought conjured up—*all* of it was deposited upon Jesus, as the one perfect man who ever lived gave His life blood as payment in full for all the evil actions of mankind before and after Him.

There is a true church in the world. It is one that extends this same love. It does not bow to the whims of society. It is not judgmental, but it does hold to the truth of the Word of God. It is not self-serving. It is designed, instead, to serve. It does not place loads of expectation upon its people. It removes loads of failure and a lifetime of hurts. It accepts with open arms all who come and welcomes them to be healed and have their lives transformed.

Healed . . . that is the way to live and that is the way to run. I have found that I cannot run if I'm hurt, not well anyway. But if I am healed and whole, bring the race on!

*"He gets hungry and his strength fails; he drinks no water and becomes weary."*

## MILE 13

# Nutrition and Hydration

A week after running a half marathon at a 9:59 pace (a good pace for me) and just 3 weeks into my official training period for my third marathon, I decided to take a long weekend getaway with my wife. I had been sick earlier in the week. Not sick, sick. I just hadn't felt myself since the half marathon a few days prior; not much energy, stomach a bit uncertain.

We were in Branson, Missouri, for some R&R but I could not skip my weekend run of "only" nine miles. And it was a nice place to run, too. The path behind the Branson Landing shops offers the scenery of Lake Taneycomo running parallel to it. The shops are off to the left, and along the way you run into an area for tourists with a water attraction that features the merging of fire, light, and music, complete with water fountains shooting 120-foot geysers into the air. I was set to enjoy my journey along the lake.

Three miles into my run, I knew I was in trouble. I began to slow dramatically. After five miles, I had to walk some. By mile 6 I told my wife, who was reading beside the lake, that I was going to walk out the last two to three miles because my legs were dead, and my body had no stores of energy. Here, just a week removed from an energetic half marathon, I felt almost powerless to continue.

The thing I already knew, but had ignored, rang in my head: "Nutrition and hydration are the key" to successfully completing these long runs. Without it, the will cannot drive the body long enough. It will fail.

I've encountered this phenomenon so many times, where even a 5-mile run, without proper nutrition and hydration, can seem harder to accomplish than a 15-mile run with good preparation. It is quite possibly the primary key to the entire running experience.

# 12.1

When Americans go car shopping and are looking for particular features, trends change almost as fast as the seasons. When I was growing up, nobody would have ever dreamed about a backup camera or a vibrating steering wheel that would nudge you back to center if you were about to stray off the edge of the road or into the center line.

Safety has become paramount. That's great, usually. My wife and I were once in the car with my first grandson. She had run into a store while I sat in the car with the sleeping baby, all cuddled into his newfangled car seat.

Now, I was about 20 years removed from the last time I had strapped our girls into *much* simpler car seats, devices that a normal adult can look at and figure out, even one with as little mechanical ability as I have. But the car seat which secured my grandson that night was designed for the future, and for more technologically advanced people.

Then the moment came that made the memory. He began to stir. My wife continued to shop for whatever necessity was inside that store.

Then the crying came. He was only about a year old. Papa sat beside him, giving gentle encouragement that Nana would be right back, and we'd be on our way. Within minutes the cries became screams, reaching a crescendo of ever- increasing octaves and intensity. I couldn't stand it. I had to get him out and hold him.

Now envision a grown man, a dark car in a parking lot, a screaming baby boy, and a car seat from hell. Just unplug the front fastener, like you always did when you raised children. But it won't unplug. Some safety device wouldn't let it . . . and I was too dense to figure out why.

It is like the newfangled gas cans that require a physics degree to get the gas to pour. I fiddled and wiggled and pulled. It was hopeless. By this time, he was in full-on hysteria. I was closing in on the same. Are those people walking by looking in at me with a strange look?

Ignore them. Work the problem.

I began by pulling one leg out. Here we go. Next get an arm loose. Okay. Now if I can just work his head out of this area. Oh no. Is his head overly large or is the strap tightening?

The hysteria has reached epic levels. Is he screaming that loud, or is it my screams now raising the pitch? He has become like a field of roosters at dawn. It is full-on constant noise of alarm.

Somehow, after what seemed like 15 minutes, I pulled his body from that ridiculous safety device in a manner that no child was ever intended to be released. As I held him, we probably both had a calming cry. I'm pretty sure it wasn't a bonding moment. No, I am fairly certain that if my precious grandson could have verbalized his thoughts right then, they would have been "Papa, you have some very serious grandparenting deficiencies and I'm going to make sure Nana never leaves me in the car with you ever again." Or something like that. Amazingly, he wasn't scarred (I think).

In my defense, I come from the generation where my mother's right arm was my protection if there was a fast stop while I was standing up in the front seat beside her (a criminal offense these days, but routine then). And devices were *so* much simpler when I was raising children. How times have changed.

But I've gone off course in my story. Apparently, my soul needed a public confession time. Say three Hail Marys.

My point here was supposed to be about how the features of cars change so rapidly. A 2009 article informed me that the most important features for a new car buyer began with leather seats. Sunroof was number 3. Third row seating, number 4. Automatic transmission and a tow hitch made the list. Cruise control was number 10.

Fast-forward 10 technology-laden years and the list I've just mentioned seems archaic . . . sort of like my simple car seat from yesteryear.

Now the top desires are auto-emergency braking, forward collision warning, rear cross traffic warning, Apple car play, 360-degree surround view cameras, and (of course) all activities should be voice activated.

But there is one thing that hasn't changed from the time the Model T Ford first began mass production in the early 1900s. No matter what the piece of metal looks like, no matter what fancy wheels it has, no matter how comfy the seats are or how beautiful the vehicle may be, and no matter what fancy technology is available for connecting with the outside world or avoiding collisions, it is all just a hunk of metal unless it has one very important thing. Fuel. Something that propels. Even the eco-friendly electric cars must have something to propel that hunk forward. Something must make it move.

# 12.3

Imagine the runners of the world as an animation similar to the Transformer movies.

The Goodyear tires of the car turn into the New Balance shoes. The rims are the Feetures brand socks. The bucket seats turn into the anti-chafing shorts (surprisingly important), the windshield and wipers become the moisture-absorbing shirts.

Look under the hood and you see the hemi engine block as it morphs into the beating heart of the runner. The computerized systems that link it all together and make it run in timing, synchronized, gradually fade away as the mind and will of the runner take shape.

The car—the runner—has all it needs to complete the race with endurance, if only it had one more item. Fuel.

Oh, we can push it along for a bit. It will roll. It will shine. It may look really fine. But it is not useful until oil and lubricants flow through the system and gasoline lights a spark that begins to turn pistons that push that hunk forward.

All the perfect clothing, the perfect training, and the greatest hearts of lions will fall short without one key element . . . fuel. Water is fuel for the runner.

Water is an absolute necessity to propel a long-distance runner through a race.

The body needs it for almost every process, including regulating body temperature, lubricating joints and the spinal cord, helping transport toxins out of the cells, and delivering oxygen throughout the body.

Without water, the body is unable to function correctly and will soon begin to stop working altogether. The effects of dehydration come on quickly, especially in extremely hot conditions. Without water, the body cannot produce sweat. This can lead to a dangerous increase in body temperature and put pressure on the fluid in the body, including the blood.

I recently heard a physician say that many long-distance runners who are not highly trained athletes often finish a marathon in a mild state of shock, caused by the stresses placed upon the body. Another physician I met told me that in Chicago, the yearly marathon produces a big increase of patients for the local emergency rooms. Dehydration can be one of the reasons for the emergency treatment that a few marathon runners will need. So proper hydration is imperative for a runner. But I also need . . .

*Food. Caloric intake is also fuel for a runner.*

One running site states that a marathon runner will lose the equivalent of 10 Big Macs' worth of calories. Another says you will burn enough energy to power your iPhone for a year. Hmmm.

So the harder part of the "fuel equation" is possibly the caloric intake needed to overcome the loss of 10 Big Macs and allow your body to stay strong enough to finish the race well.

I've tried all manner of things while doing long runs, including using gels that hurt my stomach and threatened a GI (gastrointestinal tract) problem. I've tried combinations of dried fruit, pretzels, honey sticks, and power bars. The list goes on. But while it is a challenge to find the exact mix that will both power your body and *not* make your body sick, figuring it out it is an extremely important part of the race.

This car needs fuel. This body needs water and calories. And when it has it, boy oh boy, look at that hot rod run!

# 12.5

Was he 80 years old . . . 85? I wasn't sure of the number. What I was sure of was that he was in charge on this day. His son was there (age 55?), his grandson, his grandson's father-in-law (me), and another friend or two; and all were looking to the man with the grey hair as he extended his arm toward the cement truck.

The truck was backing carefully down the hill as the elderly gent provided direction. His extended fist formed, and the truck promptly stopped. The man then turned his attention to the chute that was protruding from the back of the truck like the trough of a water slide at an amusement park, positioning it above the forms that had been built to receive the deposit about to come forth.

We were positioned with shovels along the length of the forms, each about 25 feet long. We waited. Then the day's boss began a swirling motion with his arm. Immediately, the truck driver engaged some lever that opened the gaping hole in the back of the ever-rotating cylinder. A mixture of water and rock came belching forth from the beast, pouring down the chute and into the waiting forms. But no sooner had it begun, when our leader's fist again formed, and his arm stopped waving. The hole shut, the mixture stopped pouring, and the last of the goo came slowly down the chute.

*Why did we stop?* I asked without speaking. My son-in-law's grandfather was examining the consistency of the mix. He shouted instructions to the mixing truck driver, "Add a little more water to this mix." I don't recall all the details, only that someone *knew* what was needed and was giving the instructions.

In moments, adjustments made as ordered, the beast opened its mouth again, and out poured the froth of stuff that would become the security of my daughter's new home.

This was repeated for a couple of hours as the truck repositioned, poured, and we labored to push the heavy mess to every corner of the forms. All the while, the elderly boss was waving, making a fist, instructing each one of us, making sure it was level, and occasionally adding his own muscle to the chore.

He had the experience. He'd been here before, many times, in fact. There was no hesitation, no questioning, no discussion. And we received the benefit as we watched and learned, quietly observing the one in charge . . . thankful for his presence here on this important day.

During the 15+ years I knew this gentle man, I often observed him with admiration. His gait was slow, like one walking with a familiar companion of pain. He likely had a hard time getting out of bed on cold mornings, likely took medication for various ailments, and had certainly seen his share of tragedy, including those of a man who'd fought on a battleship in the U.S. Navy during World War II.

But his countenance was always pleasant, his words always kind and caring, and he carried himself with what appeared to be a known and humble purpose—that his final days and years were in service to his family . . . who soaked up his presence and benefited from his knowledge, just as had been done on this day.

I was blessed to be at his funeral a few short years later. He'd gone fairly quickly and had not had to tarry in misery as many do as they leave this life.

The family gathered for a simple celebration at the place where his body would be laid to rest. Because of his service to our country, an honor guard was present, guns were fired, and the American flag was carefully folded and presented to his grieving widow.

His grandsons led the affair, humbly and with gentle care, now emulating what they'd seen in the man to whom they were bidding farewell. They told funny stories and relived memories together of the man, the patriarch of the family.

Was he eighty-eight when he died? Ninety? I do not know for sure. What I do know is that the man I watched that day had something going on that I'd love to experience when I reach my latter years.

The body was worn, he ached, and he had pains . . . his physical heart was slowly failing him. But his soul was still rich and vibrant and able to affect those who came around. I guess you could say his soul was still abundantly watered, and his being was still full of food and nutrients that continued to enrich his life and those around him, up until the very end.

I watched him and I perceived that the source of his ongoing inner strength and vitality was purpose. He had a purpose to live. It was to serve his family, to love them, and to enjoy them every moment he could. This man was still needed and wanted, and he knew it. So his soul kept on running until his body gave out. He ran his race well, to the end.

## 12.7

I'm winding down this section about the soul of man and it will be completed in the next section as I tell of the experience of running my second marathon in the title chapter of the book, *Go See the Beautiful* (Mile 14).

I have arrived at the place from which I started, speaking about purpose. The story of Norma (Mile 8), who fought a brave fight against cancer, with the purpose of always being kind and spreading encouragement every day, while different from the story of this elderly man who recently died, there is also similarity between them. They are two life stories, but each were lives lived with a driving purpose wherein great value was found.

As I consider the lives of each one who may read what I am writing, I recognize that they are surely as different as the face of each human. No one has had my experiences, both good and bad. No one has had yours, both the blessings and the crushing events. All unique. And yet, we all live still.

I consider that some have not had a life as blessed as mine, including my loving mother and father, my wonderful wife of 36 years, 3 girls I adore and who love me back, 9 grandchildren whose faces I am always eager to see. It is almost too much blessing to conceive of and write about without an understanding that many have experienced things so traumatic that my story can seem to be a flaunted arrogance. I pray it is not.

But I too have experienced the hard parts of life. I have been in an emergency room, looking into the eyes of my baby girl whose eyes were wide open but not looking back after she had been knocked unconscious for several heartrending minutes and we wondered if a brain injury had occurred, tears pouring forth from us when she finally began to cry and ask for people by name.

I have seen loss of loved ones riddled with diseases that are too cruel to believe. I have felt the crush of hearts nearest to me when hurts too deep to express occurred.

All of this, the blessing and the pain, is a part of the fabric of this life for each one of us.

But our book is not yet complete. There are pages still to be written, no matter where we've come from, no matter what evil and unfair abuses have poured into our souls. If only we can get up and begin to write the new pages.

Have you read books that leave you wanting more? Alternately, have you read a book where you come to the end and say to yourself, "What a colossal waste of time. I hated it." (Hopefully, you aren't experiencing that today!)

But there are books where you become so interested in the characters that you wish they were real. And when the last page is turned, there is an odd mixture of satisfaction and disappointment. Satisfaction from the experience and what you gained from it. Disappointment because there are no more pages to turn.

There are books that start rough but end good. There are books that start good and fizzle out, as if the writer lost his way at the end.

Our lives can be the same, in every descriptive way. What will be written on the final pages is ours to direct. Oh, I know life itself may have something to say about the twists and turns in the plot. But *we* write on the pages. *we* determine how the good twists will affect us and how the incivility of others will be dealt with.

We and we alone determine the purpose of our lives, how we will respond to every challenge, whether we will rise to it or fall beneath it, and how we will enjoy the beauties all around us.

We can decide to "add a little water to this mix."

# 13.0

Anyone who has given me the privilege of reading almost 13 miles of this work knows something by now; there is a deeper driving purpose within me, one that goes beyond the 80 to 90 years we get on this earth. There is a purpose for me beyond being kind to my neighbor and loving to my wife and children. There is something greater than caring equally for every race and gender of people.

I am not writing here to convince or persuade. I am only communicating a conviction that I hold—that there is something within the soul of man that reaches for eternity. Some will say it is there, indeed, but it is satisfied in the impartation of knowledge, convictions, love, and experience from one generation to the next, and the knowledge that when we die, we do, in a sense, live on within those we leave behind.

Okay. I get that and I even agree to a large extent. Much of my purpose here was and still is impartation to those in my sphere of influence, whether that sphere is big or small.

Hopefully, it includes my children and grandchildren . . . and maybe someday great grandchildren if I am blessed with many years. Hopefully, too, it will include co-workers or neighbors or friends.

But for me, there is yet something deeper that responds to that call of the eternal. I do believe in God as the Creator. I believe He is like a father and I am like a son. And as I looked in wonder at the firstborn daughter my wife and I had "created" and love like I had never known came flooding out of my soul, so too I believe that an all-powerful God who spoke and created life, looks upon us with an all-consuming love that changes the makeup of hearts and minds . . . that literally changes our entire lives.

And if it is true, then there is a purpose beyond this life that is even greater than instilling goodness and integrity into the next generation. If it is true, then there is water and food for the thirsty and hungry soul that truly satisfies like nothing ever known.

*"He makes my feet like the feet of a deer; He causes me to stand on the heights."*

## MILE 14

# Go See the Beautiful

I have been blessed to be able to do short training runs on the gorgeous island of Kauai (the single most beautiful place in the world, in my opinion), with the blue waves of the Napali Coast beating the shores down the steep cliffs below me. I have had a 19-mile training run against a backdrop of the Rocky Mountains surrounding me as I made several laps around Lake Estes.

But my marathon run in Springfield, Missouri, somehow managed to equal, in its own way, the majesty of Kauai's coastline and the mighty mountain peaks of Estes Park, Colorado. How could this be possible in flat-land America? Simply put, it was the marvel of the trees on a perfect autumn day.

The trees were breathtaking in their array of multi-colored beauty. It was November 4 and the fall colors had never seemed quite so vivid as they were on this day. It was absolutely the perfect day to run my second marathon. I will always remember the trees.

# 13.1

My brother-in-law and I had trained for this day during the heat of summer and into early fall. But fall, that year, didn't quickly bring reduced temps. I recall long runs on very hot Saturday or Sunday mornings, with fluid refills stashed along the way.

There was the 18-mile run that included steep hills and ended with me having to walk some during the last couple of miles. I arrived at his house, our ending destination, in a mild state of shock, I think, having totally depleted my body of the necessary levels of fluid and "fuel." For probably an hour after the run, I recuperated, questioning again if I had what it took to complete my second marathon.

There was the Saturday morning when the temperatures finally fell from summer heat, and we experienced a 25-degree change from one Saturday to the next. There was no gradual change that year. It was hot, then it was cold.

And then there was our final long training run together, the ultimate pre-marathon test for us, the 20-mile run that we decided to do on a flat surface three weeks before the race. On that day, the elements threw buckets of water on us, laughing at us as we ran. The rain began at about mile 10, a light misting at first, until we were gradually soaked through. And then the heavens opened and poured out upon us, as if to say, "You can't do this. You can't beat the elements and accomplish this goal." It was perfect. Our reply was, "Oh yeah, watch us!" and on we ran, occasionally laughing at the absurdity as we went.

It was a challenge, to be sure. I look back on it now as a moment I will never forget from our marathon training together. There was pain that day, but we went on, drenched like wet dogs, surely a sight to behold for people who drove by us along the streets. *Are they insane?* must have been the thoughts. Not insane . . . just determined.

And then there was the last 12-mile run as we began the pre-marathon weeks of tapering, allowing our bodies to prepare for the soon-to-come attempt at 26.2 miles.

Something unique happened for me that day. For the first time (and only time still) in my 5 years of running, I experienced something I had only heard about, a runner's high. At around mile 10, I began to feel it, the slowing of my breathing, the steadiness of my heartbeat as my legs increased the pace. It was incredible. For the first and only time in all our months of training, I heard my buddy's breath behind me rather than it being the other way around. At around mile 11, he said, "Do you know what our pace is?" He informed me of that pace, and we were surprised at the increase as we neared our last mile of the day.

I told him I was feeling strong and like I could run indefinitely and keep running fast.

His response? "Go!" And so I picked up the pace even more. It was wonderful. Ours was not a competition. It was a brotherhood of encouragement. Whatever battle there was, was faced as a team.

As we came to the end of the final mile, I wondered how long I could have gone. I will probably never know. But it was fun, and I hope someday I might experience it again.

Training for the Bass Pro Marathon in Springfield, Missouri, brought with it all the highs and lows of long runs. It also brought the beauty of friendship along many miles of a paved journey together.

Finally, on a cool, almost cold morning in early November, our training culminated with my second marathon.

# 13.3

The morning dawned almost too cold for my plan of shorts and T-shirt. At the starting line of the Bass Pro Shops, the runners gathered, some already braving the cool temps in warm weather gear but most hanging on to their jackets and sweatpants until the last moments. I joined the wimpy crowd and kept mine on.

Our wives arrived at the starting line. We received our final encouragements from them. My brother-in-law, Christopher, became entangled in his sweats during the last few moments before the gun went off. It was a comical moment, wondering if he would miss the gun as he fought with his clothing. He finally cleared them, and we quickly joined the waiting throng. There were around 3,000-3,500 people for the event, so it was about 1/8 of the crowd I had joined for my first marathon in OKC, but it still had a fun local atmosphere.

Final moments of anticipation ticked down, and we were off. For those who don't know, there are always "pacers" in long-distance running. These are folks who know they can run the race at a set pace, allowing any who want to shoot for that pace to become their entourage. Pacers are like all people. I have been by those who offer brief words of encouragement along the way but say little else. I've also been beside those who talk almost constantly about whatever topic hits their brains.

Unfortunately, Christopher and I were about to commit the error referenced often in this book. We were running at a faster pace than we should have been and faster than my running mentor had instructed. But the cool air felt so good. The weeks of tapering had left us fresh. We remembered the great 12-mile run from just two weeks ago. We felt strong and ready. Because of that feeling, I think we both (mistakenly) thought this was going to be one of those moments when all the elements came together for a race that would be surprisingly excellent.

We soon moved ahead of the pacer, who would be finishing in the time we'd previously had as a goal. In a few minutes he was far behind us. We were on a blazing pace compared to what our long training runs had been, and we were in for a fall and a hard lesson before the race ended. That pacer would be seen by us again.

The first 7 or 8 miles were enjoyable as we ran through the neighborhoods of Springfield, Missouri, and were awed by the stunning beauty of the trees in all their glorious colors. I recall one block where enormous trees provided a canopy over the yards and streets. It is hard to describe how amazing it was with color splashed all over the ground and yet the trees seemed to be holding about 90 percent of their leaves.

"The trees! The trees!"

Those words from a children's book I had read to my girls possibly three decades ago went through my mind. The book described trees more beautiful than the character had seen in all his life. That comes close to describing what the trees were like for the Bass Pro Marathon of 2018. It was like a painting and almost seemed as if it couldn't be real. I doubt I'll be graced with a marathon run exactly like that again.

Despite the inspiration of the trees, my buddy and I soon began to realize we might be in trouble due to our early fast pace. Go out fast and hang on? We hadn't trained up enough for that plan. Go out fast and crash was what was about to happen. Our first inkling of that possibility hit around mile 12.

He told me he had to make a quick pit stop at the mile marker porta potty. Only a minute or two was lost. But something about the stop affected me mentally. Running is such a mental sport.

I didn't begrudge the stop at all. I had to make one of my own in my third marathon.

And hadn't he waited on me on the day of our 18-mile run as I irrigated an unsuspecting field in the tall weeds on a country road? Hey! If you gotta go, you gotta go.

I believe it was here that a pacer went by carrying the time flag that represented what would have been our best goal of the day.

We would not see him again. The pacer whose time flag embodied our more realistic goal was still behind us, not close enough to be seen . . . yet. On we went, possibly a tad more slowly than before.

The aches and pains of the challenge began to hit with force by about mile 15. Sure, we had done a twenty-miler just three weeks ago. But that had been at a more reasonable pace and on flat roads. Today we had burned through too much energy in the early excited stages as we ran the gentle hills of Springfield. We were now beginning to pay the price.

Other runners came along and began to pass. At mile markers, we began stopping to stretch. First, it occurred every couple of miles but soon it was more frequent. I kept glancing back, fearing the next pacer would go by. Finally, he did. We would not see him again either.

We began periods of walking followed by periods of jogging. Soon the walking gained frequency and the jogging decreased. One or the other would say, "Let's start again at that car" or "Let's run until the next mile marker" and we'd urge our desperate bodies on again.

By mile 23, Christopher was experiencing great pain in multiple parts of his body. We were at a place he had never been before, and I'd only experienced once, back when I walked much of the last half of the race at OKC. We were still ahead of my OKC pace, but not by a lot.

I don't recall much of the last three miles other than a feeling of pain and disappointment. Disappointment because I had yet again ignored advice and was paying the price. Pain was to be expected, but the addition of disappointment made it seem worse.

And yet, we went on. With the pain and disappointment were also a measure of enjoyment and a sense of accomplishment. We were now to the point that we would almost certainly finish, as the last two miles approached.

Seeing mile marker 26 was like seeing the gates of heaven. As we came to the turn with the finish line just ahead, we began to turn on the speed, possibly approaching the speed with which we had begun our race those 5 hours earlier. It was a great feeling and the strongest finish line burst of the 4 marathons I ran for this book. (It was not my best overall time. Marathon 3 has that distinction.)

Together we crossed, arms lifted in victory, eyes searching for our wives among the small crowd of supporters still gathered.

Months of training had passed. A hundred training miles of conversations about life had occurred. A common goal had been reached. A battle of mind over body had been fought. And we had won . . . on a gorgeous day in Springfield, Missouri.

## 13.7

My dad has a saying; most dads have a few. One I'll always remember from my dad is to enjoy the journey. It is the outlook of the optimist. Thank God for people who look out on life and see the possibilities rather than the troubles.

My wife is like that too and I am blessed because of it. I have relayed the following story to a few who know us. It is 100 percent true.

We were driving into town one day, in no particular hurry. About five miles from the outskirts of town, we both glanced out to the right side of the car and saw a house that sits all by itself in the middle of a huge field. Very few trees were there because it had only recently been built by a banker in town. It was luxurious and oddly placed.

On this particular day there was something even more unusual. Cars. Lots of them.

There were probably 20-30 cars lining the drive up to the little mansion. What could be going on there?

Simultaneously, my wife and I made a declaration of what must be occurring.

Out of my mouth came these words, "Somebody died." At the exact same second, she shouted excitedly, "It's a party!"

We looked at each other with wide eyes and burst out laughing. Because in that one moment of time, our general outlooks on life were declared. I tend to look at the negatives of life. She tends to look on the bright side. That is why we were made for each other. It is also why we have friends. It is because of her. People love her. I do too.

And really, who do people want to be around? The doom and gloom sort that always complains? Or those who see the beauty of life and the potential that exists in the midst of great challenges?

I likely exaggerate a bit about myself. I am not really doomish and gloomish all the time.

I love life and love the wonderful aspects of it. But what we get from it and what we portray among others is so often a choice of will, just like running a great race.

The question is, are we going to gripe about the pain of the race or are we going to gaze in wonder at the beauty of the trees, gloriously displayed all along the path of pain?

## 13.8

I work in a "Count your blessings" kind of job. That is to say, I'm reminded every day to be thankful for what I have and for the events I've *not* had to endure that so many in the world have endured.

I often wonder how people go on after a child has died or a loved one has suffered such great loss. How can you not come unhinged if you witness a tragic accident and the person killed or maimed is your dearest friend?

I'll never forget the day my wife and I took our three girls to the park for a family day of fun. As we played at who knows what (that part I don't remember from 20 years ago) we heard the unmistakable roar of a motorcycle group coming our way down the road that runs beside the park.

In an instant, our enjoyment of the scene changed to horror as one of the cycles misjudged the steep turn of the approaching intersection and his bike fell over and was immediately run over by a trailer being pulled by a vehicle coming from the opposite direction. It was almost like slow motion and at the same time it happened shockingly fast.

We watched the chaotic scene with sideways glances as we tried to protect our girls from seeing anything too gruesome. Soon a helicopter arrived. There was a passenger on the back of the bike who I believe may have survived. But it was all too clear that the driver didn't make it.

Life's joys turning in a moment to one of life's greatest griefs. And many of the friends of the deceased watched it occur or arrived very soon after to discover it.

On the other hand, as I work to help people who have had their lives shattered by unimaginable grief, I am also amazed by the tenacity and resilience of the human spirit. I have seen people of faith exhibit something even deeper than resilience. It is hope in the everlasting, hope that there is something greater than these brief days on this little round rock suspended in space just three blips over from the sun.

Pain and joy. Beauty and loss. These we can all experience on this earth.

Pain and loss, we will all most certainly experience. There is really no choice about that. It will be thrust upon us at some time and place, possibly coming suddenly, unexpectedly like a thief in the night, possibly coming often and with soul-crushing force.

Joy and beauty are also there for the taking for all who choose to do so. They are all around us if we will only look and reach out to take them in our arms.

And beyond this earth, there is something greater still . . . beauty and joy without pain and loss. This is the promise of our Creator for those who will receive it by faith.

## 14.0

*What is that just ahead?* I couldn't quite make it out. But it had my attention.

I was on an early morning 3-mile run down my country dirt road, getting my miles in before work and heat of the day.

It was a good run. I had just made the halfway point and was turning around to head back home. And then I saw it in the dim light.

I had surely just passed it moments ago but hadn't noticed. Now there was no mistaking that a small animal was on my road probably 40 yards ahead. I slowed my pace and then it hit me. The tail was long and straight up in the air. Surely not! Yes. Surely so. It was a skunk.

What to do? If I chose to go the opposite direction, it would mean I'd have to run two and a half miles around the 4-mile section, which included multiple steep hills. I didn't have time to do that and get to work on time.

I decided to slowly, cautiously, continue forward while keeping my eyes glued to my new companion. The only thing worse than being late to work and running extra miles would be . . . you guessed it, being to work on time but smelling like a skunk.

The creature kept pace with me. He didn't dart off into the weeds. Instead, he kept running about 40 yards in front, but he did so like a drunk man. He was all over the road. This way, that way, back and forth. But always progressing forward.

I'm sure it was thinking, *"What the heck is following me!"* But on we both went as the light continued to grow in the early morning sky.

I guess this odd companionship continued for about a half mile, when suddenly the drunk imitator zipped off to my right and into the fields. I slowed, trotted carefully forward, came to where I thought it must have left the road, saw nothing, and turned on the afterburners, sprinting as fast as I could for at least a hundred yards. No smell, no spray. Our paths had crossed and uncrossed, leaving no stains on either of us.

I look back on this now and see this as another "verse" in my running story. It was the day that could have gone awfully awry but instead only added a touch of zest from the department of the unusual. It added to the fabric of this beautiful run we call life.

Who knows what will come tomorrow? Will there be beauty or fun or frolic? Will there be a touch of pain or sorrow? Will there be the unexpected or will it bring the repetition of an ordinary day?

Or maybe the real question is . . . what will I see tomorrow? What will I choose to pursue?

I will end here by borrowing words from my wife that were so well written and succinctly capture what I'm trying to say:

*Rus and I love to hike. Perfect date: Fancy dinner? Nope. Movie theater? Nah. For us, it's throwing backpacks in the car and heading out to the trails. Arkansas is our destination of habit. But my heart is in the mountains out west. Rockies, Cascades, Sierra Nevada. Earth-pounding waterfalls and breathtaking overlooks are the rewards of hard work. Muscles straining, lungs burning, and heart racing as we hike those unending inclines. And when we find that flat spot, oh it is heaven. We take advantage and stop to grab some water, Rus sometimes pouring a little on his head. We rest for a minute, encouraging each other that we can make it, that we are doing it, and we feel refreshed and keep moving. And this, my friend, is life. As the scripture says, when we are in His will, on His trail, if you will, He will make our ground level. We all have things we're facing that cause our muscles to scream, our lungs to burn, and our hearts to beat just a little too fast. It's hard. But then, God sends us His good Spirit and for a moment we find rest and refreshment on level ground. And His Spirit whispers, you can do this. You are doing this. And on we go. Life can be hard, but those waterfalls and views are not seen by taking the easy path. Go see the beautiful!*

# Training for the Jack & Jill Marathon
# (May the Reader Understand . . . the Storms of Life)

*"I again saw under the sun that the race is not to the swift and the battle is not to the warriors, and neither is bread to the wise nor wealth to the discerning nor favor to men of ability; for time and chance overtake them all."*

## MILE 15

# *Running in the Rain*

S o this happened one day . . .

One Saturday morning in late December between Christmas and New Year's Day, I set out for a 5-mile run during a period when I had no marathons on the horizon. The weather in Oklahoma on Christmas day had been an incredible sixty-five degrees. But the weather was just about to turn. Sixty-five degrees had given way to the high fifties; still excellent! But rain was in the forecast and, after a full day of rain, colder weather would return.

I awoke at a very late hour, doldrums keeping me in their clutches. I sat for a few minutes contemplating. I knew rain was coming. I glanced out and it looked like it might start at any moment. When it began, it was supposed to be an all-day drencher. I pulled on my running clothes and began the stroll down the lane. The air was pleasant, the wind almost calm. Perfect! In fact, I began to think I had overdressed with my sock cap, gloves, running pants, and long-sleeved shirt. It was warmer than I had expected, maybe mid 50s still.

Within 5 minutes, my gloves were stuffed in my pockets. Within 10, the sock cap came off my head. Within 12, the cap was put back in place as mist began to fall.

It was a pleasant watering upon the earth. I ran on, enjoying it. As the miles went by, the rain increased in intensity. Soon I was drenched. But it was still not an all-out rain. Rather, I would call it a light rain, the kind that annoys you when driving because it is not quite enough to keep the wipers from screeching with each pass of the blades. But for a runner on a 55-degree day, it was almost nice. I'm sure the neighbors who passed me that day thought I was a bit nuts, but I really didn't mind.

On this day, the rain was pleasant.

## 14.2

On another day, this happened to a lady I know who qualified for the Boston Marathon. It seems that many of the prestigious marathon events are scheduled at a purposely iffy time. Temperatures for Boston's premier event in April may be in the 40s or the 60s. The same could be said of the New York City Marathon in early November. But 40-60 degrees sounds like the perfect range for a marathon runner—not too hot, not too cold. Unless . . .

Unless you add to the cool weather a bone-chilling rain.

Boston, April 16, 2018: forecast: heavy rain and wind, high of 50, low of 35. The day would bring pictures of runners draped in make-shift plastic rain coverings (like clear garbage bags) splashing through flooded streets . . . trusting their training, forging on through what looked like misery. This is when people call runners crazy.

The lady I know used Facebook to inform her friends about her race, or "the hurricane" as she called it, but it was the "after race" portion of her story that got my attention. She mentioned going inside a theatre-type building being used as a "warming station" where people could change out of their wet gear. Some were crying because of how cold they were. Hypothermia was a real issue.

Her story became one of survival. Even though she was surrounded by hundreds of other people, she realized everyone was stripping out of their soaked clothes so they could put on something dry. What to do? She began trying to open her bag to get her dry clothing out but realized her cold hands would hardly function. Finally accomplishing it, the choice faced her: modesty or survival? Quickly, she began doing something that most would never do. . . but had to be done on that day. She changed clothes among a host of men and women who were doing the same. What would you choose? Head down, move as fast as you can, get warm, and survive.

It was the rule of unintended consequences striking with full force. But on this day, rain became dangerous.

## 14.3

On yet another day about 30 years ago, this happened.

I floated in a canoe down a main thoroughfare in our town, rowing to the building that was the home of my pizza restaurant, which was now submerged in 5 feet of floodwater after days of a nonstop deluge from the skies. We made the evening news, the story of my pa and me floating down Steve Owens Boulevard in Miami, Oklahoma.

Some days later, the flood waters receded, and we went in to survey the damage. The stench was what hit you first. The floor was still damp and in places small pools of water congregated. "Watch out for snakes" was a bit of advice I paid attention to and, thankfully, didn't need. But as we looked around, I noticed that the water had displaced enormous machinery. So began a cleanup of a mess I will never forget.

On this day, rain's abundance was destructive.

## 14.4

One more day. One more rain.

As I've related elsewhere in this story, one rain I'll never forget is the 20-mile rain run. That's what I'll call it anyway.

The sprinkling began turning to rain as my brother-in-law and I filled up our water bottles and prepared to head out for the final 10 of our 20-mile run. We had started on some dirt roads out in the middle of nowhere, heading back toward Miami, Oklahoma. As we began drawing close to the city, the rain increased in intensity. Soon it was a driving rain, pouring down on us. Nobody stopped to offer us relief. We had water bottles and running belts so we must have looked like we were stupid enough to be doing this on purpose.

Were we miserable? Not according to my recollection. We laughed about it. It was cold but not bitterly cold. If not for the rain, it would have been perfect.

Without verbalizing the sentiment, we simultaneously determined to push through this driving rain and enjoy it, almost as if we were doing our last 20-mile training run in symbolic defiance of all the elements that had come against us over the last 4 months of training.

On this day, rain was a nuisance—and a symbolic enemy to defeat.

## 14.5

Rain is wonderfully neutral. It is sought out as relief. It is cursed as a cruel destroyer. But it is not the rain, not really, that causes our responses. It is the element that precedes the rain, comes with the rain, or follows the rain that really makes the difference. Rain itself is just a part of everyday life.

"I love the rain" can be declared on a quiet Saturday afternoon at home, curled up by the fire with a cup of hot cocoa in your hand. "I sure wish the rain would stop" can be verbalized during a cold spring morning run. "I hate the rain" can be forcefully shouted as you clean floodwater from your home.

It doesn't really matter what we think of it. It won't be shy to come again, just in the nick of time to stop a forest fire or just when you've put up your tent and are trying to start your campfire.

But be sure of this—rains will come . . .

## 14.6

"It rains on the just and the unjust," a wise person once wrote.

Who among earth's human inhabitants can escape daily trials? The flat tire on a cold morning; the slow driver in front of you when you're in a hurry and have no way to pass; the air conditioning unit that goes kaput and will cost $5,000 to replace just when you'd saved enough money for a nice summer vacation. These, and a thousand other aggravations, are a part of what we call "daily life" or things that "rain on our parade" literally and figuratively.

But these aggravating occurrences are not all that life brings, are they? It also brings hard and unexpected events at one point or another. Has anyone ever lived a life without encountering health issues of a loved one? Words we push to the back of our minds, hoping to never hear about those closest to us, or ourselves: cancer, Alzheimer's, or any neurological and disabling disease such as ALS or Multiple Sclerosis.

And there are unexpected tragedies as well. I have referenced seeing my baby girl knocked unconscious. We left the ER that night and had her sleeping in our bed so we could check on her routinely in the night. She awoke as our normal baby girl . . . the highest high. And yet we know that, for some, a tragedy occurs and the child doesn't survive or is never the same again. There are indeed times that we look at what has occurred and wonder how a person can still be standing after the volume and depth of loss they have experienced—after a tornado, or news from war, or a phone call about a car accident in the middle of the night.

These disturbing events are part of the weaving of our life's story. As surely as the rain, we will experience some variation of these kinds of things and the loss that is associated.

But we can also experience amazing events of life: wedding days, babies being born, silver anniversaries, 75th birthdays. We may live to enjoy grandchildren or great grandchildren. We may watch as our children become healers or encouragers to the wounded. We may have the greatest joy of all in seeing them walk in truth and with wisdom in a precarious world.

Indeed, life pours down with an indiscriminate mixture of so many things, some difficult, some wonderful. We never know what is coming next. And it often seems unfair. Life may bring a torrential thunderstorm to my door at the same time it is bringing a cool mist to your summer day. Random, unfeeling, sudden. Life is like the rain.

Yes, storms will come . . . but they will also pass.

## 14.8

. . . or so my wise mother used to say. And she was right. The hard and the bad will eventually fade as we face, and walk through, the tough things that life throws at us. Sunshine comes after rain.

The last section of this book (miles 8-14) was about the things that are done to us, both good and bad, by people; things that have affected, and possibly still affect, our lives. It was also about how to deal with those wounds and how to heal . . . and about the things *we* can do for good.

In this section I intend to run away from what people do to each other, while we run toward what *life* does to us, through no fault or virtue of our own. We will examine how our response to life is just as important as our response to people.

You will notice that many of the miles in section three are titled with a phrase that concludes with "and go on." This is because there really is no other choice that is fruitful. Going on is easy when life surprises us with good things—a big bonus, a promotion, a new grand-child, an apple fritter on Friday. But when life is tough, when the storms seem strongest and the temptation is to fold up and quit, that is when the choice gets much harder. Go on? How? Is it even possible? The answer is, what else is there to do? Would quitting solve anything really? So . . . go on. Pick up the pieces and somehow, go on.

There is a poem mounted in my home. It was written by my baby girl (now 30 years old) about a moment in time with her two sisters. With her permission, I'm adding her poem to my story:

*My lane has many memories,*
*Through sun and snow and wind;*
*Walking with some cousins,*
*A few times with good friends.*

*Once with a young man,*
*Many times alone;*
*One time with a group,*
*But the best that I have known.*

*Were walks beneath umbrellas,*
*Raindrops all around;*
*Falling from heaven's glory,*
*To glimmer upon the ground.*

*But rain made not the moment,*
*Rather a joyous laugh and dance;*
*The delight to become a memory,*
*One day a backward glance.*

*It was the company beside me,*
*Faces with smiles bright;*
*That surpassed the sun's own radiance,*
*And brought new meaning of light.*

*It's a memory I'll hold forever,*
*Through years it shall remain;*
*On a country lane with sisters,*
*Dancing in the rain.*

The poem may not mean much to a reader who doesn't know my girls, but possibly you can grasp the relationship of sisters that is referenced.

A few years later, after one had married and left home, they happened to all be together in our home again one day when a light rain began to fall. Suddenly, one rushed out into the rain with a shriek, a moment later to be followed by two laughing sisters as they ran into the rain and danced a playful dance together. The photos my wife and I took of that moment (which used to be so routine in our home) now sit beside my daughter's poem hanging on our wall. It was a moment when rain was not just good, it was the prompting of blessed memories of a relationship that will withstand any storm.

The last piece that hangs beside these mementos is a plaque we found one day that read simply, "Life isn't about waiting for the storm to pass, it's about learning to dance in the rain." So a photo of girls dancing together, a poem of remembrance, and a plaque determining purpose when something other than an enjoyable rain hits us—these hang side by side as a reminder to me of the blessings and the struggles, both very much a part of every life.

Enjoy those pleasant rains of life, the random things that bring beauty and pleasure into our existence. But also determine to take on the storms with the same purpose that we have during the cool rains; to take whatever this day brings, and go on. *For it is what we do with the next day, after our best day, or (more importantly) after our worst day, that is the key.*

# 15.0

As I began to turn my attention to the possibility of running a third marathon, I was captured by the magnificent beauty of the mountains of Washington state and the downhill Jack & Jill Marathon near Snoqualmie Pass. With its pounding waterfalls and rushing streams, it seemed the perfect place to run.

I began my training during the late winter months of 2019. I experienced cold month running. Soon the cold gave way to April showers, so I experienced running in the rain.

Straining against spring winds was also a common occurrence. But all too soon the heat and humidity of a Midwest summer descended upon me with a vengeance. Then my long runs occurred in the stifling heat and humidity of early morning hours, sweat dropping off my body even as I started my 4:00 a.m. pre-run stroll.

I experienced the entire gamut of conditions that nature's elements could offer. These are part and parcel of the runner's parade of antagonistic forces, each in their own way attempting to beat into our brains that today's run is not worth the sacrifice; that there are better and more enjoyable things to do; that resting on the weekend is a much better way of life than running two or three hours in the cold or the heat or the wind or the rain.

Well, rest is for sissies. Today is for running. And there are mountains to see!

*"From whose womb has come the ice? And the frost of heaven, who has given it birth?"*

## MILE 16

# Through Every Cold Spell that Lingers, Keep On

"Did I just frostbite my stomach?" These are words most of us will never utter in our lifetimes.

It had been one of those winter mornings with cold so intense that temperatures in the teens would be the high for the day. And it was time for my long run. What to do?

I don't enjoy running in extreme cold. Cool is good, nice even, after you get going. Temps in the 40s are perfect for a long run if there is no wind. Temps in the 30s, bearable. Below 20 degrees . . . no thanks. I also don't like running with several pounds of clothes on in an attempt to combat the invasive, cold air.

But alas, I'd hit one of those weekends where the severe cold was not going to lose its grip for the entire week. It would be stinking cold, ridiculously cold, and *You have got to be kidding me* cold. Take your choice.

My choice was stinking cold, and I wore an extra layer to keep the cold at bay.

For pants, I chose my running tights and thick sweatpants. Gloves, sock cap, and my thickest running socks rounded out my gear for my first real winter run. It would be 6 miles, so I'd not be exposed for too long if it was worse than I imagined. Three miles out, three miles back. Easy, right?

Stepping into intense cold brings that breathtaking "Oh gosh, why am I outside, this is stupid" moment. But I know (or think I know) that it will be better when I'm running. After all, don't I usually pull my gloves off after a couple of miles in the "normal" winter cold of 30 degrees? Yes. It will be fine when I get going, surely.

And it was. After a mile or so, the body heated up with the exertion. My nose was cold. My face was cold. But everything else settled into feeling less than miserable. It was still a tad uncomfortable, for sure. But it was bearable.

Around mile 3, at the furthest point from my house, I noticed something that began to make me slightly uncomfortable. My sweat seemed to be initiating a *freezing* feeling to my core. I got the sensation that the warming trend of my body had reversed, at least where my stomach was concerned. My chest was getting colder too but my stomach was feeling intensely cold.

It became painful. I increased my pace. Couldn't quit. Must endure. Must finish. But I knew now that the warmth was not going to come back. It was cold and getting colder.

When I arrived back home, I quickly began to shed the clothing, knowing I needed to get dry. After my last layer of shirts came off, I glanced at my stomach. What?! Purple! And then the thought came: *Is it possible that I just frostbit my stomach? Is that even a thing?*

I've heard stories of mountain climbers on Everest who are cold for so long that they lose fingers and toes, the extremities. Even parts of noses have been lost, I think. Here, all of my body seemed to be fine except my stomach. *So what happens if you frostbite your stomach, I wondered?*

I wasn't really concerned. But as the day went on, the odd coloring didn't leave. I think it became less intensely purple, but a certain deep red hue remained for hours. I got warm. But my tummy stayed very embarrassed about what I'd done for most of that day.

There was no permanent damage done. But I realized that one could get a bodily injury from intense cold if exposed to it for too long . . . even if he is running with extra layers.

I also came away with this lesson: Running in the intense cold can leave a mark that you will remember.

## 15.2

Although I pledge to turn to lighter fare within a couple of miles, I will be addressing in this mile (as well as miles 17 and 20) some of life's dealings that are the most difficult of our human journey. I could certainly focus my writing on the fun or the funny (like purple stomachs, I guess) but the primary aim here is to delve into topics that are real, into things on this life journey that challenge us to the very core, and the choice presented to us to (1) fold up and quit, or (2) somehow find a way to go on in spite of the trauma life at times brings.

I will also say that it is unlikely that anyone can ever know how they'll respond to certain losses until the loss has occurred. And anyone who has not experienced a particular loss should probably not opine on how to react. I will try not to break that rule.

Who can know the feelings of losing a child early in pregnancy? Who will understand the loss of a child because of an odd illness or a tragic event? Who can fathom the depths of anguish when military officers stride to your door to present the solemn news of your greatest fear? Only those who have lived it, suffered, and somehow had to find a way to go on.

The story I am about to tell is true. It concerns that unique bond between a mother and her child. It will deal with questions and challenges to one's faith. And it will deal with fears of the greatest loss, then fears realized. But when we are through, it is my hope that it will provide a way through, or at least a glimpse of a light at the end of a great, dark tunnel and a way of victory over some of the greatest pain imaginable.

I ask, then, that you walk with me back in time to the late 1960s and early 1970s, and into yet another period of tremendous upheaval in our country as demonstrators marched in resistance to what was thought (by some) to be a great evil. And yet, it was a time where brave soldiers (many of whom were drafted into service by their country) struggled, fought, and died . . . in a place far from home in the jungles and tunnels of Vietnam.

## 15.3

It was the summer of 1967. A brand-new car would cost you less than $3,000. Putting fuel in that car, 33 cents per gallon. A new home would average $25,000. A first-class stamp was 5 cents. Vin Diesel and Julia Roberts had just been born.

The United States Supreme Court declared that it was unconstitutional for any state not to allow interracial marriage and the high court's first African American justice, Thurgood Marshall, was confirmed. America had not yet reached the moon.

In 1967, Muhammad Ali was stripped of his boxing title for refusing to go to war in Vietnam. Public support for the war fell below 50 percent in the United States. President Lyndon B. Johnson engaged in an effort to prop up support for the war, but over 100,000 people marched on Washington DC that October in protest. By the next year, Johnson's support and credibility had waned due to what came to be known as the "Tet Offensive" as North Vietnam launched one of the largest military campaigns of the war, hoping to crush the hopes and efforts of American troops and its allies with a series of surprise attacks against military and civilian command and control centers throughout South Vietnam.

Leonard Elzy Eulitt (or Lennie, as everyone called him) had just completed his master's degree in history at the University of Arkansas, just about two hours away from his parents' country home in northeast Oklahoma. He was in his early twenties and was gentle by nature, the studious sort.

While his three younger brothers enjoyed hunting and fishing and all the outdoor games that young boys can dream up, Lennie was, for his mother, the child who enjoyed shopping and the gentler things of life.

Lennie's mom had four boys and one daughter, but her daughter had sustained a permanent brain injury, either in utero or at birth. Sadly, she would never progress past the mental capability of an infant. So of the five children, Lennie would become the closest, in many ways, to his mother.

Lennie would also be the one to go to college and earn degrees. History was his passion.

While other young men his age were out partying and chasing girls, his spare time found him at the library, looking up battle scenes.

His bedroom was a trove of memorabilia of the Civil War, the paths of the troops, maps marking the spots of key battles. On weekends, he would travel to battle sites within driving distance. He would sit for hours and learn from elderly folks who gladly granted him time, sharing stories of a generation or two just passed, stories of battles and of lives changed.

To be a teacher of history was a goal he was about to accomplish with his master's degree just completed. He had paid his dues, but it wasn't like a down payment to him. He loved it. He was ready to begin his career and really, to begin his adult life. Everything was in front of him. Possibly, he was about to find part of the purpose of his life.

But that summer, the next of history's wars found him.

## 15.4

What kind of chill blows through a mother's heart when she first hears the news that her son has been called into a mortal conflict in a land halfway around the world? How cold is that moment? How bracing is that wind?

During a time of war, there are surely few more odious words in the English language than *drafted*. At least, this would seem true in the heart of a mother of boys in the 1960s. But millions of mothers experienced it. Dixie Eulitt, Lennie's mom, was one.

During the Vietnam War era, between 1964 and 1973, the U.S. military drafted 2.2 million American men. It is not the first time in U.S. history that the draft was utilized. But it was certainly a controversial time for it.

In March of 1965, President Johnson sent the first U.S. combat troops into South Vietnam with the stated purpose of fighting the spread of Communism from the North. The casualties of this long war were extensive and brutal due to guerilla warfare. This was also the first war to be televised in detail, sparking anti-war movements and weakening the morale of Americans fighting there. Vietnam also became known as "America's Longest War." It is also possibly the first war where the U.S. did not accomplish what it had set out to do. The Communist North eventually took control of South Vietnam.

But no matter the politics or the stated goals of any military conflict, there is always one common denominator—unspeakable loss of life, bravery of soldiers who often come back scarred for much of their lives because of the horrors seen or experienced, and the resulting loss felt by those who loved them most . . . spouses, children, and certainly mothers and fathers of children who died when their entire lives were in front of them.

On March 8, 1965, the first Marines landed in Vietnam. It would be March 29, 1973 before the last soldier would depart. During those eight years, 58,200 U.S. soldiers died in battle. Of that number was Lennie Eulitt, age 24, with a master's degree in history.

## 15.5

*"You will never know how much we miss you and how hard it was to say goodbye tonight."* From Dixie Eulitt's January 9, 1968, letter to her son, Lennie, on the night she watched him depart following three weeks of "leave" after boot camp and advanced infantry training.

Each night she wrote words of the day, words of normalcy to a son going into chaos. It is what a mother does.

"*We went shopping today.*" Or "*Saw your grandparents today*" or "*It sure was cold today. How is it there?*" The mundane, the usual, the familiar.

"*Came by Bob and Robin's today and showed your picture. I asked Lisa* (eighteen months old) '*Who is that?*' *and she said,* '*Nennie.*' *I was surprised she'd remember you, no more than you were around. She kissed it.*"

But with each day's entry, the mother's heart eventually affected the pen strokes. Occasionally a note of pain bled through.

"*I prayed God would help me hold up while you were here so it would be the best three weeks ever, and He did. I enjoyed every minute you were here. I am beginning to count the days until we pick you up again. We love you with all our hearts. More tomorrow.*"

The size of the letters grew until she worried they would be too big for the envelope. After several days she decided it was time to mail it out. Often, she inquired as to anything he might need. What could they send?

And then there were the prayers, whispered into the air every day, uttered earnestly each night, asking God for protection for her firstborn son. She let him know that she was praying. It is what a mother does.

"*I pray for you all during the day, and every night from 11:30 to midnight I'm on my knees asking God to take care of you. I know He will. I read Psalm 91 and it lifted me up. Read it, and believe every word of it, and trust God, and all will be all right.*"

Each letter held words of encouragement, words of love. It is what a mother does. "*You will never know how much we miss you and how proud we are of you.*"

But I have gotten ahead of myself. This captivating letter exchange between mother and son began many months before he arrived in Vietnam. At boot camp in Fort Polk, Louisiana, it was already in full swing.

* * *

"*Dear Folks,*" Lennie's letters began every time the same way.

His letters described new experiences of a 24-year-old who had grown up with a fascination about war, its history, its causes, and effects. Now he was living it, although he had never expected to do so.

The letters contained drawings of the base, with arrows at key spots, such as his own barracks. In this way, he made his folks familiar with exactly where he was on his new plot of ground. "I sleep here. The mess hall is here."

The letters described the grind and the challenge of each day, the aching muscles, and some of the youngsters who were struggling with the drill sergeant's commands. He explained what a day in the life of a draftee was like; awake at 5:00, morning run at 5:30, breakfast at 6:00, drills at 7:00, classes from 8:00 to noon, and so on, ending in the exhausted collapse into bed each night, falling asleep in seconds.

He portrayed the image of what he was learning—indeed, what he was training for, in an area that simulated Vietnam:

"*There is a jungle-like austerity, dusty roads, mock villages (including roaming cattle), and tunnels for tactical training. Top physical fitness is required to live and fight in dense and sometimes almost impenetrable jungles.*"

Routinely, his letters became personal, thankful: "*Thank you for the pictures and for the album. Your letters lift my spirits.*" (After graduation day from boot camp on October 13, 1967): "*You'll never know how much your visit meant to me.*"

As AIT (Advanced Infantry Training) began at Fort Polk immediately after Boot Camp, his descriptions of the necessary training grew more ominous. "*Classes are now on field radios, anti-personnel mines, first aid, pistol training, anti-tank weapons, grenade launchers, maps. We are taught what to do if captured, and how to survive alone in the jungle.*"

He described drills of being turned loose in the hills at night with a map and a compass and instructions to avoid certain "enemy" positions. His mission was to navigate the traps and get back home safely. He was one of the first who did so. But in the middle of the night he was awakened to join others to go out and search for brothers who had not come back, who were lost in the woods.

Some of these letters explained the necessity of training for warfare, surely stoking fear in his parents' hearts. But there was another component in his letters. It was comfort. Here was a young man who wasn't requesting comfort, wasn't complaining, didn't engage in self-pity.

Rather, he extended comfort and encouragement to his parents, aware of the weight of worry that they bore.

"*I've been told 2nd-hand that most with 5 years of college get some clerical spot.*

*Hoping to get that spot and be stationed in the U.S. during my two years of service.*" Often there were references such as these. "*If I have to enlist for an extra year to get the clerk/typist job, I will. I was given a recommendation because of all the typing I did for the company at basic.*"

As for self-pity, he wrote this: "*Army life is dull only if you make it so . . . some of the guys never cease to complain and they are the ones who are learning the least.*"

As his graduation from AIT drew near, at which time he'd get three weeks at home before learning his ultimate destination, he began to draw his folks into the potential reality of his participation in the war, while continuing to hold out hope for them that he might get a company clerk's position. And yet, he maintained a sense of pride of being a part of a prestigious group if he was so assigned. He stated:

*"I have realized that I likely won't get an administrative position and will likely end up in Vietnam. I hope you won't feel bad about my assignment. Whatever the Lord wills, I will do.*

*The company commander told me to let people know wherever I go about my educational background, saying I'll probably get a good position."* But he continues, *"I am assigned to the First Air Cavalry. If I had my choice of any to be stationed with in Vietnam, this is the one. The unit has a high degree of pride and I would be proud to serve with it."*

Final letters from Fort Polk announced that if he was commissioned, he would be stationed in Saigon for 12 months. He concluded: *"I can't believe I'll be home in 2 weeks. This Christmas will mean more to me than any Christmas before."*

\* \* \*

Knowing what I knew before I began to read these letters didn't prepare me for the emotions they would create. I had never known this man. To me, he was only the uncle of my wife, a man who died in the war. My wife had seen pictures of herself as a one-year-old upon his lap, images that left in her mind a vague impression that she could, in fact, remember him.

As I got to this stage of my journey through the letters, knowing what was coming next, it felt as if I was treading on hallowed ground. I was partaking of the last communications of a mother to her son and a son to his mother and father, each knowing that the horrific danger of his situation meant that the next communication could be their last, even though they both tried to keep a veil of normalcy in the correspondence. Being, myself, a father of three girls, it became very real; this bond, this holy connection between parent and child . . . when a child is in the throes of a great danger that is not of their own choice or their own making, yet a danger that they cannot escape.

Thus, we get an inkling, an inkling only, of the emotion behind her words upon his departure for Vietnam: "*You will never know how much we miss you and how hard it was to say goodbye tonight.*"

* * *

Lennie's letters begin again. January 14, 1968—From Cam Ranh Bay, S. Vietnam.

"*The flight from Washington took 14 hours. It is 70-75 degrees at night, 90-95 during the day. I probably won't be here long. I am writing this letter from the Red Cross Recreation Center, sitting beside Korean soldiers and a boy writing a letter in Chinese or Japanese.*" (Their son is now in a different world.)

Even in this place of abject danger, he again reverted to words of comfort. "*This is one of the safest places in Vietnam. The President landed here when he visited the troops a few weeks ago.*" But his note from January 24 kept them grounded in reality, informing that he'd probably be sent out to the company in the field tomorrow. He concluded: "*Thank you for your prayers every day.*"

He wrote again on January 29, noting he had moved to a newly established base camp, flown in by helicopter and then driven by truck. He'd been busy. He had been on two "noncombat" patrols to check the terrain. Then humor or wistfulness found its way into his letter: " . . .

came upon 20 people working small rice paddies. Herds of water buffalo are grazing nearby. You would hardly think there was a war going on in this country at all." And quickly personal again. "*I'm thrilled over my two letters."*

There was one more letter written by Lennie to his folks, dated February 8. His mother and father have long since passed and his brothers cannot find this last letter. But it was referenced by his mom as having been received.)

The last days of Lennie's life are marked by letters from his mother, letters that were returned to sender because the intended recipient was deceased.

All her letters were still of hope, concern, and love. Samplings:"*Doesn't seem as though you're in a very safe place—paper told today about communist attack on An Khe."*

*Seems it can't be just a little over two weeks since you left. Seems more like 6 months to me. If the rest of the year goes by like this, I'll be a hundred years old when you get home. Ha!"*

"*As soon as I wake up each morning, I start asking God to keep you safe and to not let you go through more than you can stand. He is able."*

Finally, this:

February 7, 1967: "*Got your Jan. 29 letter. Sure sorry about where you were sent. The Lord is just as able to take care of you there as any place. But I can't help but be terribly worried. We have been seeing and hearing about all the fighting in Hue. A soldier reported he was in some pretty fierce battles and seemed almost hopeless at times. I know God draws us closer in times of trouble and He must have a purpose in this. Keep holding onto God's hand and He will lead you thru it all and my what a great thanksgiving we'll have when you get back home."*

Final words: "*God bless & keep you safe. Love and many, many, many prayers. Mom.*"

The Vietnam timeline at this point would read something like this:

January 14 – arrived in Vietnam

February 7 – last letter is sent to Lennie—but never received by him

February 8 – last letter from Lennie is written to folks

How cold can the cold be? Cold enough to freeze the soul.

## 15.7

"Yours was the hand that held mine first."

These are words my daughter wrote and left behind for me on her wedding day. My darlings, my daughters. And yet my three love-lies were only mine to guide for such a short period. I adored them then. I adore them still today. It is a holy love affair that uniquely exists between moms and dads and their children. There is nothing quite like it.

So as one daughter recognized the passing from one stage of her life to another—to a better and more fulfilling and purposeful stage for her (although it was a painful parting for both of us), she wrote to comfort me, the "first" man in her life. She had the wisdom at her young age to see what she had, what she was leaving, and what she was going toward, and to recognize the value of each. And she noted in her parting letter that there would always be a special place in her heart for the one whose hand had held hers first. Precious words.

Each of my girls has written things to me upon one occasion or another that have brought tears to my eyes, and can bring them to my eyes still. And now many years later, each has formed that same unbreakable bond with children of their own. They are now the ones whose hands encompass the tiny hands of children, who comfort them when they are hurt, who hold them when they are afraid.

Because of the depth of that God-given, God-created bond, it is hard to imagine the shattering cold that must impact the heart of a parent when their precious one is suddenly taken from them in death. Having never experienced it, I can only wonder what cruel agony this occurrence must bring.

* * *

I will not linger long at this place of despair. But here is what I learned: On February 14, 1968, possibly the worst experience a mother can have occurred as men from the army walked up the pathway to her door and knocked.

Dixie's youngest son, age 14, was home. He recalls these events as if they happened yesterday. He was sitting in the other room watching Roy Rogers and Dale Evans, who were singing about grass being greener, when the melody was interrupted by something strange. He heard his mother crying. He went to investigate the reason and learned that his brother had gone missing in action.

At this time, the second oldest boy in the family was working at the local BF Goodrich tire plant on the evening shift, building tires. As he walked out of the plant that night, the guard handed him a message that he needed to call home. The news received of his missing brother, he and his young wife and their baby girl (now my wife of 37 years) headed to his folks' house to spend the night.

What happened next was a week of sleeplessness, prayers, and vows being made.

My father-in-law made a pact with God during those few tortured days, promising that he'd end his ways of rebellion, come back to the church, and serve God, if only . . . if only God did His part and brought his brother home alive. They all waited for the news.

Until, on February 20, men returned. It was confirmed. He had been killed in action during the Tet Offensive. The local newspaper published the story of yet another local boy lost in the war:

"PFC Eulitt exposed himself to enemy fire in battle and succeeded in locating an enemy emplacement. He neutralized the position with his grenade launcher, killing two enemy soldiers. While in an exposed position, he was mortally wounded by shrapnel."

Another newspaper article informed the public that the day before he died, he'd sent a last letter to his folks (the letter we could not find for this story) informing them that he was located four miles west of Hue, overlooking the city, and was scheduled to move out the next morning. The article noted that Hue had been the scene of intense fighting in recent weeks.

Later, there was an article in the paper showing Don and Dixie Eulitt receiving the Silver Star for gallantry in action, posthumously, for their son. The looks upon their faces contain a sadness that is beyond my ability to describe.

## 15.8

Again, I will not dwell long here, but it is this arena that much of this book is about. How do we fight on through the waves that sometimes upend our normal existence? How do men and women face trauma beyond description and keep living a life that is fruitful and even joyful? There is surely a choice in the equation.

I came to know the great lady who was Lennie's mother, and my wife's grandmother, many years after these events. I observed her from afar during church meetings as a young boy. About fifteen years after these events, I came to know her more personally as the lady who was always kind to everyone, helpful to everyone, and always serving those around her, traits that she passed to her sons.

But she and those sons went through some tough months and years, as would be expected. It would be abnormal not to do so.

The youngest son described the years of anger and rebellion that ensued for him after his oldest brother died. Of how he too joined the military and hoped to go to Vietnam to exact some vengeance on the ones who'd done this awful thing. Too late though. The war was just concluding, and our men were being called home. Still, he struggled on, battling through addictions of various sorts, angry at God and the world.

My father-in-law, also continued for several years through a place of rebellion. It was not necessarily in anger at God for not taking him up on that bargain he'd offered. He was simply following through on the impulses of his youth, making unwise choices that so many make.

Until a time came when he and his wife changed, from the inside out. Now the years have passed, and they have become like a rock of safety that their children, grandchildren, and great-grandchildren look to for words of wisdom during their own times of struggle. Get a piece of the rock! In fact, they have a piece of a different "Rock," a saving Rock who has established their way through every storm of life that now comes. Still, there is a choice in the equation.

The youngest brother has also come to that place of safety and now encourages anyone who will listen that there is a better way to live, and that is found only in Jesus. It took years.

It took lots of pain. And finally, the choice in the equation to live, to really live, rather than continue on in a living death of pain, anger, and bitterness.

But what about that mother? What about the one who'd brought Lennie into the world and who'd bonded with him like no other, and who'd assured him of the saving power of God even in the midst of the war? What about her faith and her choice in the equation?

For a while, it was despair. She couldn't eat. She couldn't sleep. The sons recall that physicians were involved, so great was the concern for her as she continued to lose weight. Her face bore the struggle. And yet, she did not waver in her faith. She mourned but she did not waver.

In fact, in time, she turned her pain into a plea to others who might enter into battle. Here is a part of a poem she wrote and produced and sent out to servicemen.

Message to servicemen from "Len's mom"

*To the dear ones that fight for their country in a land so far away,*

*Will you take just a moment, dear soldier, and hear what a mother must say? I had a dear son that went over to that country so far away; And while there, he was called home to heaven. The angels came for him just southwest of Hue. So I'm pleading now with you, dear soldier, trust Him (Jesus) while you may; invite Him into your heart, dear one, just let Him have His way.*

I do not know whether it was months or years before she regained some semblance of her former self. But on she did go.

The family has discussed the possibilities of the mercies of God occurring even in the midst of this death. God doesn't intervene in every action of mankind. He doesn't stop wars. He doesn't stop disasters. He has allowed man and nature to take their course to a very large degree. So what of this mother's prayers? What of her faith? Were they useless or were they, in fact, powerful?

Lennie was described by all who knew him as a young man with a tender heart. There are many stories about what war like Vietnam did to soldiers. They were men who came home to a hateful nation, hatred for actions in which they had no choice. And yet it seems that some of those men hated themselves for what they had no choice but to do, for the horrors they witnessed and the horrors they caused in their acts of survival.

So some of the family believe it may have been the merciful response of God to allow Lennie to quickly die in battle rather than return to a life filled with nightmares and memories of death. Who am I to question? And who is any one of us to do so?

A phrase comes to mind as I consider the task of mothers, fathers, wives, and children who must somehow determine to continue living a productive and joyful life after a loss of this magnitude. It is "faith that moves mountains." The phrase is associated with an exchange between Jesus and His disciples after they'd experienced a great failure. He said, "If you have faith the size of a mustard seed [Note: it is the smallest of seeds yet yields a huge plant], then you will say to this mountain, "Move from here to there" and it will move; and nothing will be impossible for you."

It occurred to me that these words could be applied to this kind of turmoil (or mountain within the soul) that parents deal with in the loss of a child.

Is it impossible to move on? Is it impossible to deal with such enormous sorrow that brings constant unyielding pain? Does life no longer make sense? Is it not worth living at this moment? And is living with a sense of purpose and joy completely unthinkable?

Or is there a place in the healing process where we can reach for something beyond ourselves, where we muster up only a grain-of-sand worth of *umph*, where we get out of bed and see the sun still rising, and without any remaining reserves of our own ability, we simply whisper, "I will trust what I cannot understand"? I will leave this, too, with One who is higher than I am?

And is it possible that we are then met—rather, that mustard seed of faith is met—from a power from on high who brings comfort we could never imagine might exist in this place of death? Where the mountain of confusion, doubt, and despair slowly disappears . . . and the fog of our lives clears just a bit as we place one foot in front of the other and discover we *can*, in fact, go on?

It is my assumption that this is what Dixie Eulitt did in the months and years that followed the death of her son. Because the lady I later knew was a woman of strong faith and outstanding character and one who never conveyed to me anything other than that. My only regret is that I didn't take the opportunity to ask her myself exactly how she managed this transition and how she lived the rest of her life with the grace she always exhibited.

## 15.9

(Author's note to the reader: As I wrote this chapter, I was awakened one night with words swirling in my mind, "oh precious blood that flowed." I got up and wrote mile 15.9 as a representation of the loss a mother may feel when faced with circumstances such as these. I pray there will be healing in the words for any who have experienced something so heartbreaking as the loss of a child in battle.)

## Ode to those who served and died . . . and to those who bore them

*I felt you first,*
*Felt your life inside of me.*
*I felt your kicks, your rolls, your turns,*
*It was a wonder, don't you see?*

*I knew the rhythm of your beating heart,*
*Only inches away from mine.*
*My life for yours, my body sustaining,*
*With all you would require.*

*And if the choice was given me,*
*That fact would never change.*
*For I would always give my life for yours,*
*There could be no other way.*

*I saw your first smile,*
*Or at least a smile it seemed to me.*
*I heard your first laughs,*
*The purest sound that there can be.*

*I saw your first steps,*
*I clapped and shouted with praise.*
*I saw your first fall,*
*And with my hand I helped to raise.*

*I felt your first tooth,*
*As it was breaking through.*

*I stayed awake when you would cry,*
*I did all that I could do.*

*Each "first" was given to me,*
*A blessing I won't forget.*
*First victories, first defeats,*
*I saw them all . . . and yet,*

*One day you would go past,*
*The place my eyes could see.*
*You left, you grew, you went away,*
*To where I could not be.*

*But you can never go so far away,*
*That your mother's love won't reach.*
*No land is far enough away,*
*To miss my silent prayer's beseech.*

*I saw you go off to fight—to serve,*
*In a place you did not know and had never imagined you*
*would be.*
*I heard your country jeer and mock,*
*They did so ignorantly.*

*From afar they could not know,*
*The bravery you showed.*
*Facing fears, going on,*
*Deep in problems others sowed.*

*But did you think of yourself first? Oh, no.*
*In each letter that was clear.*
*You wrote to me, day by day,*
*And sought to ease my fear.*

*But then they came, then they came!*
*Men I did not know.*
*Telling me, breaking me,*
*They used the word hero.*

*How could they say such words?!*
*They do not have the right.*
*Where were they when you were born?*
*They did not see my fight.*

*My fight to bring you up for good,*
*For a future and a hope.*
*Not to give that life, that precious life—No!*
*This was not your scope.*

*How have you gone where I cannot go?*
*How have you gone where I cannot go?*
*I would give my life for yours, you know!*
*How have you gone where I cannot go!*

*Oh, righteous blood that flows, on a small battlefield it*
*was poured.*
*My son! My son was given, how valiantly you warred.*
*In a land not your own, your body no longer whole*
*Oh, righteous blood that flows, crushing now my soul.*

*Where shall I turn? How can I go on?*
*This death now killing me . . .*
*Darkness, despair, confusion,*
*How can I be set free?*

*When through the fog comes something,*
*A light. A glimmer. One piercing gleam.*

*My mind brings back a memory,*
*Of a road One other had seen. Hark!*

*Oh, righteous blood that flows, on a great battlefield it*
*was poured.*
*A Son! A Son was given, how valiantly He warred.*
*Upon a cross for all mankind, to make this cruel world whole,*
*Oh, righteous blood that flows, only Yours can heal my soul!*

## 16.0

It is my sincere hope that I have, in some small way, honored the life of a man I never knew; a man who held my wife (his niece) upon his knee when she was one year old. A man trained for battle, spending one last Christmas at home before leaving to begin the last month of his life on this earth.

It is my hope that I have honored him, his family, and people like him who died in service to their country . . . but really in service to their brothers on a battlefield, as a representative of the family and nation from which they came.

It is my deepest hope in this mile, that a life like his would, therefore, continue to be known and continue to plant seeds even now, these many decades after he has gone. That he did not live . . . and die, so young in vain. That the reader would know and understand that a gentle man, a kind man, served and died for us, for freedom.

Leonard Elzy Eulitt. (12/15/1943-02/09/1968). He lives on.

And warmth replaces the cold.

*"And the rain fell, and the floods came, and the winds blew and slammed against that house; and yet it did not fall, for it had been founded on the rock."*

## MILE 17

# *Through Every Wind that Assails You, Keep On*

*(This mile is dedicated to the people of Joplin, Missouri, and to the tens of thousands left behind to mourn, remember, and rebuild.)*

I ran the Joplin Memorial Run (half marathon) for the second time in May of 2019 as I was preparing for the Jack and Jill Marathon that would commence just two months later. Whereas my first attempt, which occurred in May of 2017, took place in surprisingly cool temperatures, my second run was not to be so nice. Instead, it was hot and humid.

I was in better shape in 2019. But the elements on this day negated my training just enough that my 2019 attempt failed to match my 2017 attempt by four seconds. Four seconds! That's a little hard to live with.

I started out faster than I should have . . . yes, a common theme in my running experience. I had the 2-hour pacer just in front of me for a good part of the first half of the run. This would have meant a 9:09

average for the entire course. That would have been a great improvement on my usual 10-minute pace.

But at about mile 6, I realized I'd not be breaking that 2-hour barrier on this day. As the heat and humidity took their toll, my energy waned, and the pacer was eventually lost to my sight.

It is surprising what a mental game running is. A week before this JMR, I had increased my training regimen to 15 miles (in perfect running temps), and I had kept the 10-minute pace for the entire 15 miles. Now I was walking up hills while running a distance of 2 fewer miles . . . and didn't care enough at the moment to summon the will to maintain the pace.

I have two other memories of this race:

I ran for several miles in the vicinity of a gang of college guys. I'd be in front just a bit, then they'd speed up and lead for a while. This seesaw affair continued long enough that I overheard bits and pieces of the craziness that can be college life. I must admit, it was at least entertaining. Their manner for the run seemed almost like a party. They were relaxed, jogging along with seemingly little effort, laughing, and regaling one another with stories of conquests, or jabbing playful insults at each other. I was happy with the distraction of their company.

The finish line is my other memory. My wife couldn't come to this race and, with no buddy racing beside me, I was about to finish alone for the first time ever. But this race will always be special to me since it commemorates a day that will forever be burned into the memories of the citizens of Joplin, Missouri.

## 16.1

When it seems that the days go by with determined monotony, with sameness that sometimes drives us crazy, suddenly—like a flash of lightning separating the sky—everything changes and what once was, will never quite be the same again. In the days that immediately follow, people are shocked as they try to regain their balance. In the weeks that follow, they begin to look back with longing, for a return to normalcy and that very familiar monotony of their old everyday life.

Recently, I had the great privilege of speaking with three people who faced the sudden dire circumstances of a tornado as they were going about their days in regular fashion, thinking about graduations, working normal jobs, hanging out with friends or family. And then everything changed.

It was a moment in time, here and gone; but it changed so much for so many after that "flash of lightning" moment came crashing into town.

## 16.2

Five minutes before the F5 tornado hit their area, Sandy's mom and 11-year-old niece had arrived. They, along with Sandy's husband, were gathered in Sandy's home along with Deuce (Boxer and Rhodesian Ridgeback mix), Seek (a Maine Coon cat of about 20 pounds), and Baby Cat.

They realized something major was occurring and were about to head to the bathroom for shelter, when Baby Cat suddenly escaped out the back door. Sandy took a step toward the outside to try to retrieve Baby Cat when her husband, in a moment of real clarity concerning the situation, intervened and called for all to "get to the bathroom now!" That action was most likely a life-saving decision.

They all huddled inside the tub. Sandy's niece was positioned nearest the faucet, then mom, then Sandy, and at the back was hubby. Seek was positioned in Sandy's arms, and Deuce was on the bathroom floor. It all began to happen quickly. Glass was heard breaking. An odd thought flew through Sandy's mind in the midst of the crisis—that they needed new windows anyway. She heard her young niece crying and repeating over and over that she didn't want to die, asking if they would.

Suddenly, the bathroom tiles began popping up and Deuce jumped from the floor into the middle of the pile of humans in the tub. In that instant, Seek jumped or was sucked from Sandy's arms as the tornado began to rip the home apart. Debris began falling from above. The thought went through Sandy's mind that they were probably going to die. Her husband then attempted to shield everyone by lying on top of the group.

Sandy's comment afterward: "It seemed like it lasted forever but not very long." Incongruous thoughts are surely allowed in a moment like this, when you enter a place that may be the last seconds between life and death, between this realm and the next.

\* \* \*

Just a few short blocks west of Sandy's home lived J.D.

It had been an enjoyable Sunday for J.D., hiking with friends near the cool rushing water of Wildcat Glades. He lived in a Joplin apartment building on 20th and Connecticut Avenue. The friends decided to head to the local IHOP just a block off of 20th Street on

Joplin's primary thoroughfare, Range Line Road. It was nearing 5:30 p.m. as they entered the parking lot.

J.D. noticed a man sitting in his vehicle. The man alerted J.D., as he walked by, that a tornado had been spotted and was said to be headed their way. The group quickly headed for the safety of the restaurant. Within moments, the winds began increasing in intensity. J.D. stayed briefly at the front door, holding it shut while the winds were pulling on the doors, attempting to jerk them open. As each person ran from the parking lot to the store entry, J.D. released his hold and allowed them to quickly come into safety.

As the events unfolded inside the IHOP, someone began marshaling everyone toward the middle of the restaurant, near the kitchen and hallway. It was suggested that the women and children head to the relative safety of the walk-in coolers.

J.D. would later recall that he didn't really have time to be afraid. He wasn't thinking about life and death. He was simply reacting as the challenge unfolded.

He began seeing ceiling tiles moving. Debris from outside began slamming against the large exterior windows. Ventilation tubes began falling from the ceiling as windows shattered. In seconds, the restaurant contents were literally being tossed around. And then it passed. J.D. looked up and realized the north wall of the restaurant was gone.

He was able to exit by the rear of the building and had his first glance outside. It was stunning. No matter which direction he looked, he saw utter chaos. It seemed at first glance that everything was destroyed. A thought popped into his head: "It feels like the end of the world."

\* \* \*

Before the tornadic winds approached the IHOP where J.D. and his friends were, or even further east where Sandy and her family were waiting in her home, the once-in-a-generation storm was making its violent march down Twentieth Street, coming out of the west. It would cut a swath through the city that was as much as a mile wide in places. Directly in its path was a girl named Lucinda.

Born and raised for the first 15 years of her life in Mexico, Lucinda had lived the last six years in America but had always enjoyed dual citizenship, with a Hispanic father and an American mother. She worked as a server in a local restaurant.

On the night of the storm, she had just been released from a double shift. Noticing storm information on the TV screens at the restaurant only caught her attention in a passing way.

Storms and Midwest go hand in hand in April and May.

She was planning to attend a graduation party that night as she drove toward her friend's house on 20th Street. The weather seemed somewhat cloudy with moments of sunshine breaking through.

Suddenly, as if out of nowhere, hail began to pour out of the clouds. It was Lucinda's first clue that something bad was occurring. As she pulled to a stop by her friend's house, things started to happen quickly.

She saw a man standing outside point toward the sky and immediately turn to run into his house. She began seeing things flying around her. The rain-wrapped tornado was approaching without warning.

Lucinda was simultaneously confused by what was occurring but instinctively aware that she had a moment to make an important decision. Stay in the car with the dog she had just picked up for a friend or grab the dog and make a beeline for the front door, which was about 15 feet away? She grabbed the dog and made a run for it.

Her friend's house had a storm door that Lucinda pulled open. But when she attempted to open the entry door, it would not budge, as if an irresistible force was holding it shut. And then it hit.

Lucinda found herself pressed between the screen door and the entry door. She pounded and screamed and tried the doorknob repeatedly. Still, it would not open.

In the next moments she saw an arm reaching out toward her. But the arm was not coming from the door. It was coming from a window positioned just beside the door. Her friend had broken it out and was reaching his arm outside, blindly grasping for his trapped friend. He too had been unable to open his door.

Lucinda had another decision to make. With the ferocious storm now hurtling debris everywhere, should she leave the crushed semblance of protection between the two doors and try to enter through the broken window, or stay where she was? Again, an instant but correct decision was made. She stayed.

Moments later the door flew open. To this day, Lucinda cannot explain why it wouldn't open initially and why it suddenly did open. The only reasonable explanation, she surmises, is that the tornado itself formed some kind of suction on the entry door and the vortex that had held it so firmly had finally given release. Either that, or an unseen hand protected her until it was time for the door to open.

She fell through the door and onto the floor. Lucinda recalls only that her friend grabbed her and pulled her to safety in their bathroom as the storm unleashed its power. Nobody here knew at that moment that the large Mercy Hospital facility just a few blocks down the road had already been pummeled, and that injured and dying people would soon be discovered everywhere.

# 16.4

It was over for the people in Sandy's house. Something was lying on top of them. A neighboring gentleman walked into the remnants of their home and pulled the shower wall off of them. Possibly it had been a shield from harm. The tub participants begin to step out, look up, and see . . . that their home was entirely gone.

In this case a picture truly does describe the loss. A photo at the end of this chapter depicts what the family members saw when they stepped forth from their own personal ark of safety. Only the bathtub remained in its original place. Everything else was destroyed.

The neighborhood around them was similarly decimated. They walked down the street and found random unmatching shoes for their bare feet, as they cautiously moved through the destruction.

A church was still standing down the way. They sat inside briefly and noticed a woman in the church sitting alone with a little dog; she was shaking, crying, not speaking. Soon Sandy decided she had to get out and walk. Amazingly, family members came walking up the same street they were walking down. It was her husband's parents, and a joyful reunion ensued.

But they had lost everything. Everything! The only belongings they had were the clothes on their backs. Sandy and her husband didn't even have socks or shoes, other than the unmatched shoes they'd found scattered in the neighborhood. How seemingly tenuous this life can be.

But the next day dawned, and with it an amazing bit of good news was added to the disaster. They discovered Baby Cat inside a vehicle that had a window broken out. Baby Cat was unharmed.

And then there was Seek. That cat had been a source of pure delight to Sandy, who has no children of the two-legged variety. Seek was nowhere to be found. Flyers were put up, the neighborhood checked, and social media was utilized. Every possible lead was checked, to no avail.

"Things don't matter," Sandy would later declare. It is a cliché but it is true for the few people who've actually lost everything in a moment of time but who still do have the lives of their loved ones. And that was true for Sandy . . . almost.

For animal lovers, this may be understood. "Seek was a part of my soul," Sandy would say. Was she thankful for the loved ones who were unharmed? Yes. Yet with this one great loss, a time of depression hit her like a cruel fresh wind of the storm, battering her soul like the flattening of her home. The loss of Seek was almost more than Sandy could bear.

* * *

J.D. scanned the chaos and destruction within his vision. In moments, his keen mind took in multiple things as people crawled out from the destruction. Some looked devastated. Some seemed pumped up, as if on an adrenaline high, running around with no apparent purpose. There was a range of emotions all around. His thoughts singled in on his goal, to check on his sister and see that she was okay.

As J.D. and his friend made their way north past the zone of destruction, relief began to set in. His sister was far to the north and the storm seemed to have stayed on its easterly course. After being assured of his sister's wellbeing, his second goal kicked in, to check on his apartment down 20th Street- the bull's eye of the storm.

As a runner, J.D. practically sprinted through the flooded and littered streets. On more than one occasion, he paused for his friend to catch up. Upon arrival at the apartment, the news was not good. Just like at the IHOP he'd recently left, a wall was missing from his home and almost everything inside was either sucked out or filled with the gritty mess that the tornado had hurled through the town. All clothing was useless and couldn't be cleaned enough to get the grit out of the fibers. A total loss. So just like Sandy a few blocks east of him, J.D. was left with the clothes on his back and a few things that had been left in his parents' home a few miles away.

In the days very soon after, as the news of loss of life hit home, J.D. discovered that three of the children he'd helped as an employee at the Boys & Girls Club had not survived the storm. Never having experienced the death of a close loved one before, this sudden tragic loss of small children he knew fairly well shook him deeply. Things were just stuff. But here, for the first time in his life, was true loss.

\* \* \*

Just blocks away from J.D., Lucinda and her friend emerged from the house and took stock. Where she had previously been standing, pinned between the two doors, a tree had fallen. Her car had been picked up, turned, and deposited about twenty feet away.

Her friend's brother was supposed to be working at Mercy Hospital, just blocks away. They decided to check on him and headed out on foot. At one point, Lucinda realized she was walking on carpet that was still intact on the foundation of someone's home that was no longer there. She was literally walking *in* someone's house, a house that now only had a foundation.

The scene at Mercy Hospital was chaos. Injured nurses, some bleeding from their heads, were still trying to help their patients get to a place of care. Heroes. The hospital itself was standing, sort of. So much was missing or destroyed that the entire complex was later demolished and rebuilt on a new location. The old grounds now stand as a memorial to lost lives and have been made into a beautiful and peaceful place with paths on which the community can walk, jog, or sit and reflect at the summit where the hospital once stood.

Lucinda and her friend made their way back down the street. They found her friend's brother. He was okay.

The following minutes passed in somewhat of a dreamlike state with random things occurring. By chance, they ran into some additional friends who'd not been able to get into town by vehicle because of the mass destruction.

Lucinda realized her earrings had blown out of her ears. Suddenly it was all too much—the car, the dash to the door, the arm out the window, the path to safety, the destruction everywhere, the condition of the hospital, the patients, the caregivers—it all collided within her stomach. She threw up in an alleyway. She realized she must be in a state of shock.

Someone took Lucinda to her parents' home, which was safely positioned outside the path of the storm. She no longer lived with her parents, but her room was still available. Yet she chose not to sleep in her old room that night. Instead, she lay down in the floor of a different room. Everything seemed to be spinning and it all seemed so surreal.

# 16.7

Sandy's depression endured. She would go days without washing her hair, a thing very unlike her. Seek had been sucked from her arms but Sandy blamed herself anyway. Guilt is not always reasonable. But it can sit heavily on the shoulders like a rod of iron, weighing body and soul into the ground.

Then a miracle occurred. October 9, almost 5 months after the storm, a neighbor from three blocks away called saying she'd seen a cat nearby that possibly matched the description of Seek. Sandy immediately began crying. At the neighbor's house, she called out for Seek. A cat of about 3 pounds came walking out of the nearby woods. He was skittish at first but then came to Sandy. It was Seek! She couldn't believe it. Seek had somehow survived on his own for almost 5 months, possibly trying to make his way back home from wherever he'd been blown.

He appeared to be barely alive nutritionally, but otherwise unharmed. Over the months to follow, Seek was brought back to full strength and the family was once again whole.

Sandy looks back on the time and says: "When you lose everything, you realize it is not that important; those are things. Losing pieces of your heart, that is what you can't replace." She is more thankful now than she was before. It is a change that likely occurs when the reality of life and death slams you in the face with the ferocity of an F5 tornado.

One cannot look at the photo and hear this story and say it was not a miracle.

Yes, lives were lost all around. There was excruciating loss that cannot be described with words. And yet, in places, there were miracles. Who can say why this person was saved and yet other lives, other loved ones, were lost? There is no answer to the questions of why. None that I know anyway. And yet, as surely as you cannot deny the loss, you also cannot deny the miracles.

Here the miracle occurred in a tub. "No, little niece. You are not going to die. You will be safe in this tub, with my husband protecting you."

Something from that powerful photo took my breath away and brought tears to my eyes as soon as I saw it and thought about my friend. Before this book is finished, I will revisit that image . . . destruction all around, debris raining down, *but those four people in the tub . . . not one of them with even a scratch.*

\* \* \*

J.D. also entered a dark time in the weeks and months after the great Joplin tornado. Or maybe it lasted a few years. He recalls speaking with the parents of two of the three children who had died. They were brother and sister. J.D. used to pick the brother up from school. It was all too real. It hurt him in a deep way.

He looked to art as a way to express his feelings. Looking back at some of those pieces he painted, he sees the darkness in what came out as he dealt with the trauma of that time. And yet, something began to slowly change in him.

Eventually, J.D. came to realize that life throws very hard things at you at times, things not of your choosing. But you do have a choice in it. Will you become stronger or will you stay in a pity party? He determined it was not his job to question why things happened. Instead, it was his job to figure out how to come out better on the other side.

About three years after the tornado, J.D. met a young lady who had walked through very similar events. The tornado somehow connected them. The young lady brought a special gift with her as well. The two soon became married. In full review, for J.D. *the tornado events went from trauma to teacher to triumph . . . and a new life.*

* * *

Lucinda lay on the floor of her parents' house, trying to get the world to stop spinning.

And somewhere in the quiet calm that follows a storm she heard life-changing words as if spoken by a real voice in the room. The words echoed in her ears, "*A child will come from this!*" What?! *What a really weird thought that was,* she said to herself.

She recalled a feeling of being protected, almost as if a hand kept her pressed safely between the two doors. She then saw all the destruction and injury around her; saw what might have happened to her had she stayed in her car or been unable to get into the house. And now strange words, as if spoken quietly into her ear.

A few weeks later, on July 4, she was a mess; she had lost her job, she realized her life had been reckless, and she wasn't feeling well. Her sister asked if she could possibly be pregnant. Could she? She got a test and it turned out positive. Lucinda freaked out. She recalls watching fireworks that July 4th, tears streaming down her face. She didn't know how to tell people, especially her parents.

She soon went to a women's clinic and the confirmation was made. She realized, by the timing, that she must have been newly pregnant on the day of the tornado. The words she heard the night of the tornado came flooding back into her mind. Had her life been spared . . . *for this child*!

Today, through tears, Lucinda tells her powerful story. She says the tornado was, and is, a turning point in her life. She went from wandering aimlessly and being in a relationship with an abusive man to realizing that she was meant to be this girl's mom. *"It happened in a terrible way, to help me for the better."*

Lucinda does not believe the good things in her life would have happened except for this abrupt experience where her life was saved for a purpose. Her daughter became her purpose.

And with that purpose came an inner drive to excel in everything she did.

How odd it is, this horrible Joplin tornado of 2011. Losses that are incalculable still exist. And yet for these three, it marked a positive redirection of their lives. And that is, after all, the intention of this mile . . . of this book, really—that through great struggle, if we determine to learn and go on, we can win the day, *that through great loss, we can also find the meaning and real purpose of our lives.*

Oh yeah. Lucinda's story ends as a love story. She married J.D. And Lucinda's gift to him was a little girl named Rosa Maria . . . who got for herself a changed man and a wonderful daddy.

The writer wonders, *What will be the purpose and path of Rosa Maria's life, a life that J.D. and Lucinda were preserved for, a life they are now privileged to shape and watch unfold.*

## 16.9

I have never attended the walks of remembrance that precede "memorial" races. After hearing the stories of my friends who survived the storm, I now wish to honor more perfectly those who did not survive and, in so doing, I hope to honor their memories along with the loved ones who suffered in ways that are hard to imagine, unless you too have experienced the loss.

A part of my friends' stories included seeing people in those first minutes and hours after the tornado struck, people who were so shaken and traumatized that they could only sit in shock. Not having experienced these kinds of losses, I am wary of putting forth platitudes about what to do next, after an unspeakable loss has occurred. I only feel that somehow, in time, we must go on. And that the person who has left this life *wants* loved ones to go on living and not to settle into a life of despair.

My friends encountered the very real possibility of death. They came face-to-face with it. Some didn't have time to think that it might be the end. Others *did* have the thought. Each responded differently, just as the makeup of each life would indicate. Some people come through a life and death experience, it seems, with a time of shock that can lead to depression. Some go into a period of darkness as the reality of death hits home. Some almost immediately take stock and realize that life is so precious that it must be lived, must be taken on in a better way than it had been in the past.

And so, in one way or another, each of these friends of mine look back at the strongest "winds" that hit their lives and realize that something changed within them for good.

And this must be the response, I carefully suggest. We must go on. We cannot quit no matter how hard the winds of life suddenly blow.

A picture of my first marathon flashes again into my mind, of running against 20-25 mph winds on the back half of the OKC marathon; of seeing a lady kneel in the street; of stopping to check to see if she was okay; and of her words, "The wind! It's so strong!"

In a few moments, she summoned her strength and got up. And went on.

# 17.0

On a day two months before the Joplin Memorial Run of 2019 . . .

The long, cold winter months were about to pass into spring. It was March 9, 2019. A mere five days ago, our dogs had been in the garage because of ten-degree temps and a harsh wind making it feel below zero. And here, on the cusp of the "lion" of March becoming a "lamb," the weekend arrived with a 65-degree day and a 33-mph wind . . . and time for my 6-mile run as I began preparing my body for the coming four months in which I would undertake the training for my third marathon. But on this day, the wind assailed me.

With gusts in the 30-mph range coming from the south and west, I either had a great friend tossing me around the outdoor path or an enemy so strong that I had to lower my head, shorten my stride, and force my way forward. For one brief moment, I actually lost my balance enough that my foot went off the concrete path. I felt battered and worn and wondered if twice as many miles on a calm day would have caused no greater loss on the stores of my energy than this windy 6-mile battle.

This run was not the destructive sort. It was just the aggravating sort. In fact, for running, wind is almost always my enemy.

But can I overcome it? Can you? Absostinkinlutely! We can!

*"But as for you, be strong and do not give
up, for your work will be rewarded."*

## MILE 18

# When the Road Seems Monotonous–Go On, It Will Change

Mile 16 was cold, dealing with the loss of children. Mile 17 was windy, blowing unexpected and traumatic disasters our way. Mile 18 was going to be the third in a row of difficult forces thrown at runners and our lives but, alas, my soul is tired. That's what happens when facing strong elements. We need a break. We need some cloud cover and a cool breeze. We need times of refreshing.

So I am postponing my third straight difficult run. It will come at mile 20 after we've had a bit of a rest. In mile 19, we will jazz things up a bit with the unexpected and bizarre events that runners encounter. But for mile 18, let's take a brief run down a road that runners regularly experience . . .

Boredom.

What is as far opposite as can be from the adrenaline high that surely accompanies a battlefield or a tornado? It is running the same 3-mile stretch of ground day after day after monotonous day. If variety is the spice of life, then unchanging, constant, same ole same ole is the saltless potato of life, often leading people to apathy or restlessness. Unchecked, it can also lead to very bad decisions and a lot of permanent problems. But let's start this run slowly.

## 17.1

During the weeks and months of marathon training, over 75 percent of the mornings start the same way, especially during hot summer months. Wake up earlier than you want to wake up. Pull covers back, slide legs out, feet hit floor. Brush your teeth and begin to pull on running clothes, eyes still bleary, mind not yet fully engaged.

Grab your keys to drive to your running trail, or possibly begin your short trek down the lane, flashlight in hand to make sure you don't step on any snakes on your way out to the road you'll use while your neighbors sleep.

Stretch just a moment. Glance at the sky and see the beauty of the first glimpse of dawn breaking the eastern sky. Click your watch. Begin to jog down the same trail you've jogged hundreds of times before.

Your flashlight is still in hand, but you know where the divots are in the road. The flashlight is actually for protection, so any early drivers don't make you into a divot in the road. (And to watch for snakes, of course.)

During a period of my third marathon training, I headed to Mercy Park, the site of the hospital that was destroyed, as referenced in the last mile. I love the path that circles a pond at the middle level of the grounds. The pond sports two huge fountains that constantly shoot into the air and on a windy day the mist gently floats over you, feeling just like those memories of reaching the base of your favorite Colorado waterfall.

Many people come here to walk, run, or take their dogs for a stroll. During my training runs I became accustomed to some of the same people arriving at 5:30 or 6:00 a.m. Small pleasantries would pass between us, or maybe just the nod of the head, or "It's a hot one today."

During hours of darkness, small lights mark the way. On many occasions I have watched the morning sky brighten just enough that the sensitive lights would shut off, giving way to the rising sun.

This can be part of a runner's day. It is peaceful and even restful in a way. But do it a hundred times and the choice presents itself to you. *Will I continue to look for and find the beauty of this day even though it seems the same as the last hundred days, or will I give way to the dissatisfaction of continual sameness?*

Wash, rinse, repeat. Isn't this so often our lives?

## 17.3

The Missions Half Marathon took place about a month before my 2nd attempt at the half marathon distance of the Joplin Memorial Run. My boss and running enthusiast encouraged me to do it because, in his words, "It is for a great cause."

On this occasion, I was to have a special treat. My son-in-law decided to join me. I'm an *old man running* and haven't ever been the super athletic type. He is young, has probably 1 percent body fat, and is the very description of the athletic body type.

We have a good relationship, and being able to run the race with him was an enjoyable idea. Oh, I knew I would be eating his dust within about 10 yards of the gun going off. But we were in the race together and he would be at the finish line with my wife, my daughter, and four of our precious grandchildren. Also, the route was an out-and-back route so at some point along the way we would be crossing paths and would get to shout encouragement to each other for at least a half a second. Nonrunners likely think this is silly. Runners love the sight of an encouraging friend on the trail.

The April morning dawned with a brisk chill in the air. It was the perfect temperature for running and almost a carbon copy of the Tulsa half marathon I'd done in November of 2017.

Just cold enough that nobody in their right mind would stand outside without long sleeves, long pants, and a jacket. But just warm enough to make a half marathon perfect for shorts and a T- shirt. It was in the 40s and calm. We stayed in the car until almost time for the race to start, then we peeled off the outer layers and went to work.

I had never seen or heard of the path we would be running on that morning. It was fine.

It was entirely flat, which runners love. The weather was perfect. But I must say, it was the most mundane long race I have run to date.

I think it is an old railroad line. It is made up of small white rock or packed dirt. There is a line of trees and bushes lining almost the entire course. Run out six and a half miles to a cone and run back. No scenery really. Just a path and no view outside of it. Even the runners fell into a boring pace. The fast runners obviously led the way and the slower runners seemed to settle into one slow pace. I'm used to passing a few people and being passed by many. It hardly happened at all on this day.

I fell in behind a guy about my age who was running at my exact pace. I was attempting to beat a 10:00 minute pace for the entire course and he was doing the very same thing, purposely or not. I didn't have the energy or drive to pass him, and he didn't leave me behind. So, for miles, he was my only companion- or, rather, his backside was. We weren't side by side. I was about 5-10 paces behind him for most of the first half of the race.

Until something really exciting happened. He stopped at one of the only porta potties on the trail to use the restroom. Woohoo! My scenery changed! Now it was just me and myself, running alone for the rest of 13.1 miles.

My actual exciting moment came at about mile 5 when my son-in-law, who had already hit the halfway cone and was on his way back with a pack of speedsters, came into view. We waved, shouted, and then he was gone. I was glad to see him doing so well.

He would end up hitting his goal of somewhere around a 7-minute per mile average. It was a great race for him. And I would eventually find my way back to the start/finish line and see my crew waiting and cheering. That was the highlight amidst the sameness of the track. It was, indeed, a fast track. I made my personal record for a half marathon, but sadly I have lost the time. I only recall that it was below the 10-minute per mile average by just a tad.

The race itself was a good memory because of my son-in-law being there. And I'm happy to have done it because of the cause it was supporting. But as races go, for my taste . . . as one who's now experienced 25,000 people in Oklahoma City, the fall colors in Springfield, Missouri, and the beautiful mountains in the state of Washington, it just didn't bring the excitement that a race can bring. Others may have a different opinion about the trail. That was mine.

It was more like a morning training run kind of race. Or you could call it a "real life" kind of race. Real life isn't usually about parades and mountains and waterfalls. Those are the special treats that people save up for and dream about. Real life is usually about sameness. Occasionally, it is downright boring. If we let it be.

## 17.6

The age is usually anywhere from 40 to 50. Realization hits. This is it. I'm not going to be rich. I'm no longer going to get out of bed without that nagging pain I never had in my knees during my 20s and 30s. My appearance is changing and . . . hmmm . . . my wife's appearance is changing a bit too. And where did this mole come from? Is it cancer? Is this all there is to life, to *my* life? Did I hit my peak 10 years ago and everything is only going to get worse from here?

There may be 50 questions of this type. Notice they all center around self. But then, we are selfish creatures, aren't we? Self-concerns, selfish ambitions unattained, self-driven dreams unfulfilled.

This is all life is and it is all it is ever going to be! Same job, same house, same wife.

I'm sick of this dead-end job. I'm tired of waking up every morning at 6:30, toiling for much less than I'm worth 5 days a week, getting home and finding I no longer have energy in the evenings, and hearing about chores that need done around my house, which always seems to be falling apart.

I'm tired of this old house. And the bills my home seems to generate keep me from enjoying the weekends I now live for.

Weekends are often lousy too. They are usually spent mowing, weed eating, keeping the beat-up car running, and doing a list of "honey-dos" a mile long. What about fishing and boating and hunting and golf? When is *me* time? Not this weekend, that's for sure.

Somewhere in the mix of all of this, or of things similar to it, the boredom and frustration of life create a crossroads of sorts. The popular title is "mid-life crisis." Truth be known, most of us come to a form of this crisis in our emotions and our thinking. Men seem to struggle with it more than women.

But there doesn't have to be a true crisis. It can be looked upon simply as part of the fabric of life and the blessing of growing old with someone. Or unchecked, it can become a danger zone for relationships and marriages. It can become a pit of financial outlays that will wreak havoc for years to come.

A new boat could help this feeling, especially if I have a new Ford truck to pull the boat. Why should I wait? I'll be paying on stuff the rest of my life anyway, so I might as well enjoy the journey, right?

Maybe some new clothes, a new hairdo, and a new *me* style. That will make the ladies turn and look like they did when I was twenty-five, surely.

And now that I'm thinking about it, what I really need is out of this 20-year commitment to this lady who has grown so used to me that we hardly even talk anymore. Why should I live the rest of my life without ever knowing what it would feel like to enjoy that young flirtatious girl?

New toys, new companions, new me, and a great life *can* still be mine! Right?

I know this all sounds very simplistic. But I wonder how it is that committed husbands and wives of 20 or 30 years can suddenly ditch each other for someone new. It surely doesn't just happen without any forethought. I wonder if part of the problem can begin in the dissatisfaction with the monotony of life and the thought that we somehow missed what we should have had, so we have only one more chance to strike out into the great unknown and, possibly, if we're lucky, find it—happiness—at last.

I believe this a great lie. The fruit of the lie is awful pain for those who stand in the wake of the tidal wave of selfishness that ensues when one person decides this boring life must change.

Or how about another alternative? Instead of freaking out by acting on your midlife crisis adventure, you can simply give up and stay in the worn-out ruts of the paths of your life. Just get old, get fat (literally and figuratively speaking), and stop caring.

Surely there is a better response to life's doldrums than these.

## 17.8

Turn your focus out.

I am not questioning the truth that life can seem the same for a long time or that the sameness can feel to us like being dragged through the same mud every time we wake up. It can be that way at times. But what I know for sure is this: hold tight and it will change. Sometimes it will bring change we like; sometimes change we don't want so much. But change will come if we wait for it.

The point, though, to successfully navigating the sameness and dullness of life is not simply to weather the storm and wait for it to "get better." Instead, it is to change focus. Look outward, away from self.

I grew weary in my past job of twenty years, making pizza dough twice a day every day, making pizza sauce, preparing for the lunch rush, dealing with employee problems, day after day for so many years. I can grow weary in my present job of seventeen years as well, sitting at my desk, looking at records until my eyes cross, dealing with problems of one variety or another that come any time people are involved in anything.

So I could look at life's concrete squares underneath my feet. Or I can look at the difference in each day's sunrise and see which of those people I come in contact with today might need an encouraging word or a kind smile. I can think about new ways to make my wife's life more enjoyable *this* day, even though we've already had over thirteen thousand days together.

There are so many ways to find and spread the beauty of life in the midst of the routines of our days. Look outward, not inward. That is the way. I am convinced that this is true.

## 18.0

This is a short mile. I see no reason to belabor the point. It is a simple choice of viewpoint and purpose. But as mentioned, when we least expect it, change *will* come. (Was 2020 proof of this premise, or what?!) In fact, each day is unique if we look for it. I have run down my lane many hundreds of times. It is packed dirt and rock, with a stretch or two of asphalt if I run very far. Same ole, same ole.

When suddenly, down that lane does appear . . . *What in the world?!*

*"When you walk, your step will not be hampered;*
*and if you run, you will not stumble."*

# Barking Dogs, Attacking Birds, and the Occasional Cow

Is that a cow?

I was running my 9-mile run early on a Sunday morning, jogging around the dirt roads by my house. Suddenly, I came upon a large cow with horns standing in my way, obviously having escaped her fence and now standing separated from the herd. She saw me and took off running... away from me. *At least not an attack cow with horns,* I thought.

As the fearful beast trotted on in front of me, always keeping a good twenty yards between us, I realized I might run her all the way to the paved road where cars speed by at 55 mph, which is only a mile and a half away.

Just as suddenly as the cow appeared and began running away from me, a choice appeared to me. As I slowed my pace, I quickly considered three options.

Option 1: Turn right at the next mile section of dirt road, which was only a half mile away, meaning the cow would still be a full mile from the dangerous paved intersection of highway speeds traffic.

Option 2: Continue to run the cow all the way to the dangerous intersection, where I usually turned north, with the knowledge that an accident could occur, or where she might just keep running for miles in front of me. Obviously, I couldn't choose this path.

Option 3: Turn around and completely mess up my route, which would also mean I couldn't do a circular route and would have to get to some spot and just stop and turn around. I didn't like this choice at all. Running is a very mental sport. I already had my psyche prepared for a circular run.

Option 1 would seem the natural and best choice. It could still be accomplished in a circular route, albeit one that would be a bit altered. But there was one problem with option 1. A couple of years ago I had ventured down that road for the first time and had been chased by vicious dogs. The owners came screaming after them as if they knew I would be eaten alive if they weren't stopped. I vowed never to run down that road again and I had kept my vow, until this moment.

Time was up. I had to choose. Isn't that the way with choices sometimes? They are thrust upon us without the benefit of time to carefully consider the options and figure out a wise choice. Every parent knows these moments intimately.

My moment had come. Being the brave soul that I am (insert laughter from my wife and daughters), I decided to chance it with the dogs. Was my heart beating a bit faster or was it just the exertion from the long run? Hmmm.

As I approached that evil-dog house, I began running as lightly as an overweight male can run. Suddenly, bursting from the thick woods that sat just to the left of the dirt road (and just beside my left arm since I was running as far away from that house as humanly possible) were what must have been a flock of quail. I just about jumped out of my shorts, and maybe those shorts were a tad damper for the remainder of the run. But it was only birds.

At the house, one old dog slowly pulled himself together and got up to bark benignly from his porch. They must have gotten rid of the killer demon dogs. I'm not sure if this dog was barking at me or the birds. He quickly sat back down. My heart rate didn't.

A horned cow on the loose, a flock of quail, and an old farm dog on a porch . . . these teamed up to make a memory on a day that could have been a boring, long-run day around my very familiar trail. What a great day to be alive!

## 18.2

Another day, another early morning run, this time at Mercy Park.

I was making my first of three passes around the pond, which would complete a mile of my 3-mile maintenance run. One time around, and I barely noticed the jabbering of the birds. It was normal for birds to nest in the area. I paid little attention.

A second time around, and what can only be described as a blood-curdling squawk just beside my right ear—I mean *just* beside it, not from up in the trees—made me jump and left goosebumps running along my body. What in the world?!

I thought for a moment about birds distracting humans from nests by acting injured and leading them away from the nest. But there was no acting injury in that squawk. There was a mortal warning. Get away now!

Still, I reasoned to myself, the park has walkers and runners all the time. Birds would never attack. I'd never seen them bother anyone before. Plus, I'm a man. They are stupid little birds. Insignificant in strength, comparatively. Right?

I kept running but must admit that I was glancing around for a few strides. It unnerved me a bit. Should I alter my course? No. Surely not. I ran on around the pond, close to completing my first mile when, suddenly, it attacked!

"Oh, come on!" I can hear you saying. But it is true. Without warning and without a second squawk, the bird made an attack dive and pecked me on the crown of my head.

(In the next instant, I turned, sighted the bird, quickly whipped out my 9-millimeter Glock, and dispensed of the offending bird in a shower of feathers, then blew on my gun and holstered it with a nod.)

Okay, that is the dream scenario I thought up later. Reality was . . . I was stunned. Now my running wasn't the normal jog. I was truly running! Looking all around, waving my arms, my pace markedly increasing. I took the first turn possible off the pond loop and got the heck out of there. Attack birds! You've got to be kidding me!

Girl: "Mommy, why is the man doing that?"

Mother: "Doing what, honey?"

Girl: "Look. He's running kinda crazy and waving his arms all around his head . . . at nothing. And what is he saying?"

Mother: "I'm not sure, dear. But let's go *this* way."

Or so I imagined the conversation might have gone with anyone watching me that day.

The truth is the peck didn't hurt much, not really. It was kind of like you would think a peck might feel. It was enough that I kept feeling to see if he'd scratched me enough to draw blood. I was expecting to see red on my fingers but didn't. So it had not hit me that hard. But it was a shocking experience.

I have run at Mercy Park possibly a hundred times and that is the only time I've been pecked by a bird. I have, however, experienced another squawk in my ear and that time I didn't make another circuit. I heeded the warning and went another way. Stupid birds.

And yet, it made another memory and wove another thread into the story of my sometimes-monotonous runs.

## 18.4

For anyone who runs through the residential streets of a city, they have doubtless encountered many dogs that sound as if they'll tear you limb from limb if they can only get outside of their containment and get at you. For anyone who runs multiple miles on country roads near their home, they will certainly have come upon many canines who are on the loose and come bounding out to meet you with the same ferocious, challenging barks. And you will have approached those, the first time, very cautiously.

In the mile sections of dirt road around my house, I am quite familiar with all my furry friends, some of whom treat me like an invader from outer space and others who treat me like a long-lost buddy. I've never been bitten (most dogs are nicer than birds), although I think the dogs I was wary of in my cow story might have done so if they'd gotten to me.

But I know them all now because of my many runs on these roads. The ones who treat me like the enemy do so every time. Especially so with one dog that lives a mile and a half away from me at the home of a friendly neighbor who has been in my house in his capacity as a plumber.

I think this particular dog is a cross between pit bull and some other breed. He comes roaring to the road with teeth bared and a bark that could kill. He gets close at my heels and approaches with sincere intent, or so it seems. But one pause from me and he immediately turns back. He's a barking dog. That's all!

I cannot count the times I have run his way but whatever the number, it is the same number of times that he's come after me in this manner. I've tried treats. He ignores them. I've tried gentle talk. He barks all the more. I've tried authority; he doesn't care. He has a job to do and he is doing it with great dedication.

But do you see what he is? He has no bite. I can run there every day without concern. In fact, he adds interest to my day. There is no danger here. It's only a barking dog.

## 18.6

Have you ever noticed how many potential "mountains" turn out to be mole hills?

We have, at this time in history, dealt with a true mountain-sort of problem in the experience that COVID-19 brought to our world. It changed the way most people live even if you think it is all a bunch of media hype and not a real problem. I am not going to comment on my beliefs about this virus because I am not intent on making enemies out of half of the population. I will take stands where I need to take them. I see no use in a stand on this issue for the purposes of this book. However, it cannot be argued that it has changed the world in ways surely few of us ever imagined.

But I believe the majority of problems that come at us in daily life and seem insurmountable, are not. It seems there is almost a yearly warning from people in authority about some new thing that is going to get us. They are almost always wrong in the direness of their predictions. They are mole hills, those possible viruses that will be unlike every other virus. They are usually only barking dogs . . . although a barking dog does need to be approached with caution if it is a dog you haven't encountered before, right?

The same can be said of diseases. Cancer is a big one. And thank God for the internet! I now know that almost every ache or pain my body feels has a possible origin in cancer. Just google it. You'll find out. The truth is it is usually just a barking dog. Yet this dog, cancer, is one that bites with awful precision when it does bite. It is possibly the biggest health fear of our time.

I have been blessed with excellent health. I do not take it for granted. I am thankful. No broken bones, no diseases, no major ailments of any kind. But I know this can change in a moment. One day that ache may, in fact, be cancer related. It may be a dog that bites.

I recently had blood work that led to the concern for the possibility of cancer. More tests led to more concerns. Needless to say, it had my attention. After years of excellent health, was it all about to change? Would my intention to run another marathon turn into a fight against a killer disease?

Such things can lead to great fear. It is understandable why it is so. Cancer kills. Cancer treatment is often brutal and devastating, killing good things in the body as it attempts to kill the cancer. Who wouldn't be afraid of that mess? But oftentimes, it bares its teeth and slinks away when you face it, barking a final warning as it goes.

What about other life problems? Does my son have a learning disability? Am I going to lose my job? Is that storm going to yield a tornado? Are we going to have enough money to fix the roof? Will we be able to get presents for the kids for Christmas?

Problems in life are as numerous as the dogs in the neighborhood, and as loud.

Sometimes when one dog starts barking, every dog in the neighborhood barks. Have you noticed that? There are times it seems that every bad problem hits us at once. Is it all falling apart? Is life as I know it about to come crashing down? Where can I go? What can I do?

And fear feeds upon itself in the symphony of the neighborhood hounds. But wait.

Usually, they are only barking dogs. Usually, they will not bite. Hold strong. Be steady. Go on. It may be just a barking dog.

## 18.9

Some dogs bite. I know this is true, and that bite is not to be belittled. In fact, I am about to run back down an emotional road, in Mile 20, with a discussion of an attacking beast that challenged me deeply.

But while the possibility of biting dogs is a real concern, isn't it also true that we often waste energy with the fear associated with dogs that bark but don't bite?

I suggest that we give attention to the molehills, but that we not allow ourselves to be dominated by them; that we do our best to forsake the fear of them because so many of them simply do not grow into the mountains that we fear they may become. In fact, if anything, fear only adds to the size of the hill, a hill that may never materialize at all if we simply face it as a possibility we will determine to run through, even if it does bite.

Skunks, attack birds, the occasional stray cow . . . and barking dogs. This is part of the tapestry of life. As is the comforting presence of a spouse of 37 years, the sight of grandchildren building a fort out of sticks in the front yard, the unbridled joy of a toddler's laugh, the security of a parent's love, and the unparalleled beauty of the Creator's brushstrokes across the morning sky.

It is all a part of our lives. And we run in its beauty with determined joy.

## 19.0

About two days after I had written this mile and had sent the first draft to my girls for their input (as I always did during the writing of this book), I received the following text from my wife. It was about one of my girls who had been dealing with a potentially serious medical issue. My daughter sent this text to my wife, who then forwarded to me:

*"Earlier this week I woke up and I heard the words, 'Don't be afraid, que ladra.' I had no idea what that meant but I heard the phrase twice more. It sounded like a different language. I got up and looked it up in Spanish. It is translated 'that barks.' So 'Don't be afraid of that which barks'? I was still confused and blew it off. Then (later that day) I read dad's Mile 19. Don't be afraid of the barking dog. 'It's just a barking dog!' I think the Lord was using that to speak to me about these things. I don't know how many times my symptoms have lined up with some very serious condition. I need that reminder. Don't be afraid. He is my refuge in distress. It's not a biting dog, but it sure, sometimes, sounds like it."*

This is a very real application of what this Mile is about. There are so many times that things come at us that cause great concern. The truth is, even if that dog appears to bite this time (i.e., the cancer scare turns out to really be cancer, or the migraine turns out to be a tumor), this is still just a barking dog to those who find their refuge in the Lord. There is no place, in life or in death, that can separate us from His love and His care. Simply put, there is no bite that can separate us from Him, and every mountain is only a stroll into His glory.

*"Though youths grow weary and tired and vigorous young men stumble badly, yet those who wait on the Lord will find new strength. They will fly high on wings like eagles. They will run and not grow weary. They will walk and not faint."*

## MILE 20

# *When Heat Waves Hit, Endure*

Heat and humidity sap the body's strength and reservoirs of energy like almost nothing else can. Cold can be brutal, wind may resist your every step, and rain can be annoying, but heat will tear you down, chew you up, and spit you out. It exhausts the body like no other element, leaving you weak and unable to continue if not dealt with in the right way.

For our 36th anniversary, my wife and I had a wild hare moment and decided to jump in the car to head to Estes Park in Colorado, where our honeymoon had been all those many years ago. Being in the middle of my training plan for my 3rd marathon at the time, I had to work a couple of runs in around the amazing hikes we took that week. Here I was in the Colorado mountains, a month before a marathon that would occur in the mountains of Washington, so I decided to use the last morning before our departure to get my 19-mile training run in, taking advantage of the 40-degree morning rather than doing it on the 80-degree mornings that I knew awaited me when I returned to Oklahoma. And, oh the difference it made.

Running nineteen miles anytime is going to be a challenge for me, despite the years of training. But what a joy to be able to run those laps around Lake Estes with the majesty of the Rocky Mountains all around and the cool mountain breezes softly blowing across my tired body.

Fast forward a week later to my next long run, just 12 miles - but back in Oklahoma where it was going to get "down" to 80 degrees by 10:00 p.m. and still hover around 75 degrees when I started my run at 6:00 a.m. Ugh. It was awful by comparison.

I felt good to begin with. I now know all the keys to long runs, keys I didn't really learn until after my first marathon was over. So I had prepared myself with lots of hydration and a good carb buildup. But by mile 6, I was blown out. I was shooting to maintain my 10-minute pace, and did so for the first 6, but after that, the heat and humidity bore down on me with a force that zapped all my energy and most of my will power. I stumbled through the last 6 miles, barely keeping my average at 11 minutes overall.

Exercise in the heat can debilitate. It pulls the life from inside you as sweat pours over your body, doing its best to regulate the core temps and keep you alive. Will drags you on.

I have many similar examples of experiencing the change in seasons. And in every season, the body will adapt, especially if we take the necessary steps to prepare the body for what is coming, making the crucial adjustments along the way. If we do, even in summer's heat, what these bodies can train up to is incredible. Oh, the heat will still be hot. The humidity will still be stifling. But these bodies can endure.

If we will, they can.

# 19.1

As I write this, twelve years ago today, my mother died. It was July 23, 2008. She was far too young, having just reached the 65-year mark. The last few years of her life were lived in what can only be described as a prison whose walls continued to close in until she could no longer move or speak. She could only exist.

However, there is more to the story than that. I will attempt to tell it here because it is a story many will relate to.

To be with my mom at her peak was to experience vitality and spunk. She had a zest for life and for engaging people with her wit. She loved a challenge of the mind but only for fun, never for superiority or power. She enjoyed people of all kinds and because of her basic goodness and acceptance of people, many were drawn to her for comfort and counsel.

I recall having to share her at times with kids who were troubled. At other times, I shared her with young ladies who were trying to learn how to be a wife or a mom. She offered herself freely in those days, always willing to listen, encourage, and care.

If you were a person who had been disdained or shamed because of your actions, she was liable to walk up to you, kiss you on the cheek, and tell you how much she liked you. It didn't matter that everyone else in the room avoided you. She didn't care about that. She cared about you and what you did next . . . after your failure or your shameful event.

One extended family member of mine, who had experienced this unconditional acceptance and love, stood beside me at her graveside and told me what he had done that he was ashamed of, and then he related to me what my mom had done. He told me about that kiss on his cheek when he was at his most vulnerable. "She was a rare gem" was what he said to me. I wholeheartedly agree. For I, as one of her two sons, experienced the strength of her support and the stability of her wisdom for the first forty-four years of my life. Far too short, but I am thankful for every day.

My father and she were a wonderful team for forty-seven years. They had problems, like all couples do, but they weathered them all. Their favorite spot together was the Colorado mountains. There, the zest for life in my mother was like that of a young gazelle. She bounded up long and steep mountain trails, testing the endurance of those who followed her, smiling as she went. Occasionally her arms shot into the air and a shriek of joy escaped her mouth because of the wonder of the encompassing beauty.

There was nothing quite like the cool Colorado Rocky Mountains for my mom and dad, the crisp air, the rushing streams, and the pounding waterfalls, their joy.

Then one day, a hot wind imposed itself upon their beautiful lives almost as if a crack in the earth had opened up and steam belched forth from the pit of hell itself. And in a moment, almost in the blink of an eye, everything changed.

## 19.2

For most children, a day comes when their parents begin to slow down. That time didn't occur in quite the normal fashion for my mom. She'd worked beside me for almost twenty years in the fast-paced environment of the pizza business, in a venture that had been started by our family in 1983. For my mother, being in the food business was among the last things she would have chosen. But supporting her husband and sons was near the top of her list of priorities. So she sacrificed and played her important role. On the busiest day of the week, she would be beside me in the kitchen with a ticket rail full of orders to be made, saying "Oh Rusty, oh, Rusty!" as we met the rush and overcame it time after time.

Fridays were my long days, usually working at least a twelve-hour shift and covering both the lunch and supper rushes. I would grab a few minutes in the afternoon after we had cleaned up from the lunch rush and restocked supplies in preparation for the coming supper rush. And here, my mom was at her finest. After having worked the lunch rush, she refused to go home for the evening until she knew that her son had eaten and had restored his strength and energy for what was to come. She was all about health.

She often had gotten up early in the morning to prepare something ahead of time so that when those few minutes of respite came, the crockpot was ready with our healthy food, something that would truly strengthen rather than just filling the stomach with fast food.

Toward the end of this twenty-year period, just as I was really burning out with the food industry, and just before my brother would bail me out with an offer to work for him, my mom began to slow down just a bit. She was meticulous by nature, so even when she began to step back from Friday rushes, she maintained the bookkeeping and, in so doing, managed to keep at least one responsibility off my plate. That was always her way. Support. Strengthen. Encourage.

I guess the first winds of change began to come in ways I didn't recognize. I have read an account of events my father put together that informs me that she had begun to have some health struggles for as much as two or three of the last years of our business. This knowledge surprises me now. But a warm current of health troubles had begun to blow through their lives as the beginning signs of the changing season.

It wasn't until a year or so after my departure from our business that things became noticeable to those other than my dad. Whereas her walking pace was always one that was a challenge to keep up with, she almost suddenly began to slow down, and he noticed that her feet began to shuffle.

She began to experience weakness in her knees and balance problems. While on a morning walk, she stumbled and fell on her face. Her balance became worse in marked increments. Her penmanship became almost illegible. Her overall pain levels increased. Her social life came suddenly to a halt, the hot winds of change now fully coming to bear.

After going from specialist to specialist over the course of several months, a diagnosis was made at Barnes Jewish Hospital in St. Louis: Progressive Supranuclear Palsy, a progressively debilitating disease much like ALS (Lou Gehrig's disease). I had never heard of it.

But, it was like a death knell when the words were first uttered. Burned in my memory is the moment of walking into my brother's office having just heard from my dad, conveying to my brother, while trying to keep myself from breaking down emotionally, that our mother had a diagnosis, a nightmare declaration, and hearing the words "life expectancy" for the first time ever uttered about a person I loved so dearly. Five years maybe, he said. As the days unfolded, she didn't even accomplish half of that . . . mercifully.

A walk was about to occur that would lead over a cliff in a matter of months and the mom I'd always known would change into a person I could almost not recognize. Her energy changed, her mental capacity changed, her cognition altered, and every attribute that had defined her life would flee.

Her muscles grew increasingly weak. Once I had to rush to keep pace with her. Now I held her hand as we ever so slowly walked around a field. I recall that day. She said to me, "I hate what has happened to me. But I can hate it until the cows come home and it won't change anything." She was full of sayings like that. I was glad to hear the saying because that was a sign that part of my mother still existed. But soon the weakness increased so that there would be no more walking, only sitting in a wheelchair and being moved around. This woman, who would set the world on fire with her liveliness, was now confined into a chair with her legs barely functioning.

Possibly the worst change she experienced was to her mind because it had always been so sharp. Early on, her speech slowed dramatically. Soon she became almost entirely non- verbal, so much so that if a word or phrase did suddenly come from her mouth, all those around her almost jumped with surprise. Interestingly, the phrase would be on topic, proving to us yet again that some part of her was still there, functioning but trapped and without escape.

Her personality soon changed too. An awful effect of the disease is a loss of expression. Her face no longer smiled. It no longer frowned. It was just there. She seemed passive about everything. Amazingly, other than the one comment she made about hating this until the cows came home, I never heard her complain. My father is witness that the opposite of complaining actually occurred.

As a person who had often spoken about never wanting to live as a burden to anyone, and who had now become absolutely dependent for every life event (eating, moving, etc.), there was a time when she described having amazing joy inside, in spite of what was happening. One could only imagine it as being the grace of God upon her, even though it was the same God who was allowing this awful course of events to unfold.

And therein arose a bit of a struggle for my own faith. How could God so do?

I find now, looking back on this time, that almost all of us can question a Creator God about this thing or that. How can He allow this child to be abused, that person to be killed, that war to be started, or my mom to be so debilitated? The question is wrong, though. I see it now. God has not set the universe in an order so that every evil and every trial is eliminated, and only good things are experienced. Quite the opposite. In this short life, we get the full range of opportunity to experience good and evil, beauty and horror, joy and anguish.

In my view of the world, there are reasons for this that I will not get into now. Nor will I venture yet into the saving grace that I believe can await on the other side of the veil of these short years on the earth.

But for my mom, it seemed to us who looked on to be the worst kind of hell to live through. It was a hot summer wind that took our breath away and before it was over, its suffocating humidity would almost destroy some of us.

My dad has written very personal notes about this time in their lives. Therein I discovered something that pierces me in a place of some of my deepest shame. I struggled to deal with seeing these changes in my previously very independent mom. I struggled with the embarrassment of being with her in public at a restaurant during the last year or so of her life.

There is a moment; I see it vividly in my mind's eye. We were at a Chinese restaurant. My dad had gotten her plate and gone to fill his own from the buffet. I sat there beside her, my brother and sister-in-law across the table. Her arm came up halfway to her mouth with food and stopped. My dad wasn't there to help. I'd never helped my mother eat, not ever. She who'd raised me and cared for me now needed my care for one moment, for one simple act. And I failed her. Soon my father returned, and she still sat, looking at the food half raised to her lips, with her son doing nothing to assist. Surely a part of her still existed inside that brain. Surely, she knew. But I tried to dismiss it, this horrible show of my bad character.

And now I see these words in my father's journal during that last year of her life: *"This condition is something Becky would have hated more than anything, not being able to care for herself. However, along with her growing problems, she has become quiet and somewhat unconcerned. She has a firm faith in God and is entrusted totally to Him. She looks forward to two things during the week. One is seeing her family and having lunch with them."*

Oh. What kind of worm am I?

And yet, in the midst of even this, he declared that she found joy. He finished the above entry with this: *"She even says she has a great joy deep inside while all this humiliating stuff continues to take her quality of life."* I cannot imagine it. And yet it is true. In the stifling moment of their lives . . . she found joy.

## 19.5

When she was gone, my dad felt a moment of great joy. Her suffering was gone. It was over. The love of his life was finally free.

He spoke during those days about powerful moments of connection with his bride. Of lying beside her, not talking (she couldn't talk anyway), and staring into each other's eyes for long periods of time . . . speaking to each other like only a husband and wife can do.

But not many moments after she was gone, the inevitable occurred . . . his feelings of great loss and an undying pit of loneliness flooded in, soon followed by something akin to despair. Some of the loneliness had begun while she still lived, of course.

Some of the loss of all the life they'd enjoyed had already hit home many months before she died. He missed his "Rebecca" and any communication from her, even so much as a grunt in response, gave my dad a moment of joy, like one gasp of cool air to his heat-worn soul.

But after she was gone for good, now what?

As summer turned into fall of that first year, barely three months had gone by and he was already feeling a loss of motivation to do much of anything. He could try to stay busy during the days, but why? There was nobody to enjoy any accomplishment with. And the nights were only dark and alone. Even as the fall turned into beautiful colors, depression hung over his head at all times. A dread of winter was coming on, missing her . . . missing her . . . having had no idea how much he'd taken her presence for granted.

"*She was the life of this house and the light of my life, and I knew it but did not really appreciate it like I do now. How will this get better? I do not know what to do.*" Words from a journal he wrote on October 20, 2008, words that ring true for many of us. Do not waste the precious days of this life with the one you've been blessed to walk this path with (my words, not his, although I think that is what he'd say).

His words on that day become very indicative of where his mind went during this brief period of time. My father is a man of faith. He had spent the biggest portion of his life serving people, teaching people, helping people through their own hardships of life. If anyone stood firm, he did. He has been my example in these things. And through this great storm of his life, he amazed me as he exemplified absolute selfless love in serving his wife. And yet, when she was gone, he wrote:

*"I am caught in between. I would really like to just step over on the other side and grab her into my arms, but I know that is not the right way to think and I must not keep on giving in to that feeling. I have been asking the Lord to keep me in the center of His plan, not mine. I have experienced enough disappointments and hope to see Him move me toward something useful and fulfilling. I just need to know what it is! So for now, I 'feel' lost with regard to purpose or direction."*

I recall him saying things like this, of wanting just to pass on from this life, wondering what reason there was to remain now that she was gone.

I get it. I cannot imagine life without my own lovely lady, with whom I've shared everything these last 37 years. What would life be like outside of that relationship? I can't think of it.

But this is the thing we all know. For all who are joined together for decades, for all who complete one another's sentences, for all who know what someone is thinking before they say it and who can read the looks of whimsy or anger or hurt or despair; for each of us, this moment is coming. It is a part of the consuming bitter heat that life throws at us all somewhere on this journey, no matter how much we fight to keep it at bay.

It will come for one or the other of the two. And one will live on and wonder, *why?*

*Why should I go on? What is my purpose now?*

## 19.6

Not quite a year after my mom was gone, my dad discovered something. Life would never be the same, but it could still be good. He remembered a basic understanding on which his life and faith had rested, that God is good, regardless of what we are experiencing. He is good and has our good in mind.

He began to release the loss and the pain and hopelessness and began to face the possibilities of a new day.

Much to my brother's and my surprise, our good ole dad recalled a conversation with a man about a Christian singles website. After entering a lot of information into the site, he was shocked to discover that in six days he had 75 women who were "compatible" who wanted to correspond with him. Time to narrow the parameters. He very soon narrowed the field down to only one he really wanted to talk to. I will call her Jane to protect her privacy. I hope she doesn't mind. Within 5 months, they were married!

I will be honest. I was shocked and dismayed after seeing my dad only ever with my mom. I thought he had lost his mind. But I was dead wrong. Eleven years have now passed, and my dad has indeed found a new lease on life and a breath of fresh cool air has blown through his days.

As might be expected, Jane is a lady with spunk and zest. Whereas my mom used to hurry domino players or card players along, I discovered in one of our early sessions of game- playing with my dad's new wife that we were being hurried along to play. Ha!

One might expect some turmoil with them. They seem to have none. What we have discovered is a lady for my dad who exhibits all the kindness and grace our mother used to extend to others.

Jane has been for my dad exactly what he needed for the enjoyment and reward of his last decades on this planet. Again, he has purpose. Again, there is life and joy. And we are all greatly blessed because of it.

Death, so traumatic . . . life, so good. Let us live while we can, eh? I also realize their story will not be everyone's story. Some may be appalled at the thought of marrying again. Many will live on in the joy of serving their children, their grandchildren, their fellow man. They will absorb the loss and find a way to still gain meaning in life. Or they will not, if they choose not to do so. As with all things, the choice is ours.

## 19.7

Just two days after an awful July 5, 2020, run of 7 miles, I had my routine morning 3-mile maintenance run on another hot day. But on the day of the prior 7-mile run, I'd also mowed the yard for two hours in the scorching heat and I'd gone to visit family that night, staying up 2 hours past my normal 9:30 p.m. bedtime (yes, I'm old).

I awoke at 6:00 a.m. for a morning run.

I discovered that my body hadn't yet recovered from the hard day, but I pushed myself out anyway. Determination is the only way on these days. My first mile was sluggish at about a 10:14 pace, my second mile was only slightly faster and then . . . I found my legs and energy and pushed my third mile in at a very fast pace (for me) of 8 minutes, 30 seconds.

I wonder if that is the way of things with the loss of one so dear as my mom was to me and my brother . . . and even more so for my dad, his spouse of 47 years.

Do we discover that our souls are worn to the point that we need days, weeks, or even years to recover? Until one morning we get up and find we still have legs and still have wind and there is still a race we can run. And we push ourselves and find once again the joy of the race.

The loss for me was hard. I wish she were here for key moments of life, or just to talk during the mundane ones. I miss her sharp wit, fun sense of humor, and uncanny ability to provide a word of perfect wisdom at just the right time.

I still think about her. But I found my stride fairly quickly after she was gone. I had to. My wife was still with me, needing me. My girls (although grown and married) didn't need to see a dad in despair. So I got myself together and went on, as my mother would have wanted me to do.

For my dad, it took much longer. But those fresh legs for running he did find. And he's running well still today.

## 19.8

My mom encouraged people to overcome their failures and their weaknesses. She had a phrase or two that would commonly come from her mouth when she was trying to guide people to overcome. "Slay that giant" and "Be ruthless" were the terms. She wasn't mamby pamby. She was gentle but strong. "Let's do this! You can!"

As I wrote about my shameful behavior in her last year of life and how I failed her, I had to take a walk to work it all out in my emotions. What kind of a son does that? The worst kind is the answer. And now, twelve years after she is gone, there is no way to ask her to forgive me. I can speak it into the clouds and hope that she hears. I can tell my dad, who will respond only with kindness.

And then I recalled how she responded when others were caught in the midst of their failure and shame. I know now what she would do if she were here today . . . if I could speak to her now. She would sense my shame. She would know. And before I could speak, she would come up to me and kiss me on my cheek. She would say, "I love you. You've always given me such joy." Grace is what she would exhibit.

That is the love and grace with which my mother lived her life. That is the love she always gave me and would give me still.

Even in her absence, even twelve years later, I am still learning from her as I recall her ways. I am learning how we should treat those who fail miserably, how one should run in the heat and humidity of life, and how one should thrive and endure, come what may.

## 20.0

I didn't get to tell my mother goodbye, not really. By the time we knew what was happening, she'd already changed mentally. So the opportunity never presented itself for long talks about anything and everything. An end came and it was brutal. But even in that, there were moments of joy and moments of sacrificial love.

I recall what I later referred to as the "passion week" as she began a 7-day ordeal of no longer getting food or water after my dad finally decided there was no use trying to force food into her body because it only choked her continuously. She was ready to shed the shell of this life.

And in those days, I watched moments of sacrificial love by many people: by my Aunt Gail who came to care for her around the clock alongside my dad; by my brother who sat beside her and read comforting words to her from the Bible; and by my dad who would practically never leave her side, aching with her every ache, and rejoicing when she was finally released from that jail cell of her body.

I watched men and women come to pray over her, sing around her, and say final words of love to her. They didn't see a broken and defeated body. They saw past that, into the spirit of a woman with great compassion and abounding grace.

The following words were written by my mother during one of the deepest trials of her own life, many years before the events described in this mile. She later cross-stitched them onto a canvas, a canvas which is on the wall in my office at work. It is titled, simply, Grace.

*Your grace is sufficient is what they say,*
*To bear all the trials that come my way.*
*Okay! I agree! That sounds good to me.*
*But what does that mean when I'm sad as can be?*
*What does that mean when my heart cries in pain,*
*When it seems that life will never be right again?*
*What does that mean when I'm confused in my mind,*
*When all circumstances say there's no way I can find,*
*To get over this mountain I find in my path,*
*To get through this valley of blackness and wrath?*
*Oh God! I just can't! I cry deep within.*
*You can! Yes you can! Your voice sounds again.*
*Grace was the gift that cost my Son's life,*
*His death on the cross purchased the end of your strife.*
*I'll make your low places high and your high places low.*
*Now lean hard on Me and we'll conquer that foe.*
*Listen, just listen, I'll whisper the plan.*
*Trust in Me, child, we will take that land!*

I will allow my dad the last word here. He deserves it. He wrote: "*She was my soul mate, my friend, and my lifelong sweetheart. She was the most loving, honest, freedom-loving spirit ever created, unique in every way.*"

These are words of a warrior, my dad, who went on, after the greatest loss of his life. Of a man who decided to live and found in life a new breath of fresh air, much to his great surprise.

"*This too will pass*," my mama used to say. The heat will pass. It will. What must we do? Endure. And go on, until the cool breezes of fall begin to blow again.

*"God is our refuge and strength, a very present help in trouble.*
*Therefore, we will not fear, though the earth should change*
*and though the mountains slip into the heart of the sea."*

## MILE 21

# Up Every Hill, Down Every Valley, Don't Stop

When the boss and running mentor I'm calling Joe first mentioned the Jack and Jill Marathon to me, I was intrigued. Then I went to the website and I was hooked. Count me in.

Training began in mid-January. Training ended in late July. It began in the dead of winter and ended during the heat of a Midwest summer. During these long months I was destined to experience the gamut of the elements, from extreme cold to extreme heat, from cool breezes to fierce spring winds, from bright sunshine to driving rains. I would get it all.

I had good experiences during the months of training. I had lousy moments as well. I had ups. I had downs. I had "I can't wait" moments. I had "Why am I doing this?" moments. And on I trained. Occasionally, I went to the website and looked at the video of a previous race, seeing the beauty all around, the waterfall, the mountain streams, the tree-covered mountain, the mystery of the tunnel through the mountain. I gazed at it all and dreamed of my own run down that mountain and across one more marathon finish line.

The half marathon I ran in April, when my son-in-law joined me, was an up—good feelings all around. The half marathon in Joplin a month later was a suddenly hot day and I performed poorly. It was a down. Ups. Downs. This is the way of spring. But the way of training in summer is mostly downs, at least it is for me.

I remember getting out from under my covers at 3:00 a.m. on more than one Saturday morning. But I could not beat the heat of June and July in the Midwest. You walk out the door at 3:30 a.m.; it is dark, stars in the sky, crickets cricketing. It should be cool, right? Instead, a wave of heat and humidity smacks you right in the face. But I was not alone. Unseen people were joining me.

## 20.1

Standing in the very long line to the pre-race restroom on July 28, thirty minutes from the start of the Jack & Jill Marathon . . . wondering if the line would move fast enough for all of us to get our last shot at the restroom . . . I'm listening to conversations all around. It is cold here. Someone said it is in the forties on top of the mountain today. Yes! I think. I love the cool after feeling the sweltering heat over the last two months of long training runs.

I heard the young lady in front of me telling three others that she is cold, and that her 20-mile run had been in her hometown in Arizona . . . in 86-degree heat! She said she got out of bed at 3:00 in the morning! Ha! I was *not* alone! But where I faced 76 degrees and humidity, she faced 86 degrees. (A dry heat in Arizona though, right? Wimps! Come to Oklahoma!) And then I heard her comment on the run. "It was 86 degrees at 3:00 a.m.! It was stupid!" She said that last part emphatically. *"Stupid!"*

And there you go. Marathon runners are stupid, or so some may think. The thought once again went through my mind, *Do people who run marathons know they don't have to?* The answer to why we do it is probably quite varied, and my answer is possibly discovered somewhere in this book, but suffice it to say that at 3:00 a.m. on a summer morning with 76- degree heat and 99 percent humidity, that's a down feeling. It is pain leading into misery. It is not any fun whatsoever until . . . you finish. And then satisfaction leaks into your drained body. And somewhere from inside the exhausted being comes a whisper, "Good run! You did it!" And the down becomes an up.

Your day is better. Slower maybe. Less energetic the rest of the day. But it is an up. You have just faced a mountain of challenge in the pounding heat for 20 miles. You overcame again. A definite up.

I am writing these words on my 55th birthday. Talk about a temptation for a down! I received an email about being a senior citizen. Senior citizen?! That is crazy. I still feel like I should be in my thirties. Old people are senior citizens. Not me. But hey, I just ran a marathon two days ago and set a personal record by twenty minutes! Take that, you awful "down" thought. This is an up!

Ups, downs. Ups, downs. Cold and harsh winds, cool breezes, humid sun-scorched heat, breathtaking mountain runs. This is running. This is life. I don't care how cold, how hot, how humid, how windy, or how rainy it may be. I'm going to run today. Those things will change.

My determination will not. Those things are outside, pressing down on me. But there is something greater from inside that resists the outside pressing and then takes it on, tussles with it, and gradually gets the upper hand. Which then finally owns the day and turns to look back at the finished fight with the laugh of a warrior—bloodied yet strong.

## 20.2

The drive to the starting line at 5:30 a.m. was fantastic. The first light of dawn begins to stretch out over the mountains as you drive. Wisps of clouds rest here and there near the mountain peaks. Trees are painted thickly into the hillsides. It is nature at its best—fresh and new.

I took in a few breaths of anticipation and let them out slowly. My faithful companion was driving me to the starting line. She glanced over at me and said a few encouraging words. She believed them. I was unsure.

I began to toy with the ideas of ignoring the counsel I received from the experienced runner, Joe. He knows I burned out at the end of both prior marathons and he witnessed one burnout firsthand. His counsel was to avoid the temptation to start faster than I'd trained for, enjoy the race, *then* try to finish strong and hang on for the second half. When will I ever learn? He was right the first time. He was right the second time. He'll be right again today.

*But it's downhill,* I tried to convince myself. *He knows that,* I reminded myself. Back and forth I went. It was like the shoulder angel and shoulder devil. Follow counsel or think about counsel being wrong and doing my own plan because I've got a great plan and that counselor probably doesn't know how hard I've trained and, and, and . . . When will I learn? Not today apparently.

I tried for the most part to follow (after again starting out a bit too fast) but I wasn't fully committed to it, and the result betrayed that truth in the end. It was a better than normal finish but still not the finish I wanted and not the result he said I'd have if I followed his counsel. Urg! Follow the counsel of those who have gone before! Follow it fully, completely! I believe in this.

We arrived at the starting line parking area about 45 minutes prior to the start and not a moment too soon. The first thing I noticed was the long lines to the restrooms and porta potties. As the line very gradually moved, nervous folks of all ages chatted, glanced at watches, and worried. Soon a person stepped out and announced that door number 6 has a toilet that is no longer flushing. People continued to enter. With about 10 minutes to spare, I'm in.

My wife joined me on a quick walk to the start line. And then we both got a new experience.

As I've mentioned, this was a mountain race. There were trees and bushes everywhere.

There was a narrow path that was the trail, and all around was nature. And then it happened: People began to give up hope on the restrooms and they used the restroom afforded in creation—trees, bushes, any hiding place they can find. I've never in my life been standing in the midst of a thousand people while just fifteen yards away people are lining the trees or wading into the bushes to use nature's restroom. Necessity, the mother of invention? It is also a thief of normal modesty that humans have (or at least, used to have). I turned away, thankful at least for the trees and the bushes.

# 20.3

The race begins in the unincorporated mountaintop community of Hyak at Snoqualmie Pass. It ends in the valley town of North Bend, population 6,821.

The race trail is used for all kinds of activities. Even while running the marathon, there were bikers, random joggers, families exploring the mountain trails, and climbers taking on sheer cliffs. As we ran, a few of the families stopped to encourage us on. This was a first for me, a marathon that didn't stop everything else in its path. Here on this mountain, all could come and go as they pleased as a thousand people came running by.

And so the moment had come. It was a moment I had been waiting for and training for over the last seven months, a moment conceived of even months before that—the start to the downhill marathon in the mountains of Washington. It was not like my first in OKC, where I stood grinning like a fool. It was not like my second in Springfield, Missouri, where I stood beside my friend and brother-in-law to experience the challenge *with* someone racing beside me. I did think back for a moment to all the training and early morning choices to get out of bed to run in some uncomfortable element. But mainly I was just thinking, *I'm ready to do this,* and was glad the time was now. The run began.

Within a half mile we turned into the Snoqualmie Tunnel, which was a fascinating and memorable experience. Runners had flashlights or headlamps, as instructed. Without them, we would have been in pitch black. It was two miles of concrete overhead and dirt below.

Occasionally we came to pits in the road where the dripping roof had created small pools of water or washed away little portions of roadway. Each step forward brought the potential of a turned ankle or a shoe/sock/foot soaked for the remainder of the 24 miles of the marathon. Neither was an option we wanted so the lights were focused downward, the eyes maintaining alertness to any changes in the next few feet. Occasionally, I took a quick glance up but quickly looked back to the path.

At one point, possibly a mile into the tunnel, I glanced up and saw a light far in the distance that I knew must be the exit point. *How far?* I wondered. A half mile, a mile, more? Our GPS watches were useless inside. So I could not be certain of pace either, in spite of the importance that pace has for a successful long run.

"Start slow, at 11 minutes," my boss had instructed. Eleven minutes? Heck! I could be going at a 10-minute pace or a 12-minute pace. I simply wasn't sure. But after what seemed like a long time, the end of the tunnel approached. The light became greater. And in a few more minutes I was through, into the fresh air and the beauty of the mountain. All in all, I have to say that tunnel experience was not only unique, but it was yet again a life lesson to draw from.

## 20.4

Lights at ends of tunnels are nice references that encouraging people may use when a friend encounters prolonged difficulty. But really? Isn't it more to the point that the tunnel is long and at times pitch dark, and the only important thing is that a person take the next step even though "this little light of mine" is only shining on that next step and doesn't penetrate far enough into the pit of darkness to ascertain whether there is danger just a few feet away?

The tunnel experiences of life are surely almost never a rewarding time in and of themselves. They are desperate times; times of great confusion and turmoil; times of doubt and times of fear; and yet, they are also something else . . . they are times when men and women learn what they are made of and what is in the fabric of their beings.

They are times when faith becomes reality because the eyes cannot penetrate the depth of darkness far enough to trust in what they can see. Blind faith? No. Faith because there is no other choice but to believe, unless it is to quit and die. And then one day, when darkness and uncertainty have been constant companions, a light is seen somewhere in the distance. And the step quickens with the glance.

But even then, the focus of our eyes must quickly revert back to this day, this moment, this bit of work that must be done because the light is still far off and the dangers are still very present, just a step in front of me. But now hope alights and joins faith. Now I see there *is* an end. I just have to get there.

And I ask, where would we be without that hope and that help? Because just as surely as a mountain in Washington, Mount Saint Helens, suddenly blew its top, shocking the area and bringing devastation all around, so it is almost a certainty that all humans will, at some point or another, experience volcanic-like shock in their lives where they do not know what is happening, which end is up, and when the sudden trouble will end. What then? Loss of hope? Loss of a future? Loss of a way? Or is there a place of help in the midst of trouble; a place so certain that it will not move even if the mountains are falling into the sea?

There is an end to every tunnel . . . with one requirement only. That we keep going forward rather than sitting down in defeat or in fear of the next step. Even if that next step brings a turned ankle or a wet foot, even if it brings cold that chills the bone and chills the soul, as long as the next step is forward and not backward, the tunnel's end *will* come. It is never forever.

Out of the tunnel and into the light again, I saw a sign that spouted a familiar saying: "If you are going through hell, keep going," a useful sentiment to the deep and depressive darkness of some people's tunnel experience. Keep going. This too *will* pass.

## 20.5

Breaking into the light again, I was feeling great but wondering if my pace was too fast. My counsel had been for 11:00 minute miles for the first half marathon distance. I discovered at the 3-mile marker that I had a 10:20 pace. I tried to slow down. Feeling so good in this cool mountain air proved to be a challenge for my slow-down determination. I wanted to obey! I really did. But I felt so good.

Here was an *up* feeling. Mountain beauty, trails into the forest, sounds of rushing water, cool weather after all that hot and humid training, a feeling of great health and invincibility, thoughts of a great race result, better than I'd even imagined—all of these waged war against the voice of experience, the voice of counsel to go slow in the early miles and save strength for the battle to come. My slow-down efforts, therefore, were only partially successful. By mile 7, my watch informed me that I was at a 10:34 pace. Too fast according to the counsel. Would I pay the price? I wasn't sure. But for most of these 7 miles, I was on an *up* feeling part of my race. Most, I say, not all.

After mile 6, a problem arose. If not for this problem my pace at the 7-mile timing mat probably would have been sub 10:30. As people run a long run, they've had to learn how to replenish the nutrition their body needs to continue to endure the strain of constant running. I had accustomed my body to Strawberry Newtons, pretzels, energy gels, Gatorade, and water for the sustenance of long runs. But I violated a cardinal rule of running. *Never try something new on race day.* It was a rule I knew and should never have violated.

A prior racer at this event had mentioned a person handing out fresh strawberries during the race. This kind of thing is common at marathons. In my OKC marathon, I'd been handed a piece of an orange at about mile 22. I took a bite and it was like a jolt of energy going into my sapped body. With those two pieces of history in my mind, I added something new to this run. I took three strawberries and two orange slices in my pack of things to draw on during the run. When I downed pieces of those during the early part of the course, it had seemed fine.

But at mile 6, something happened that I'd not experienced in my last two marathons or in hardly any of my long training runs . . . gastrointestinal distress. That is, in layman's terms, a tummy ache. And it didn't go away. I hadn't really had much to eat at the time: a couple bites of strawberry, a couple Strawberry Newtons, a few sips of Gatorade and water. But something wasn't mixing quite right. I realized that for the first time on a marathon, I'd need to stop at a porta potty station along the way. Darn! Time would waste. Time I'd gained in my too-fast start.

Soon, however, I didn't care about the time waste. I began praying for an empty station along the way. It's funny what we pray for. As ups and downs go, this was a down . . . about to go down hard and fast. (Sorry about that.) "Lord, would you clear the way? Would you cause that next station to be empty of people? Please, Lord!" My first shot at answered prayer was another down. It was busy and someone else was waiting to go next. On I went. I could not afford to waste that much time.

As the next miles went by, some spacing began to occur. I could look 30 yards ahead and 30 yards behind before seeing another person. And then, holy cow! I ran by a guy who popped up from squatting behind a rock. His GI issue must have been worse than mine. Oh, Lord! Let the next station be empty. At mile 9, it was. Finally. Thankfully. This was a definite *down* of my marathon experience.

Then I was out into the fresh air again, feeling much better, ready for some more *up* feelings in this amazing venue.

I could not be sure of the overall timing at this point, but I again determined to try to keep the 11-minute pace. My thought of an astounding finish, after all, had been washed down the drain, so to speak. Miles 9-12 were pretty nice. Lovely scenery all around, peace and quiet, time to pray for my family, time to enjoy this once-in-a-lifetime experience. I also began to think about conserving energy for the last half, the half where I intended to run a 10-minute pace for 10 miles and then "speed" at a 9-minute pace for the last 5K or so. These were *up* thoughts and *up* moments of my race.

The half marathon mark came. My watch dinged with the announcement of my overall pace of 10:48 per mile. I had slowed down, and my average was now within shouting distance of the 11-minute counsel I'd been given. An *up* moment it was and now it was time to turn it on.

A great bridge over an expanse of mountain approached. I could hear the roar of rushing water beneath, catching glimpses of it as I ran. I increased my pace. I was passing people along the way. *Up. Up. Up.*

Mile 14 was complete, and then it came from nowhere. A *down*. My energy level began to wane. I slowed back to my near 11-minute pace. I tried to add energy with the foods I'd brought. More strawberry. A piece of orange, a bite of this and that. At miles 17 and 18 it hit again, more stomach gurgling. Oh, no. With depleting energy, renewed stomach issues, and the distance now fully hitting my body, I began to truly struggle for the first time.

I used my cell phone to record video entries. . . wondering aloud if I could just somehow manage to keep the 11-minute pace and sustain the run, truly running for the next 8 or 9 miles. Funny how 8 miles can at times in the training seem like such an easy run and then at other times, at the end of the actual race, it can seem like an eternity in distance. Eternity now, it seemed. At mile 19 I made the usual declaration of 'never again' will I do this crazy thing. Down.

The mental side of the race came into play again at mile 21. I'd managed to get through the marker of 20 miles with an 11:01 course pace. If I just had had enough to maintain that pace for 6 more measly miles. But at mile 20, I experienced more downs, and began my first very small allowance of . . . walking. Ugh. Was it the lack of nutrition in my body that caused my mind to be weak? Was it the GI issues? I'm not sure. It wasn't a long walk. I soon started again. But now the miles went by at 12 minutes or 12:30 and I knew I was very unlikely to meet my secondary goal of an 11-minute overall pace . . . and there was no way that I'd shock myself and complete the downhill in 4.5 hours. A 'down' it was.

And then at mile 21, along came a pacer. He was a 4-hour 50-minute pacer. Not the 4:30 dream or the 4:48 hope, but still within striking distance of 4:48. Who knows, maybe he's even a couple minutes fast.

"I'll follow him!" I told myself. And so I ran. I stayed with him for at least a mile and a half, getting ever so close to the finish line now. A brief *up* it was. I was hanging. I could do this to the end. It is a mental game indeed.

Then a water station approached. Everyone needs water. It is an absolute must on this course of 26 miles. The body cannot survive without it. I stopped quickly and what?! He kept running! The dude didn't stop for water! Brutha! Wait for me! But he didn't wait. As I filled my water bottles he kept right on, as did his other groupies who were making his pace their goal.

I quickly filled and looked ahead, and he was surely already 30 yards away or more. Distance passes quickly even at a slow pace. And there was not within me the will to chase him down. I had outpaced him for almost the entire course. Yet here in this moment, I could not convince myself to pursue. I gave up the chase for his time and recalibrated to a finish of less than 5 hours . . . *must* do less than five! And I lost him in the distance as I again felt the defeat and walked for a tenth of a mile. *Down.*

At mile 23, I was now only 5K away. I was jogging again, aware of every pain all through my body but mainly in the lower half. *Why is my hip hurting like that? My calves are hurting too. My quads are feeling the toll of the gradual downhill course.* Blisters that have been my constant companion since mile 6 (I chose the wrong shoes after all) were now screaming for attention. I ignored them.

I passed a lady on my right who has been in a regular seesaw battle with me. She was walking now. I commented to her that it is only a 5K now so that surely wouldn't be a problem for us.

"Right?" She gave me a weak smile. She didn't pick up my encouragement. I would not see her pass me again. On I ran. *Am I up? Am I down? Unsure. I'm simply going on.* Mile 24 is here. Two to go.

Pain, determination, misery, an end getting very close yet seeming still so far—these thoughts and feelings were all my constant companions. *Up, down. Up, down.* Thus my feet and legs went (up, down), so my feelings went (up, down), so my thoughts went (up, down); this is what the race provided. Ups and downs. *This is my race. This is our life. And on I go.*

Mile 25 arrives. I expect a feeling of euphoria. I don't have that, not quite. I know I'll finish . . . of that there is now no doubt. I've seen others recently taken off the course in pain, young men, younger than I. I've seen others struggling to walk. People who were once surely far ahead of me are limping as if their feet will no longer carry them. But I will finish; I will cross that line.

A dull determination has set in. It is an odd mixture of misery and expectation. A lady stands just a tad past the 25-mile marker. She's just standing there doing absolutely nothing. I ask if she is the 1-mile marker. She looks at me and gives an odd chuckle but no response. I guess not. On I jog. At what I guess is a half mile from the end of my misery a lone man is standing. He's clapping, shouting to me that I'm almost there. I see his medal. He has finished and decided to come back for a friend, maybe, or just to be an encourager to those still to come. I appreciate that he is there, his voice telling me that I am about to accomplish my goal. An *up*.

And then I turn the corner in the woods and see it. For these long months I've envisioned this very moment. The finish line in sight! The ups and downs of cold mornings and hot mornings, of triumphant training runs, of excited expectation . . . all coming down to this moment. What do I feel? I realize that I'm whispering to myself, "There it is, there it is!" I am *so* desirous of crossing that line that I could almost cry for wanting it so badly.

In races past, I've always sped up at this point. But today, on this cool race that is downhill the entire way, some mixture of the elements and events of this day had left me bereft of any energy to increase my speed. I merely continued, doggedly, fighting my way forward . . . knowing my wife was there just a few tenths of a mile away.

The mind again—I began telling myself (maybe I said it out loud) that this distance is the same distance I've run literally hundreds of times in short training runs around a pool at Mercy Park in Joplin, Missouri. It is about 3 tenths of a mile (.3) in distance around the pool. One more time. That's all it is.

Cheers begin. I'm approaching alone. None are near me on either side. My name is announced as I approach. I see my wife filming as I pass. My arms raise weakly, halfway into the air. Finished. It is done.

Water is handed to me. A medal. I struggle to my wife, struggle to sit down, collapse and feel a tad sick, lightheaded, almost like I might pass out. The struggle was real, but it is done. I overcame and it is done. *Up. Up. Up.*

## 20.8

### (About 6 years prior)

I'm standing at attention in Busch Stadium in St. Louis. My brother is beside me. My father is beside me. We're attending a game together for the first time in years. We've enjoyed Cardinal baseball for years. My brother and I grew up playing whiffle ball, pretending to be the great Bob Gibson, blowing fastballs by the wimpy hitters. One of us always represented the superior St. Louis Cardinals.

In recent years, we'd allowed the busyness of life to get in the way of making the time to get together to enjoy a ball game in St. Louis. But on this night, we'd made the time and amazingly, something special was happening; something that hadn't occurred in St. Louis for 30 years. A no-hitter was in progress. The rookie and rising star, Michael Wacha, was on the mound, attempting to keep the Cardinals in the running for a playoff spot with just a few days left in the season. And this rookie had the gall not to allow a single hit to the Washington Nationals for eight innings. By inning six, the crowd was fully into it. With each out, the crowd roared louder, anticipation growing.

By the ninth inning, I don't think a single person in the stadium was seated. The roar was deafening. First batter out. Roars. Second batter out. Crescendo is being reached. Are the concrete pillars shaking? I find that I too am screaming at the top of my lungs, but I can't hear a thing coming from my own full-throated roar. This is not like me, and not like my brother or dad. But we've joined the moment, with nothing left in volume reserves.

Not in thirty years has this happened for a Cardinals pitcher in Busch Stadium, not since Bob Forsch in 1983. Not in many years have we three been here together, brothers and dad. And it is happening *now*! Emotions soaring, mouths open with voices joined in approval all around—the pitch is thrown. The batter makes a weak connection. The ball bounces in front of the pitching mound and *up* over the head of Michael Wacha, at 6'6" a giant of a man on the mound.

Yet the ball just tops over his outreached arm and behind the mound. That image is burned into my mind, ball over outstretched arm. Second baseman and shortstop converge. One of them grabs, fires to first . . . too late! An infield hit. The no-hitter is destroyed. The crowd is momentarily stunned in disbelief as the roar is hushed. How could this amazing moment be defeated by such a weak hit? My emotions go from absolute excitement to utter disappointment. In one instant, we saw history about to be made—and then dashed. *up*, way *up*; then *down*, way *down*. And that is the way of emotions.

All this for a ball being hit by a bat and a man running to a base. Nobody died. Nobody was about to be saved from an injury or from certain death. Nobody lost a job, nobody was robbed. Nobody was married and no child was born. It was a baseball game that made no real difference in life and death terms, in terms that really mattered to the 45,000 people there that day. And yet, the emotions ran sky high and then went way low.

My wife is a birth Doula. Many may wonder what that is. I guess you can call it an experienced encourager of a mother in labor. She knows so much about labor, delivery, the best helps and positions, that I'm simply amazed. Sometimes she's listening to and watching births on her iPad. Agg! I can't take it. It is *too* emotional, too traumatic, too real. She soaks up every moment with joy. Her face is the picture of ecstasy when the moment of delivery finally occurs. She might cry. And I think she's told me that she does cry with every birth she attends.

As real as any emotion can be is the joy of delivering a child after enduring a struggle that men cannot even begin to fathom. And yet the emotion can change very soon for young mothers, I'm told. Post-partum depression, I think it is called. A real emotion that (once again) men cannot begin to comprehend . . . and one also likely linked to hormones that men don't share.

So the emotions can run from the highest high to the lowest low in a matter of only hours or days. And yet, does that even matter when it comes to what must be done? The baby still must be fed, diapers must be changed, constant care must be given. If a new mother is giddy with joy or in the depths of emotional turmoil, the tasks at hand are still the tasks at hand. The actions of love have no dependence upon the emotions (although I understand that true hormonal imbalances do need special care).

I've provided two scenarios of depths of emotions, one in the sports world that men so often cater to; one in the much more serious world of childbirth and parenthood that women more often cater to. But in both of the scenarios, the heights and depths of emotions can rule the day.

When the Cardinal pitcher lost his no-hitter, should disappointed men and women go home and kick the dog, and gripe at their family for no reason? No. Instead, a person should still be joyful, peaceful, and kind to others even if their favorite pitcher just failed. Shouldn't they? Emotions do not rule. Or at least they should not.

I have learned something I wish I had learned much earlier in life, that my emotions are to be controlled *by* me. They are not to be in control *of* me.

The struggle for some of us is in keeping our emotions from ruling our days and on "down feeling" days, negatively affecting those we love the most. Or worse yet, letting a level of slavery to our emotions become a lifestyle so that our spouse, children, co-workers, and friends are never quite sure what they will get from us day to day—either the fun-loving companion who lifts everyone with his/her smile, or the grump who spreads misery with every glance, cutting word, and harsh action.

Going one step deeper, the lesson I learned much too late in my life is that I need to live life with an ability to understand when the thoughts I am having or the actions I am taking are being derived almost solely from an emotional perspective rather than from the indwelling Spirit of God, from whom I can take a direction starkly different from what my emotions may dictate at a given time.

This assertion would begin a much lengthier discourse that is not the direct intention of this book. But suffice it to say that in this

emotional roller coaster we call "life" there are many things (and people) we simply cannot control. What we can control is our response to
those things. We can choose not to allow emotions to lead us. We can,
instead, lead and instruct them, choosing the way of the Spirit of life
rather than the way of emotions that can lead to death.

## 21.0

Whether I ever run another marathon, whether I am able to run or
even walk, that is not to rule my outlook on life. It certainly could do
so if I allowed it. I have heard people say they don't know what they
would do if they could no longer run. I want to say, "You'll get up in the
morning, put your pants on, brush your teeth, go to work, be kind to
your co-workers, and be kind to your spouse. You'll pet the dog, help
those who need help, care about things that matter, and keep right
on living your life. You will rule those emotions that tempt to make
you think life is not worth living if you cannot run, or cannot walk, or
cannot do anything you wanted to do."

I know that the pain of loss referenced in section three of this
book is real, and that emotions are real. But they must not rule. By
God's Spirit within us, we must rule those things and bring that which
would captivate us into captivity, meeting each new day and each new
challenge with one resolve: that no matter what I feel or what I see, I
will do justly, I will love mercy, and I will walk humbly before my God.

If the earth should change; if presidents and nations should
change; if it seems that problems of this life are so cataclysmic that it
is as if mountains are falling into the sea, I will not fear. There will be
ups. There will be downs. But I will not stop. I will "run" on.

# Training for the NYC Marathon (Running . . . in the World)

*"And by His light I walked through darkness."*

## MILE 22

# *Running in the Darkness*

The world is gray as I run, the dim outlines of the road stretching out before me like a forbidden path into nothingness. Within moments, the outline of shapes appears, only slightly darker than their dull surroundings. They stand like silent pillars in the middle of the road maybe 20 yards ahead of me. Suddenly the pillars move. Deer. It is a mother and her fawn. They see, or hear, my approach and quickly vanish into the fields that I know are all around me.

A mixture of cool and warm air blows ever so slightly as I run. These are the moments of mercy even as they portend the coming of a scorching day. It is why I chose them.

A mile passes in the relative quiet of my surroundings; I hear the stir of cattle in the field, the distant cry of a rooster, the chatter of a bird, then two, then three, as life begins to awaken to the call.

A second pair of statues present in my way, these much smaller than the first. I can see them more clearly now. Both have spots on their backs. Where is their mother? I look around and no more bodies appear. These two young ones get to the safety of the grass and then they stop and stand still, staring at me like two sentinels on guard at the castle wall. I am the oddity to them. Everything else is normal. *Why has this strange-looking creature interrupted our morning stroll,* they must wonder? *Why is he plodding along like that, so slow, and breathing heavily? Did his mother teach him nothing about safety?*

I reach the midway point and turn to begin the journey back on this quick 3-mile run.

As I turn, I can't help but notice the sky. Dawn has been coming with increasing reticence as summer nears its last month of dominance. But its beauty has not waned.

The eastern sky begins to paint the horizon with magnificent colors and shapes. I see streaks of pink cirrus clouds and between each wisp is a pool of aqua, as if you could sit on the pink outskirts and toss a line into the perfect blue waters, catching something that would surely put up no struggle as it came joyfully to the surface.

Ever so slowly the pink begins to turn to a light shade of orange. It is just like the dial being turned on your outdoor grill, flames changing to a deeper color as the heat increases.

I glance to the west to see what the darker side of the world will show, and I gasp in surprise. There is a rainbow, it's staff-life form rising from the ground into the heavens, with only the slightest curve being seen as the bow disappears into a wall that must be filled with rain. I hadn't seen this dark intruder when I first began my run; it was an unexpected surprise.

Stretching across the vast expanse that connects the eastern sky to the western wall of approaching rain are cirrocumulus clouds, or what a child might describe as a cotton ball world. The brighter (eastern) portion of these large puffs have the familiar smattering of pink, gradually becoming white in the area directly above my head. Oddly, they still look small because there are so many of them, thousands of individual balls filling up the Painter's canvas across the sky. On I run, amazed at the variety in the display.

My destination approaches and I glance to the west once again. The bow is fading as the sky grows ever brighter. I notice the field of green to my right with large strands of brown weeds dispersed throughout. My attention turns to that field as it changes. No, the field is not changing. The appearance of it is, because at that moment, it happens: The sun reaches up and tips its supremacy over the tree line in the east.

Light begins its gradual march across the western fields, coming like a slow but determined wave across the ocean of green and brown, swaying ever so slightly in the quiet breeze as it comes. Will the light reach me before my run is finished?

I look now at the road before me, the same pavement that only 25 minutes ago had slipped away in the shadows. I see it all clearly now although my feet still fall on a shaded path. The sun has come but it is low enough so that the space I am traversing is pale by comparison to the brightening field at my right.

Then my own likeness appears off toward the west. My head and body are now dancing in the distance, like a dark imposter mimicking or mocking my every move. I try to trick it briefly, but it cannot be done. The sun will have its way.

And then it is done. My run is finished. The wave of the sun's light now reaches me fully, impacting my body with its rays. It is warm, fresh, clean. A new day has dawned.

## 21.2

Into the darkness light has come . . . piercing, rich, glorious . . . drawing man to its warmth; welcoming, no, *calling* all who dare to step forward to explore the new phenomenon. Into every corner, invading every crevice, it marches forward with boldness, laughing at the shadows that flee as a thief running from the siren. Light! Beautiful light.

Into the darkness light has come. A babe is born, a mother cries, a father swells with awestruck pride. How can this one so pure, so innocent, so dependent be entrusted to imperfect guides? And yet there is nothing like it in the entirety of creation. Those little fingers, the toes wriggling with life, a little nose the size of a tiny button, skin softer than newest silk—this miracle of light. Love dawns into the heart with power like an atomic bomb, exploding in mere moments preconceived notions of what fatherhood and motherhood would be like. Protect it with their lives? Without a second thought, yes!

And so, for possibly the first time in their lives, they feel sacrificial love well up within them. What will he/she need? They will provide it, no matter the cost, as long as there is breath in their lungs and blood coursing through their veins. The baby is a mirror image of mom and dad . . . eyes, cheeks, nose, forehead. Into the darkness light has come. Behold. It has come.

It is a great mystery, this newness of life. And yet the mystery is revealed to those who will see. How does this life come? How can one life so affect mine? What is the purpose for this small beauty I hold? Is it random or is it divine?

Recently I visited my children, who live 4 hours from my home. Because of an epidemic that had spread across our world, we'd only seen these precious ones two times during the first nine months of the year. My wife and I entered the home and hugged our baby girl, now 30 years of age. But she is still a spark of light in our hearts, just as when we first held her in our arms.

Her own 4 children were about to rouse from their rest time in the afternoon. Three beautiful granddaughters came with their love and energy as they began to regale us with stories about dogs and goats and life in general.

And then he came with his daddy, the little one, with his large blue eyes and bright smiles. In moments I could see that he'd changed from the time of our last visit. His words came with more certainty. As his sisters spoke of things he had no clue about, he began to declare, "Yeah, yeah" as he nodded his head confidently.

Would he be shy around us, having so seldom seen us in his first two years of life? The answer came quickly. He came straight for his Papa, a tad surprising for me because the grand- girls typically thrill over their Nana's presence, much more so than their Papa's. And that's okay, because I do too. Nana is *that* wonderful.

But he came for me! Reaching trusting arms up to a semi-stranger because he was that secure in his mother and father's kingdom, he welcomed himself into my space. I was taken in. And there we sat for moments, listening to his chatty sisters, his head nodding in affirmation of whatever they were declaring.

Moments later, he turned his face to mine, taking me in completely. Personal space knew no boundaries as his face came ever closer to mine. Gradually his nose was a mere inch from mine as we were eye to eye, nose to nose. Time stopped. I almost shrank back, unintentionally, as humans normally do in such close proximity. Thankfully I didn't. The thought, *What he is he doing?* went through my mind, as I chuckled.

And then he did it—his lips pursed together and he stuck them out toward my own, now almost touching. I met him in the middle. Precious, innocent, loving, crushing my heart with the tenderness of his gesture. His light invaded my space and took it by storm. If anything had been troubling me, if any work problems, home problems, world problems that may have taken up space in my mind, they would have bowed in that moment before something greater than all. Into any darkness, light came. *Unadulterated love. Acceptance of who I am.*

What brings such glory into this world? Could it be random chance? Really?

No. I confess and do not deny. I declare it is not random. This mystery has an answer.

It is before all those who would find the truth.

Into the darkness light has come . . . piercing, rich, glorious.

A Babe was born. His mother surely cried with joy and His father surely looked on with wonder. One came, completely pure, innocent, dependent on imperfect guides. And yet there had never been anything like this, from the beginning of time up to that moment, and nothing like it has ever occurred since.

Announcements were made in the evening skies as simple shepherds watched their flocks. They came to see, as did others who had perceived the event.

This greatest story ever told is surely the creation of a madman if not 100 percent true. Who would make up such a story? And how could that story sweep all the world and hold it in its grasp as *the* event of the ages . . . the event that all flock to or run from?

A Creator, who made the stars and who made man, had come into the world He created, as a baby, the most helpless form that mankind ever takes, completely dependent. What an idea! And yet, He had been declared from millennia in the past to be the Savior of the world; declared from the heavens as being the very Son of God, now existing with man. One man, declaring Himself *the light of the world.*

He came with unadulterated love. It was merciful, forgiving, welcoming to all who would come. A baby came from God with the answers to the questions of life wrapped up in the innocence of majesty. The Light has come into this darkness!

But men loved the darkness rather than the light . . .

## 21.4

About two weeks before the beautiful morning run that introduced this mile, I had a very different sort of morning run. I guess you might call it the worst and shortest run of my life.

During the summer, I do my running in the mornings, sacrificing sleep so I can run when the temperature is bearable. Some 75-degree mornings at 5:30 a.m. seem a bit unbearable, but not nearly so unbearable as a 99-degree afternoon.

As June and July give way to August, the sun begins to come up later each morning. By August, my 5:30 a.m. runs begin at 6:00, and still the darkness prevails for the first ten to fifteen minutes. To get to work on time, I can't start any later. So out comes the flashlight, serving as a means of warning if anyone in my neighborhood is heading out to work early. The flashlight also provides a lamp to my path and sure steps for my feet.

On the morning of this run, something occurred that had never happened before. I had driven to a starting point on a paved section of roadway near my house but still off the main highway that feeds these county roads. A car's lights appeared in front of me, about a half mile away. Simultaneously, someone turned onto the road behind me, coming off the main highway. That car was much closer, possibly a quarter mile away.

I was only about a quarter of a mile from my car, about where the car behind me now approached. The roadway before me was still too dim to make out clearly. I needed to do three things at once. Flash ahead, flash behind, and keep my eyes and light to the path in front of me. It was too much.

I had quickly shined the light in both directions. But the car coming from the rear was closer and was concerning me. I took a quick glance behind me to make sure I wasn't about to be run over when suddenly, I was on the ground . . . hard.

As I'd taken my eyes off the roadway, I must have come upon a pothole and a chunk of pavement that was sitting on top of the road, big enough that it wouldn't move. I can only surmise that my right foot caught the broken pavement at just the right spot so that, after my foot had planted down, it couldn't come back up. *Splat!*

It was so sudden that I was completely shocked by the impact. There had been no moment of tripping and trying to regain balance. I was simply up and running and then I was down on unforgiving pavement.

The flashlight had fallen from my hand. I quickly located it, flashed it again at both cars, still concerned about the possibility of being struck by one of them . . . and then I ran on as any self-respecting person would do. Surely it was too dark for the people in the cars to notice.

Right? Surely if they did notice, they'd see that I was upright again and running fine. Nobody would stop to inquire. Please don't do that. I'm embarrassed enough.

In moments, the car in front of me (the one that had been farther away) passed by. The car behind me slowed almost to a stop. They must have seen. They must be checking on me. Keep running. Very slowly it passed by me on the left. They gave a very slight toot of their horn and went on.

After running long enough to see both cars depart, I stopped and took an accounting of the screaming pain from my left knee and both hands, directing the beam of the flashlight toward myself. It was ugly. Blood was streaming down my leg. It felt like it was on fire. The palms of both hands had flesh ripped back from them and were streaming blood. Dark bits of gravel shredded my skin.

Briefly, for possibly 30 seconds, I thought about completing my run. I am very goal oriented. I was preparing to run my fourth (and probably final) marathon and I wanted it to be my best. This was to be a 6-mile morning run at race pace. I'd covered a quarter of a mile.

What if the injuries kept me from running for a day or two? I needed to get this run done. But what if the bleeding didn't stop and I became weak miles from my car? A vision of a sock soaked and shoe filled with blood flashed through my exaggerating mind. I took another glance at the blood running down my leg and I quashed the notion to complete the run. I turned back toward my car, moving along in the darkness, a defeated and hurting runner, unwilling or unable to complete my goal.

*What would a "real" runner have done?* I thought, as I jogged back. *"You're a failure. You're weak. You should have finished the run."*

Nice. My mind is accusing me now. But in that state, I agreed with myself. I had failed, wound or no wound . . . I had failed in the darkness.

## 21.7

Let's take a test. I want to discover what is right (or light) and what is wrong (or dark).

No. 1: It is okay for a church leader to have an illicit affair with the secretary or sexually abuse children when:

a. The other party seems to want that kind of attention;

b. Nobody is watching and people won't find out;

c. The church system puts stupid abstinence requirements on the clergy;

d. Never, these things are always wrong.

*What is right and what is wrong? What is light and what is darkness?*

No. 2: The idea of a Christian God is:

a. Unscientific. Science tells us that everything came from nothing, and life evolved;

b. Misguided. Creativity resides in man and a godlike ability to affect change resides in each of us. In a way, each of us is god;

c. Partially true. But the Bible is not 100 percent accurate because men wrote it;

d. The only truth, with the Bible being the inspired Word of God to mankind.

*Now let's examine some questions about basic morality.*

No. 3: It is okay to kill if:

a. You get really mad at someone;

b. Someone is breaking into your house and they are armed;

c. Someone has maliciously killed your loved one and justice requires their death;

d. The person is not yet born, i.e., a fetus.

Subset of questions for question 3d:

    1. Fetus is just discovered;

    2. Mother was raped or mom's life is in danger;

    3. Mom wants to, for any reason, even up to nine months;

    4. This is never okay.

No. 4: It is okay to steal if:

a. Your family is starving, and you have no way to feed them;

b. You have less than someone else;

c. You enjoy it;

d. None of the above.

No. 5: It is okay to lie if:

a. It is just a "little white lie" and nobody will be harmed;

b. It will make someone feel better if you do, or it will hurt them if you tell the truth;

c. You may get in trouble if you tell the truth;

d. None of the above, because honesty is the *only* policy.

No. 6: It is okay to be unfaithful to your spouse if:

a. They are not fulfilling your needs;

b. They've already been unfaithful to you;

c. You've lost interest in them and others excite you;

d. Never.

No. 7: Racism is okay if:

a. My name is Adolf;

b. I am white;

c. I am black and it is my turn to be racist;

d. My daddy was a racist;

e. None of the above.

No. 8: Homosexuality/bisexuality/transgender is okay if:

a. I feel like that is who I am;

b. Never;

c. This is nobody's business.

No. 9: Which lives matter?

a. Black lives;

b. White lives;

c. All lives;

d. The question is stupid and misses the point.

*Is there a right and wrong? Is there light and dark in all of this?*

*Now one more question just to stir the pot:*

No. 10:   America will be great when:

a. Republicans control.

b. Democrats control.

c. Republicans and Democrats learn to work together.

d. Never, the system is broken.

How did you score? If the test taker is also the one who grades the test, I bet each person scored 100 percent. We always agree with ourselves. In fact, if only *we* (each test taker) could be the all-knowing ruler, then goodness and light would prevail. Right?

But we know that in the real world, problems arise. Some "decent" people think differently about some of these issues. There is another small detail that comes to mind: Some murderers may have just taken the test, or some rapists and child molesters, some chronic liars, some habitual thieves. Hmmm.

The simple truth is that these issues are just the tip of the iceberg of the problems that have divided mankind from the beginning of time. While some of these topics have recently hit a fever pitch and seem to have the United States on the brink of internal destruction, I think the underlying difficulties have existed as long as man has been around. Each person wants a society that is based upon his or her own (small) understanding.

But I ask the question: Is there a right answer to these and all the divisive questions of our days? Or will mankind forever battle over their ideological differences?

It is getting downright dark outside. How can I run now?

# 22.0

*"If anyone walks in the day, he does not stumble, because he sees the light of this world.*

*But if anyone walks in the night, he stumbles, because the light is not in him."*

The recent morning runs that I described were real. Each of the particulars was experienced by me, one man, in one tiny speck of the universe, feeling the crushing pain of running in the darkness and a couple of weeks later, watching the glory of the light invading the darkness, revealing the beauty surrounding me.

In this final section, I want to look at something deeper than what we have explored so far. Let us call into view a world full of darkness and yet with pervading light that cannot be quenched.

I want to suggest to any willing to be open-minded that they consider that there are really only two kingdoms in the world: a kingdom of darkness consisting of struggles for power, wealth, influence, intellect, and taking in every agenda that burns within the hearts of governments and peoples . . . and a kingdom of light, waging its war with weapons of truth, justice, and love.

I will be suggesting that there is a King in that kingdom of light, *and it is not you or me.* I will offer a humble, yet fervent assertion that the King over the kingdom of light serves His subjects with sacrificial love. A good King. A loving King. A King who reigns with absolute justice. A King who answers, with finality, all of life's divisive questions of right and wrong and just or unjust. (It is His world after all. He sets the rules. Not you or me.)

I want to consider a King whose purity and innocence are demonstrated as a sign for all to see in the birth of children all over the world every day.

And I want to suggest that while we may be surrounded by a darkness so deep that it violates and hurts and brings insult to the very meaning of life, there is still a way to run in the light. Because . . .

*The light came into the world, and the darkness was unable to contain it.*

*"Encourage the fainthearted, help the weak."*

## MILE 23

# *You Will See Some Who Need Help Along the Way - Help Them*

It happened at about mile 10 of a 16-mile run . . .

It was one of those beautiful fall mornings, perfect for running. Finally, we had arrived at a time of year when the heat and humidity would no longer suck the life out of our bodies during long training runs. The second to last Saturday in September was bright and clear with temperatures around 54 degrees. A slight breeze blew through the streets of Joplin, Missouri. After all the sweltering runs, I almost couldn't wait to begin, although 16 miles would be our longest venture to date in this marathon training cycle. And what a great run it was!

We had a fairly quick pace of 10:20 per mile for the first eight. At the halfway point, we quickly refilled our water bottles and were off again. Eight more to go.

And so, it happened. The event of the day's 16-mile run. It was completely unexpected and yet my brother-in-law, Christopher, and I both would comment later that it was the highlight of the day.

We had been going about two miles since our refuel stop when Christopher suddenly veered sharply away from me and said "Hey, what's going on?" He stopped in the road, facing away from me.

Without my even noticing, we had come upon a vehicle stopped on the side of the road where a black man stood (his color of skin makes no difference to me, but I note it here with purpose that will become evident soon). He must have made a plea for help or had motioned for Christopher to stop. I had not seen it or heard it. I was busy talking and pushing one foot in front of the other. But Christopher had noticed and stopped immediately.

The man was beside an SUV type of vehicle, but his problem was behind it. A small trailer had disengaged from the SUV, and the connection was sitting on the ground. The trailer was full of heavy, home furnishings. He asked if we could help him lift the trailer so he could reconnect it to the SUV.

I moved to the opposite side of the connection and grabbed ahold of the trailer as Christopher took hold of the side where we'd been running. We both bent down and pulled up with all our strength. The trailer did not move even a fraction. What was in this trailer?! It may as well have been a load of granite.

Before we had a chance to contemplate our next step, a car came up behind the trailer and stopped. I glanced back and saw a servant of the public step out of his car. He was a Joplin police officer.

For a fraction of a second a thought flew through my mind. White police officer, black man broken down in the street, all the societal issues occurring at this very moment in our nation, bringing our nation to the verge of being torn apart from the inside . . .

. . . and then the smiling officer approached and asked what was going on and how could he help.

One look at the obstacle answered his question. He said nothing critical. There was no disdain toward the man who was having a bad day in the officer's jurisdiction. He only wanted to help.

"Do you think we can lift the trailer if I help?" he asked.

Christopher and I both commented that it was unlikely. The owner informed him that it was loaded with a heavy wheelchair and he had hurt his back trying to do it himself.

The officer reached to his collar and pushed a button, speaking into the transmitter.

Within moments, another car came up from behind and two more officers exited their vehicle. White men all around. More smiles. How could they help? Soon five white dudes hoisted the trailer, and the pin was placed in the hitch.

The black man, polite and nice from the outset and throughout, expressed his gratitude.

The first officer turned to him and with genuine kindness said, "I hope the rest of your day is better, sir." He then turned to Christopher and me and thanked us for stopping to help.

But my brother-in-law was not done. At the end of every run, he takes a selfie of us, which always ends up on his Facebook page, with the additions of some program that either makes us look like hippies or cowboys or heavy metal bandits or some such crazy outfit. But he wanted the selfie now, at mile 10, with everyone in the photo.

The three policemen agreed and stepped up behind Christopher and me. I didn't see where our new friend was until I saw the Facebook posting hours later. There he was with a large smile, standing at the connection of his trailer and SUV, with a hand high in the air, waving to the camera . . . standing behind three smiling policemen and two slightly worn out runners.

It is the way our interactions with each other are to be, no matter the color or sex or beliefs of our fellow citizens.

Christopher didn't mention color of skin in his post. I was glad he didn't. Why should he? Instead, he commented that a fellow human being needed our help along the road today and he was aided by some very nice servants of the public doing what they do every day. It was perfect.

After the pictures were taken, Christopher thanked the police for their service, and we headed back out to complete our run. My running mate almost immediately noted how awesome the event was, and I agreed. We discussed it for the next mile or so and then noticed that our pace was faster than it had been. He figured it was because we were running on a high from the endorphins of having been able to help someone in need.

We soon slowed down, and our bodies reminded us that we were entering uncharted mileage territory. But our spirits remained high even after the run was over.

The 16 miles were completed in relatively strong fashion. I was surprised at how good I felt. Was it the cool weather that made the difference? Or was it something more, something inward that occurred that actually changed the performance of my body that day? I don't know. But I will say I think I ran in the light that day.

And the light felt good.

# 22.3

My recent years of running had brought me to the completion of three marathons and several half-marathons.

As other priorities came to the forefront of my mind, I purposed to make one last attack on the full marathon distance and could think of no better place to do it than the biggest of all, the famous New York City Marathon, in what would be the 50th annual running of the event while being sponsored by the New York Road Runners.

But how to get in? Of the 50,000 yearly participants in the world's biggest marathon, about 10% are allowed in through the luck of a lottery drawing, with an unknown quantity of people entering that lottery each year. I entered that lottery but failed to gain access.

One can also get entry by time qualification. No chance of that for me. I am about an hour and a half too slow for that. The final viable option is to participate through a charity.

Enter the John Ritter Foundation.

The Foundation was created in 2003 shortly after the death of actor John Ritter, who died of an acute aortic dissection. It is dedicated to improving the identification of individuals at risk for aortic dissections and the treatment of thoracic aortic disease through medical research.

Because of a work-related connection I had to the Ritter Foundation, I entered their pool. My hopes were high because the minimum funds that must be raised had already been pledged to me by my generous brother, who also had an interest in helping the Ritter Foundation.

There are a host of charities that can field a team for the NYC Marathon each year. Each one has a minimum dollar amount that a participant must raise in order to be accepted by that charity. The charity screens their applicants and eventually chooses their "team" out of a group of hopefuls. I had no idea how many people might apply, but I hoped to find out by March of 2020 so I could get an early start on the training schedule I had laid out months ago for the November 1, 2020, New York City Marathon.

And then COVID-19 swept across the world. Although these feelings may seem misplaced while many people were dealing with great fear from the virus, I experienced a fairly high degree of discouragement when the email came to me from the New York Road Runners that the 2020 marathon had been cancelled. Days later, I was informed by the Ritter Foundation that I was accepted onto the team. The acceptance email went on to note that the marathon was, however, cancelled. So although I was a part of the team, my ability to participate in the world's biggest marathon was postponed until 2021. The question was, did I want to wait? And what would I do in the meantime?

I had been tracking my runs for months. I logged the mileage of four different pairs of shoes, two of which had a commemorative logo of NYC emblazoned on them. After so many months of planning and work, I decided not to throw it all away. Instead, I entered the "virtual" NYC marathon.

I later learned that the local Bass Pro Marathon planned to go forward with their November 1 race. I could accomplish an actual event with other runners while simultaneously getting the virtual NYC marathon done. Even better, my brother-in-law, Christopher, decided to hook up with me to do the same marathon we'd done together two years previously.

My race was back on. But there was a deeper purpose for the training period and for this race.

## 22.5

The formation of this book came to me in waves, so to speak. Initially, I wrote to relate to my extended family what I had to overcome to complete my first marathon. Wave one was commemoration.

The second wave began with the encouragement from my wife that possibly the lessons I learned could help people outside our family . . . that they could potentially encourage people I didn't even know.

I began with an outline largely inspired by a letter I wrote to my children just before the Oklahoma City Memorial Marathon. In that letter, I noted that each running lesson could have a life lesson. I saw the potential of giving some person, somewhere, a lift in their day as they read a story of the common denominators of the human condition and the ways to overcome our fears and our failures.

So the second wave was developing the plan and finding the motivation in that plan to get up on cold mornings when it was still dark outside to do a lonely run on a dirt road. Vision was in that wave. Commemoration came first, then vision.

The final wave brought me beyond memories and vision. It became a personal endeavor of living with a better understanding of the purpose of this short life. And it includes a hope of introducing that purpose to others.

The title of this mile gives indication of that purpose in a way, "You will see some who need help along the way. Help them."

As the calendar turned to 2020, I had a strange nudge that I'd never had before. I can only describe this as an inspiration that came from God. It wasn't something I thought up. It was that every time I ran in 2020, I spent time during that run praying for my co-workers. Every time. The prayers were also for my wife, each of my girls and their families, and the church family I'm associated with.

What was I praying for? For their good, for health, for blessing . . . but more to the point, that they would know why they were created and who the Creator is; that each of these would come to have the fullness of joy in their lives that I have experienced because of that relationship with a Father in heaven.

The final wave, then, became *for* all those my life touches . . . and thus, for every reader who may read this book. It was no longer just a practice of applying lessons to the feat of running. This last wave became personal and about individuals. I would run and I would accomplish this task . . . praying that the King of light would overcome the king of darkness who has brought deception into the lives of so many.

My hope, my prayer, is that none will be afraid to see what may be gleaned from the completion of this book's journey, with just three more miles to go. My hope is that those who read will, in one way or another, be changed.

## 22.6

In the 2016 Rio Olympics, Abbey D'Agostino of the USA was running the 5,000-meter event (equivalent of 3.1 miles, or what many know as a 5K race) as several ladies in close proximity to one another dashed along a straightaway. Suddenly, Nikki Hamblin of New Zealand and Abbey D'Agostino made history. Neither set a world record that day. But both became heroes of the games.

Replay video from the race shows Hamblin initially tripping on the foot of a runner directly in front of her. As she was falling to the ground, D'Agostino, who was directly behind Hamblin, became entangled in Hamblin's legs and twisted her knee in awful fashion as she too went crashing to the ground.

D'Agostino was the first to get up but, before attempting to turn to try to catch the pack, she glanced back and noticed Hamblin still in a heap on the ground. Abbey helped Nikki up and both began to run again when suddenly, Abbey winced in pain and crumpled back to the ground.

This time it was Nikki Hamblin's turn to show incredible sportsmanship. Seeing Abbey D'Agostino fall, Hamblin stopped to help her up. Eventually, each would finish the race, although D'Agostino was the last to come hobbling across the finish line with an obvious injury and a grimace of pain with each step. She was a full two minutes behind the first-place finisher and about twenty-five seconds behind the next to last finisher, Hamblin. They were the last two finishers in a race they'd been preparing for and dreaming of for years. In a different (more important) way, both were still champions that day.

Before the race, D'Agostino had been interviewed, as most Olympic athletes are, so personal interest stories can be seen by the millions who watch the games every four years. In the interview, she spoke chiefly of her relationship with Jesus and made comments that later seemed almost prophetic.

"I am so thankful to be here," she said. "What I do want, and what Christ has led me to want, is Him first. So I hope my experience here is a reflection of that. It doesn't always manifest in the way that we think it might. It doesn't manifest in medals all the time, although sometimes it does. *Sometimes it means coming in last place.*" She went on to state: "It's not always about winning. It's about making it to the finish."

Just a few days later, she lived out the example of grace that she had spoken of . . . and accomplished that last-place finish.

Abbey and Nikki both received the Rio 2016 Fair Play Award. Their race concluded with an amazing hug at the finish line, displaying not only sportsmanship, but genuine care for each other, even though they'd never really met prior to the race.

One other pre-race comment of Abbey: "If God allows you to see things through His lens, you will conduct yourself differently." What an amazing example. What a champion. If only our world, with all of its chaos and animosity-filled divisiveness, could see each other through that lens . . . and conduct themselves differently.

## 22.8

Here is the question. What will I do, and what will you do to help others? And will it really help them?

I have witnessed, along with most Americans, the shocking events of police brutality, where officers seemed to treat other humans inappropriately. The times shown to us by the media are when they are white officers and black victims. My own view is that there are likely actions by police officers against people of their own race that are just as heinous as what we've seen displayed so prominently. I believe there are bad policemen, bad doctors, bad lawyers, bad actors in every occupation. There are bad people or, more perfectly put, people who act in outrageously bad ways in every walk of life.

Just as we do not get rid of all doctors because 5 percent of them are bad, so we should not get rid of all police because 5 percent are bad. As my story in this mile portrays, I believe most police officers take their role in society as one of service and protection. Do people with authority abuse it? Yes, at every level. Should they be convicted and punished if they act criminally?

Yes, every time.

But should we rise up as a society and demand change by becoming criminally active ourselves? Should we burn homes and businesses and attack others even if they are peaceful and doing their job well? Here is where it gets dicey and divisive. Here is where the rubber meets the road and where we are thrust into a moment in history where it seems we are close to ripping our great country apart.

Allow me to bring the question again. What will I do? And more to my point . . . how will I act if I see the world through God's lens? What will I do if I see a battle between a kingdom of light and a kingdom of darkness? How does that apply practically?

As I run, I've been praying about this question. What is my response to the seeming scourge of this moment in America?

I will see some that need help along the way. I will help them. Are they white, black, brown, green? I don't care. I should help them. I am one man. And that is what I can do.

Doesn't it really start with each of us?

My brother, who is also my employer, made similar comments while addressing those under his sphere of influence—his 25, or so employees and co-workers. While attempting to lead his business through the perils of COVID-19, trying to help each one feel secure and safe, he also acknowledged the anger and uncertainty existing in the world in which we live. His commentary was that we must deal with each other with patience, understanding, and kindness. And his final point one day was, *"And it starts with me."*

I agree. But it goes deeper still.

I don't understand the lives of people who have a different color of skin. I have read about it, but I have not lived it. So a new prayer has taken up residence in my heart. "Lord, bring a black family into my life. Bring many of them!" A crazy prayer? I don't know, but the prayer has grown into a real desire. I want it to be. I want friends of nationalities and skin tones that are different from my own. I want to trust them, and I want them to trust me. I want to ask them to forgive what my fathers have done to theirs. I want to find a way forward together, in peace.

In my travels, and in my daily life, I have met people from many nationalities. I treasure these people. Friendships like these could be some of the more important ones in our lives.

They could change us in important and valuable ways. And maybe we could do the same for them.

I want my circle of friends to include more than a bunch of white guys who think just like me. I want every color in the circle . . . with white included. For you see, I don't hate my own kind either. I hate what any man of any race does that is evil, that is dark.

So what will I do? I will do my best to live an honorable life and seek out those who are different from me, respecting their differences. But in so doing, I will not sacrifice what I believe to be true concerning the most important issues of all: issues of darkness and light. And therein can be the greatest struggle of all.

## 23.0

My brother-in-law made a wise comment on one of our long runs. We were discussing the topic of my mile 19, which dealt with barking dogs that, usually, don't bite. He listened to my stories and the lessons I was deriving from them, and then said, "But, you know, even if the dog does bite . . . or we die of cancer or from a car accident . . . it really is still just a barking dog." I knew what he meant, and I immediately agreed before he went on to explain his thought.

"Even if we die, we are with the Lord. We go on to a better place. That dog can't hurt us."

This comes to the very point of this section and this mile. I will see some who need help. And I can help them or ignore them. But if I help them, will my help endure beyond the temporary need?

It is as if there are tiny bits of light that shine into the darkness of the chaos of this world.

Each time an innocent child is hurt, it is darkness. Each time a hero comes into the life of that innocent one and applies the salve of love and gentleness and kindness, it is like candlelight that begins to burn in a pitch-dark room. It is some light. It gives a bit of warmth. It is good.

But believing what I believe about eternity, it is not enough for me to help them for a day or a year or 70 years. It is good. It is fulfilling. It gives them hope, possibly, and can lead to even greater events for them. But for me, it is shortsighted. It is not enough. And, I believe, it can even be a trick of that dark kingdom—*that so doing will dispense with the responsibility I have to spread light.* "Be a part of a good cause. Help the helpless when I can." No, I say. It is not enough.

This wave of the running of the last stages of the race of my life *must* be for the purpose of bringing people to a place—a relationship—where no dog can bite them . . . where all dogs (neglect, abuse, cancer, war, bigotry, earthquakes, pandemics, and yes, even death) are merely barking and helpless animals, unable to pierce the hope that can exist in the heart of man.

For . . . *"He has also set eternity in their heart."*

*"And the Philistines were gathered into a troop where there was a plot of ground full of lentils, and the people fled from the Philistines. But Shammah took his stand in the midst of the plot, defended it and struck the Philistines."*

## MILE 24

# You Will See Some Stop along the Way- Keep On

About 79 percent of those who start a marathon complete it. If 79 percent finish, what about the 21 percent who start the race and quit at some point along the way. Absent an injury, why do people do this? After all the training and preparation, why would they stop?

An article I read once sheds some light on the subject. The writer suggested that the most difficult spot is around miles 21 to 23. The human body is generally only able to store enough glycogen to have enough readily accessible energy to run those 20 miles, and after that the body rapidly gets exhausted, meaning that no matter how well-trained one is, those last 6.2 miles are really difficult and require a lot of mental fortitude.

Physiological changes are sending what could be described as "life-saving" messages to your brain, informing your control center that dangerous things are occurring within your body and rest is required to save yourself. Thus, mental strength is an absolute necessity through this period of the run. When every pore in your body is telling your mind to stop, will your mind listen, or will it tell the body to pipe down and obey the brain's commands to push on?

During that phase, it's easy to get discouraged and want to quit. The focus becomes taking the next step, over and over and over again. Once you get to mile 24 or 25, the end starts to come into sight. While some runners literally collapse just yards from the finish line, unable to physically stand any longer, the mental fog usually starts to lift when you realize you have just minutes to go.

It is warfare. Our bodies and minds are at war with each other. "Quit and be safe," says the body? "Go on into the dangerous unknown," says the mind? Who will win the war? Apparently 4 out of 5 will win the marathon battle.

For this mile, we will look on those who look at life's race and decide *not* to go on.

## 23.2

The most famous "I quit" moment in my memory came during a boxing match. It was billed as "the super fight" at the time. The fight took place on November 25, 1980, at the Superdome in New Orleans.

The match featured one of America's Olympic boxing champions from the 1976 Games who had emerged as the new boxing superstar in an era that was witnessing the final days of the dominance of the great Muhammad Ali. Sugar Ray Leonard burst upon the boxing scene with a flair that reminded many of Ali.

But every hero needs a frightening opponent. As Smokin' Joe Frazier had been to Muhammad Ali, Panama's Roberto Duran added to the legend of Sugar Ray Leonard.

Duran was nicknamed, Mano de Piedra or Hand of Stone because of his raw punching power. Duran won most of his matches by KO, knocking out most of his opponents with a frightening right fist. But Duran also possessed a versatility that became a problem for Sugar Ray. Duran wasn't just a brawler. He was also a skilled boxer.

During an early 1980 match, the pair fought to a near draw. It was close but all judges viewed Duran as the winner on punches landed.

Leonard had entered the fight with a perfect 27-0 record. Duran, the more experienced of the two, had an amazing record of 71-1. But Leonard was stunned by his first loss.

Reports were that Leonard watched the fight on tape over and over for days, trying to discern why he had lost the fight. He continued watching it until he came to conclusions of what had gone wrong and what he must do to win a second match against the man who had taken his Welterweight title.

There is some debate about who should be named the best boxers in history. Many place Sugar Ray Leonard and Roberto Duran at various spots in the top ten. Duran, in 2002, was voted by *The Ring* magazine as the fifth greatest fighter of the last 80 years, while putting Leonard at ninth place. Others put Leonard slightly ahead of Duran. Either way, these arguments at least show the powerful career that each man had and their commitment to their craft. Which makes all the more amazing what happened next, when Leonard and Duran met for their rematch in November 1980.

After the first victory over Leonard, Duran reportedly spent several months partying. Leonard spent several months studying and training for a rematch. When the rematch was booked for November, Duran stopped partying long enough to train for a month. He had gained weight during his party spree though. He was a hero for the people of Panama. He enjoyed his hero status just a bit too much apparently.

To meet the weight requirements, Duran was said to have needed a precipitous weight drop for the day of the weigh-in. Although he made the necessary weight, it seemed that the experience left him weaker than he should have been to begin his title defense against the motivated Leonard.

Leonard changed tactics throughout the 2nd match and went back to his flashy style of movement and grace in the ring. Duran spent much of the first 7 rounds chasing Leonard around the ring but was always frustrated in his attempts to pin him in and unleash his typical pounding on his opponent. By the end of the 7th round, a round in which Leonard taunted and teased the slower Duran, Leonard felt sure he was ahead but not so much that he couldn't lose if the tide began to turn.

During the 8th, Leonard landed several punches, but none seemed to be terribly damaging, when the unthinkable happened. Toward the end of the round, the usually terrifying Duran simply stopped boxing. He raised his hands and appeared to say, "No mas" (No more) to the referee.

At first, Leonard didn't believe it was real. Thinking Duran was attempting to bait him, Leonard continued to try to box only to see Duran continue to raise his arms in defeat. He had simply quit the match. One of the top 10 boxing champions of all time quit.

It is not unusual to see the towel thrown in during a boxing match, but it is almost always in between rounds, as the manager assesses the health of his fighter. But I had never seen this manner of quitting, and certainly not by one of the great champions of our time in the middle of a legendary match.

The result of this decision brought major personal repercussions to the one-time hero of Panama. He had come from the streets. He was one of them. But with those two words, shame descended on Duran from the people who had loved him. Even today, it is said that "No Mas" are the two words that broke boxing great Roberto Duran. He could never live that moment down.

## 23.5

Quitting a boxing match is one thing. Quitting life is in an entirely different category. My path today runs by the topic of suicide. It is the ultimate in quitting this race of life. And the kingdom of darkness finds its greatest pleasure in this complete abandonment of hope.

Interestingly, experts believe that a completely opposite human instinct tops the charts for us. These are the top three natural tendencies of man:

- self-preservation: the interests of personal safety, security, and comfort;
- sexual or intimacy needs;
- social or interpersonal relationship needs.

Of these three, we learn that the will to survive, to live, is the greatest of all. Imagine that drive in a person that causes them to crawl down from a mountaintop airplane crash or to overcome battlefield injuries of losing legs or arms. This drive is powerful indeed.

How great, then, is the success of the kingdom of darkness if that inborn "will" can be snuffed out to such an extent that a person would terminate the very thing that all of his or her senses are crying out to protect? It is hard to even imagine such hopelessness.

In 2018, there were 48,344 recorded suicides in America, up from 42,773 in 2014, according to the National Center for Health Statistics (NCHS). On average, adjusted for age, the annual U.S. suicide rate increased 24 percent between 1999 and 2014, from 10.5 to 13.0 suicides per 100,000 people, the highest rate recorded in 28 years. These numbers are hard to comprehend. Over 48,000 people in a year?! How can this be?

I recall the shock to a small Oklahoma town many years ago, when the high school football team quarterback took his own life. His entire life was in front of him. Then it was not.

If there are more than 40,000 people taking this drastic measure each year, imagine the people in our society who suffer from a depth of depression that takes them to the brink but not over it, or who attempt it but are unsuccessful. There are surely millions who struggle with a level of despair that approaches this loss of hope and causes them to give consideration to quitting this life.

I wonder, is there an answer for the millions who suffer in silence? Is there a beam of truth that is able to pierce the soul of confusion and rend the veil of deception?

## 23.6

Please stay with me on a slightly twisted journey into the darkness.

I awoke shortly before 4:00 a.m. I don't usually wake up this early. Today my brother- in-law and I would run our 18-mile run in preparation for my final marathon, which would occur 5 weeks later.

My alarm was set for 5:40 a.m. I had almost two more precious hours of sleep available.

But then . . .

*I was dreaming.* I had gone to bed thinking about the 18-mile run, wondering if we could keep running the entire way. And I was thinking about the following week, which would involve a much needed excursion with my wife.

And then the dream...

My dream had no humor or embarrassing moments. It had only sheer horror.

Someone had been killed in brutal fashion and I was living the aftershocks. A close acquaintance had been stabbed repeatedly and the scene of the murder was something from the kind of movie I imagine exists but have never watched. Blood was everywhere.

I knew that the police were involved in an intense investigation. My mother was alive and with me, along with my only brother. Our family was in a place of great mourning. We were bewildered and stunned by the occurrence.

An odd detail came out. The police had determined what the killer had been eating prior to the crime.

Suddenly, we were at a huge church meeting. It was being held in one of those enormous churches that you see but have never gone into. It was crammed with people. And the police were there in plain clothes, as if they knew the killer was somewhere *in* the building.

The meeting hadn't started yet. I was standing beside my mother. My brother was a row away from us . . . when suddenly it hit me like a Mack truck. The police don't know it yet, but they should be looking for *me*! I was the killer!

Just like a good murder mystery, the few details began to fall in place in my mind. I had been eating the food they discovered the killer had eaten. Flashbacks went through my mind of an occurrence I'd truly not remembered . . . had blocked out . . . of wielding a knife against someone who had done me no wrong—and repeatedly thrusting it forward.

At this time in a horrible dream, we usually wake up. I did not.

I stood briefly in the midst of the throng of people who'd come to begin to worship God and I knew, for the first time, that I was a murderer in the most horrid sense. I had killed someone and only I knew it. My mother didn't know. How could she? My brother . . . surely, he could not know, could he? Could he possibly suspect it because of having seen what I ate and having heard the news of the killer's food? If he did suspect, he would do the big brother thing; he would hide it and protect. But would he? Even this?

As the shock of the realization began to set in, I knew two things. First, the police would discover the truth and they would do so soon. Second, I had to tell my brother the truth before it was revealed by strangers. And then, I would face a future that would be very different than I had planned.

Still the questions filled my mind. How did I do this thing? *why?* It was unspeakable and unimaginable. It is not who I am or have ever thought of being. And if I had done this, why had it been so blocked from my consciousness that I had truly gone along in the same level of shock as my family had? I had wanted the killer caught and brought to justice just like everyone else in my family did. And yet, I knew now, I *had* done it.

It all added up just like 1+1=734. It made no sense whatsoever. Only one thing now mattered. Only one thing made sense to me. I had to tell my brother and I had to tell him now.

I began to make my move out of the aisle of the row in which I was sitting. As I glanced back, I saw that my brother was already walking in the back of the cathedral. I approached and said only that I needed to talk to him about something important. He looked at me with what I imagined was a knowing look and led the way outside.

We were walking down the huge steps that descended from the structure when the dream struck again with an oddity. There, coming up the long steps, was our pastor and his wife from more than 40 years ago. I'd not been in his church since I was 16 years old. My brother had been a youth group leader in that church. Here they were in my dream, flung at us from the distant past.

They walked up the steps. My brother went by them as if he hadn't seen them. They glanced back as he passed. "That's Alan!" I heard one of them say in surprise.

I scooted by them, keeping my eyes averted. I could not stop to talk to these long-lost influencers of my life. I had one mission. I would accomplish it now.

My brother got to the bottom of the steps. He stood off to one side. And then, one last bit of weirdness. A cousin of ours appeared. He had died a couple of years before of complications from diabetes. He was only around 60 years old when he passed. My brother and I used to enjoy Whiffle Ball games with him and his younger brother after a workday at the sawmill where we worked together during our teenage years. He was a good guy, also gone too early in life. But now, it was as if he'd come to listen. Our eyes caught briefly, so that he knew I'd seen him and knew (somehow) that, whatever I'd come to say, would only be said to my brother. I would not let him hear. He walked past us and was gone from my dream.

One thing left to do. It began sputtering out of me as when an outside faucet is turned on and there is air in the hose, in spits and starts. *"It makes no sense. I killed him! I can't remember it at all. Really, I couldn't do this! But then I knew. The food. It was mine. The blood. I can see it now. Why? I would never.* (He was saying nothing to me. Just looking, listening, sad.) *I wouldn't! I couldn't! But I did!"*

I knew the truth. I had done it and would never know why.

## 23.8

*"What is truth?"* Words uttered by the man in the place of authority on a given day at a given time, thousands of years ago in a place called Jerusalem.

Another brutal murder was about to occur, as a man named Jesus was about to die at the hands of a mob with bloodlust in their hearts.

The man hadn't hurt anyone during his thirty-three years on the earth. On the contrary, he had defended the weak and hurting of society. He was for the widow and the orphan. He was the man who had reached out and touched—*touched*—the outcasts of society of that day, including a man with the dreaded and contagious disease of leprosy. He touched the leper with love and healed him.

And wasn't this the man who healed the sick and, if the claims are to be believed, raised the dead? Didn't he heal a man born blind, causing the religious leaders of the day to bring the parents of the man before them to confirm that this was indeed their son who'd been blind from birth?

Religion. Hadn't this man saved His only harsh words for the religious leaders of that day who walked around in their hypocritical pomp and self-righteous smugness, who failed to lift one finger to ease the load their rules placed on people? Hadn't this man called out their error publicly, even though those same men would one day lead the mob to call for His death?

His death for what? For His message that said, "*My command is that you love one another,*" and "*There is no greater love than to give your life for a friend,*" and "*The greatest among you will be the one who is the servant of all*" . . . death for that message?

Wasn't this the only Man ever born who actually lived a righteous life? And for that, He was killed—brutally beaten, spit upon, mocked, and eventually nailed to a tree?

Wasn't this the Man who looked down upon His murderers and said, "*Father, forgive them, for they do not know what they are doing?*"

When I awoke from my nightmare, I knew I had to get up and write, despite the darkness of the early morning hours and my approaching 18-mile run. For I realized that I had come face-to-face with a truth: that abiding in me, as a member of the human race, is the capacity to kill an innocent man, just like those Jews had done to an innocent Man named Jesus over 2,000 years ago.

While such an act seems impossible in my own mind, the proof of all humanity is that all of us have, in one way or another, become a part of the mob and become guilty of contributing to the blows upon His back, the spit into His face, and the application of the hammer to nails into His body.

He came *for* us and we rejected Him and killed the innocent Man of our time, the righteous Man of the ages. And still today, society fights to kill *the truth,* who came in bodily form. We are capable still of being part of the mob of darkness.

And since that time, mankind has gone down one of two paths: Either he has admitted the sin of what he has done and has cried out for forgiveness from the One whose blood provided for us that very thing—forgiveness of our lifetime of sins, or . . .

We have taken the path of the kingdom of darkness, denying that the Man ever existed, or claiming that any need of Him is nothing more than a crutch for the weak, claiming that truth is found, somehow, within ourselves or within the "beauty" of things that surround us, worshipping the created thing rather than the Creator Himself.

For one reason or another, the majority of humans have said "No mas" to the beauty, the truth, and the purpose that God has put into the heart of man. Or said another way, mankind has abandoned the very purpose for which it was created; that is, a relationship with the Creator, being welcomed into His kingdom of light. They have quit on the only race that really matters.

For . . . *"He came to His own and those who were His own did not receive Him."*

## 24.0

Speaking the truth is no longer popular. It is ridiculed. It is called hate speech. What excellent deception that a message of love is now called hate.

The world has completely abandoned the truth of Creation in favor of the lie of what is called science . . . as if out of absolute nothingness, everything that now exists "exploded" into being billions of years ago. And *that* is science? Anything I've ever seen that exploded brought about nothing but destruction. It certainly didn't cause perfect order, such as we see at work in our universe and in the tiniest cells in our bodies.

No, this is not science. I say, it is folly. It is deception. It is darkness.

The religious and the atheist *both* have quit the race of truth. And *neither* has anything that comes close to the truth that the hurting—the suicidal—of this age so desperately need.

Who will stand for truth in this day? Who will love the people of the world but refuse to fall in love with the deceiving kingdoms of this world, kingdoms that declare that hope and truth inherently reside within us—in us! In the ones who have killed one another from the beginning of time. In us! In the ones who spread hatred and hurt and anger to every corner of the earth.

In us? No. It is not inherently in us. Hope and truth are only in the One who came to welcome us into His light. But who will stand for this increasingly unpopular truth in these days? Who will declare the light of truth into a fallen and dark world?

Jesus is Light in the darkness. He is the way maker where there seems to be no way. In Him comes beauty for ashes, dancing instead of mourning, healing where there has only been hurt, love instead of hate.

*There is a child (maybe it is you) who was hurt and rejected by those who should have loved you most. Nightmares, terrors of life, hidden hurts in dark and secret places. These have occurred with so many innocent and tender lives with devastating effects, (although the wounded do their best to hide it all). But the hurts will not heal . . . so you consider what it may be like to quench your pain in the only way you know how. Unless...*

*One day, you find the Light of life and all things become new. And the hurt one will say, "I was one way, and now I am different. And the only thing that happened in between . . . was Him."*

This is God. It is who He has always been. It is who He will always be.

There is a way into this kingdom of Light. It is not religion or the hypocrisy that religion so often portrays. It is a love relationship with a Savior, with a Father, with a friend.

If all run away from this truth, I will not stop believing it. I will run on. And I will stand and defend this plot of ground with the last breaths of my body.

*"The God who has girded me with strength*
*has opened wide my path."*

## MILE 25

# *There Is Beauty Everywhere You Run*

Kauai. The Garden Island. It is said to be the most undeveloped of
the main Hawaiian Islands and the least crowded with tourists
or nightlife.

In places, it is a tropical rain forest, unbelievably lush and thick
with the extravagance of never-before-seen varieties of plants and trees.

To the extreme north, the Napali Coast provides the most beautiful and dramatic mountain pinnacles I have ever seen, with the Pacific
Ocean as a backdrop of turquoise, colliding with the majesty of the
mountain peaks. To the south, you discover the enormity of Waimea
Canyon, appropriately called the Grand Canyon of the Pacific.

The beaches are incredible and each one seems to be a unique
experience. Some are available for all to access, displaying massive
breaking waves upon the northern shores. Others are an adventure to
even get to and are, therefore, less populated.

Thundering waterfalls are spread around the island, sometimes
found after a 4-hour hike and sometimes discovered as you drive down

the road. Ocean pools in lava rock can be found, teeming with colorful sea life that has been dumped in by the most recent wave.

Extremely challenging overnight mountain hikes are available for the adventuresome.

People have died on those trails, slipping at a muddy spot, falling to the rocks far below. But the views are spectacular, unlike anything you have seen.

At certain times of the year, whales are breaching all around the island. Boat tours can be very rewarding at these times, assuming you aren't bent over the stern of the boat tossing up everything you've eaten over the last month, your grim appearance as green as the waters into which you deposit your misery.

Kauai is a beauty that is difficult to describe. It must be smelled, tasted, experienced.

Included with the memories of exploring this island are those associated with running.

Look where you are! You see ocean. You see mountains. You see abundant vegetation. These six miles are going to be great.

But there is something I failed to mention about Kauai. Rain. It rains almost every day on the north shore. This is why it is called the Garden Island. Perfect temperatures (almost always in the 70s or 80s) and lots of rain.

Quite often the rain is seen coming over the horizon of ocean waves. It pops through for 15-30 minutes and is gone. On other days, the rain will lock in and you know it will not be a beach day.

And so, it occurred one day that I checked the skies and told my wife that I thought I had time for a quick 30-minute run before some possible rain clouds made their way to our area (sounds like famous last words even as I type them). To be safe, I asked her to keep a lookout and come get me if a cloudburst did occur. She agreed.

I think I was about 10 minutes into my run when the first sprinkles began. It was perfect. Warm weather, beautiful scenery, a cooling mist. When suddenly, the skies opened up as if a giant-sized bucket of water had been tipped over the side of a cliff. It began coming down in sheets. I was drenched through and through within seconds. I kept running toward our rental cabin. Within a couple of minutes, a car approached. My darling stopped alongside me, probably attempting to contain the laughter that wanted to burst forth from her. I paused and told her there was no reason for me to stop now. I couldn't get any wetter than I already was. She headed back to the rental and I sloshed on down the road to complete my run.

It became a memory for the banks of my running experiences. Say the words "Kauai, running, rain" in close proximity and it will all come flooding back, ending with a smile on my face and a wistfulness that I could return someday and do it all again.

For me, it has been a thread of the beautiful.

## 24.3

When I was 26 years old, I had the opportunity to visit Panama and be a part of a team of missionaries to the country that resides just to the south of Mexico.

My uncle, Louis, went with me on the trip and we enjoyed a very interesting time as we were dropped off at Teen Challenge camps overseen by a local pastor. The camps housed troubled youth, some of whom were criminals who had committed the theoretically tame crimes associated with drugs. Others were accused of more serious violent crimes.

A guide transported us from place to place and served as our interpreter. We would spend a night in one camp, eat beans and rice and possibly a chicken leg. We would teach a lesson and then sleep in quarters with an occasional gecko or lizard running up and down the block walls beside our beds. Then we would head to another camp the next day and do it all again.

There was an aspect of danger here, but we didn't have any fear. Certainly, thoughts went through my mind about how safe it was to be spending time with the criminals who possibly should have been put behind bars but who were instead farmed out to these camps in the hope of rehabilitation. However, we found nothing from these young men (and women in the ladies' camp) but kindness and what appeared to be a genuine interest in what we were sharing about the ways to turn their lives around and hope for a better future.

I look back now and see my youthful ignorance and lack of understanding of what these young men and women were facing. I had no idea, really, about how they could lead a better life in practical terms. I only knew of one hope for them in spiritual terms and that that hope could also lead them to a better place in practical ways.

But the people were what made the trip. The guide was fervent in his desire to serve us and equally so in his desire to serve God. We went about as "preachers and teachers" to the residents of the camps. But I was fairly certain that our interpreter was the true preacher. On more than one occasion, I wondered if it were possible that he was repeating my words to the listeners verbatim. His efforts came out with so much more enthusiasm, so much more authority, and he seemed to carry on in much longer sentences than those I'd spoken.

Although I've used false names in my book to describe my friends and family and acquaintances, I will use his real name. I've never forgotten it even though more than 30 years have passed since I spoke to him.

As we parted ways and made our way to the airport, he asked us to remember him and to pray for him and his nation. He wanted to make a difference in his country. He was willing to sacrifice, and had sacrificed, to make it so. He had come from a desperate life. He'd been a member of those same camps as a youth. He had been one who had no hope in his life. And then he'd discovered hope at the camp. His life had been changed as he accepted a Savior into it.

From that point on, he had built a real life for himself. He had abandoned a life of criminal survival on the streets. He had a job, a wife, a family. And he was living as a servant to those who were now like he had once been.

Yes, I do remember Gilberto. I committed to pray for him. And then we left. As time has passed, he still comes to my mind from time to time and I think about him and ask the Lord to remember him as well. I wonder how he is.

For me, knowing Gilberto and seeing the people of Panama was another thread of the beautiful. I can put on running shoes everywhere I go. Or I can really "run," doing my best to bring the truth of the kingdom of light into every corner of this dark world.

## 24.5

My wife, three daughters, and I stepped onto a bus in San Pedro Sula, Honduras, with a team that included six other members from our church.

My two older girls were in their early teens at the time and my youngest was 10 years old. We had come to connect with a missionary who lives in Honduras and has done so for decades. He gathered us, and all of our luggage and musical instruments, onto the bus that he'd arranged for our transportation.

I didn't realize it at the time, but Honduras was, and is, a dangerous place. We began noticing soldiers at various places in the city, bearing arms. We noticed armed guards standing outside of businesses. We pulled into the residence of our host and saw that it was protected all around with a high block wall, and guards stood at an iron gate at the entrance of his driveway. It was almost like a scene from a movie.

Years later, I was casually checking the internet concerning the world's most dangerous countries and saw Honduras near the top. Today it appears to have dropped to around number 40, so that is good, I guess.

But even in 2020, I could still find a post from just six years prior about this country. It stated as follows: "Here's What It's Like in the Most Dangerous City in the World. In San Pedro Sula, Honduras, last year, 187 were murdered for every 100,000 people. That tragic statistic makes the city the most violent in the world. Gangs, drugs, and poverty plague every day in the Central American city of San Pedro Sula."

Had I known I was flying my family into such danger, I doubt I would have done it. I simply didn't realize that this impoverished country was so violent. And if you asked me about it later, that is not what would have been the lead in my story.

Instead, you would have heard me speak of the wonderful people of Honduras we met. Some were the poorest of the poor. Their homes had dirt floors. Tin made up the walls and the roofs. But almost without fail, the people living inside these homes approached us with the utmost kindness and with bright smiles on their faces.

We attempted to minister to them, sharing gifts with their excited children. In their simple church gatherings, we were regarded with a level of honor and respect that I wasn't used to encountering.

I would tell you about my middle daughter performing evangelistic skits in small churches or in the open square of the city with Hondurans all around in rapt attention. She was so good and expressive, able to come out of her shy shell in order to play a part that communicated the love of Jesus to strangers.

I would have told you about the trek on foot up a mountain, carrying our instruments on our way to a huge mountaintop open-air structure; it was the church on the mountain.

I would tell you about my 10-year-old daughter standing beside me in that mountaintop church with a microphone in her hand, singing to the Lord with a nervous voice, "Dame, mas de Ti" (Give me more of You).

I would have mentioned the call of Shofars being blown in that place, and their echoes blasting across the mountains as hundreds of excited worshipers ignored their "poverty" and exulted in the "true riches" of the Spirit.

I did not run in Honduras. But I marched up a mountain, taught in the public schools and on a military base (something unthinkable in our "free" country), taught in the poor valley churches and in the home of some wealthy people on a beach. In every place, I witnessed amazing kindness and acceptance from the people of a "most dangerous nation."

But what I saw was a trumpeting of great beauty.

# 24.8

While I have been privileged to run in amazing places, I have been more blessed to meet amazing people in some places of the earth that are potentially very dangerous.

The same was true of Venezuela. I discovered there an affectionate people who prefer to greet you with a kiss on the cheek instead of a handshake. I was warned this would be the case and it still caught me off guard. My visit came around the turn of the century. My wife and oldest daughter went with me on that trip, as we visited yet another missionary couple, these living in the city of Maracay.

Just as with the other trips, I was captivated by these wonderful people. My daughter cried when we had to leave. But I'll always remember her sitting in the middle of a crowd of high school- and college-aged young men and women playing cards, listening to the energetic chatter of their language. She had picked up bits and pieces of Spanish as we had traveled and tried to learn it, and she has the ability to let the words flow off her tongue sounding just like a native speaker . . . quite the opposite of my stilted "Como esta?" or "Donde esta?" In a short time of being immersed in their culture, she would have been fluent in the language. Her olive skin also causes her to almost look the part of a Venezuelan. All of this, too, was beautiful to me.

And yet, when that nice group of youngsters tried to get me to allow my gorgeous 16- year-old daughter to walk in the city with them, there was no chance. She was my charge and my treasure. I would not risk her safety even among well-intentioned people because I know the world. As beautiful as it can be, it is also broken and as ugly as an open grave.

In those days, Venezuela was prospering under a different kind of leadership than it has today. The people I saw in the city seemed to have nice clothing and each was in possession of a nice cell phone, at a time when cell phones were not yet in every hand in America.

Today, under a different leadership, the country has rampant crime and poverty. And so, at a turn of events, what once seemed good and healthy can become angry and dangerous on multiple levels. Brokenness abounds there.

But brokenness also abounds in what many refer to as the greatest country in the world . . . in my country. A nation formed as "one nation under God" is currently experiencing another time of crisis.

Although I still believe that just as the violent and poor nations I visited had people who were sweet and kind, our nation has a core of people who still try to treat their neighbors with respect each day and act with kindness to their fellow man.

So what is the issue? Why are we so off course? Where, oh where, is the beauty in the midst of all this turmoil?

## 25.0

What I am about to say may seem strange to some. You may think I'm off my rocker.

Allow it as a submission of a possibility and accept it as being the world as this writer sees it. It does not have to offend. I am not casting it into anyone's face. It is a viewpoint, grounded in a belief of what is at work in all that we see, both in the beauty and in the ugliness of our world.

It is that the beautiful sights I have seen on my travels are pieces of the beauty created by God—mountains, waterfalls, streams, oceans, and the like. But these are just a hint of the real glory, a glory that was meant to reside within man as a deposit from that same Creator. He made man in His image, with feelings and thoughts and the ability to love . . . even though He also allows us an ability to hate, since we are people, not puppets.

From the Creator came the ability to love, just as the Creator has loved, and that is beautiful. And from the same Creator came the freedom to hate and, after going down that road a few miles, the ability to steal and kill; and therein is found the horror of this world.

I believe that what we are witnessing in these days is similar to watching people in a great play. And those people are controlled by one force or another, a force of darkness (wherein hate abounds) or a force of light (wherein love abounds).

I submit that the brokenness of the world is a result of a path chosen, a wide and self- centered path. I believe it is a path that is controlled by principalities and powers of darkness and its end will be destruction on every level imaginable. It will be physical, societal, emotional, and spiritual.

The path of darkness has denied God and/or His existence. It will state, at times, (deceptively) that *we* are God. And in a sense, that is what those on this path have become. They are gods unto themselves, but the deception is that they think they can find a path of good while being a god. There is no good on this path. It will always end in chaos and destruction. Just look around at our world and try to deny it.

A well-studied co-worker of mine has a fatalistic view. He believes that the earth will only be okay once it is rid of its inhabitants. Apparently, his view is that the earth is the good thing here and the people are mere parasites upon it.

I submit that creation was, indeed, good but that all the chaos of the world is the result of the power of the kingdom of darkness. The people are not evil. They are deceived. They are lost and wandering, blindly, in the darkness and in its power.

I also submit that there is hope. Because there is another path. It is a narrow path, and it leads to life. It is a path of serving others instead of ourselves. He who would be first should be last. He who would be great should be a servant of all. Gentleness and kindness are the standard. Love, joy, peace, patience, goodness . . . these are the fruits of this kingdom's way.

And there is One who has led this way, by example. And He says . . . *"I have come as Light into the world, so that everyone who believes in Me will not remain in darkness."*

I am fifty-six years old. It is not quite the twilight of my life, I hope. Not yet. But it is closer to the end than the beginning. How much farther do I have to run on this earth? There is no way to know.

But however far it is, I want to be a son of that Light and run in His brightness.

*"Though your beginning was insignificant,*
*yet your end will increase greatly."*

## MILE 26

# *The Only Finish Line that Really Matters*

(About 2,000 years ago)

*The air was heavy with the tension of injustice.*

There had never been a day like this day. The rabid fervor of hatred was felt in the open streets, hotter than the fires that lit their clay ovens. A life that had been thrust upon them only three short years ago was about to be snuffed out, making the city electric, partly with a sense of anticipation, partly with feelings of dread.

And then the darkness came . . .

Darkness. Such darkness as was occurring at this moment was something nobody had ever seen, not even in the depths of the night, and especially not in the middle of the day as it was now. Darkness that could be felt as much as seen, if seeing darkness was the right term for it. The accompanying tension was palpable.

"Death" had been the sentence and the plan had been carried out forthwith. But He'd done nothing wrong! And deep down, they all knew it. Nobody, not one person, could give an honest account of a stray word or deed, much less anything that could ever be deserving of death. But the mob had ruled and the jealous and resentful had won the day.

"Let His blood be upon our heads and the heads of our sons," they had declared, not realizing the prophetic nature of their assertion. Yes, let His blood flow. *That will do the trick,* they thought. That will bring an end to His heretical assertions. It would be the end of it all, with the spilling of His cursed blood.

So it had proceeded. Many who had previously been among those who cheered when He came into town to help the helpless and care for those who were downcast, were now joining the bloodthirsty crowd that shouted curses at the brutally injured man.

They watched as He carried the heavy instrument of His own death up the hill. They saw when His strength gave out and He collapsed in the dust. As some shouted angry taunts, others wept quietly in fear. Amazingly, He spoke with compassion to those who wept. He continued exuding the same love the masses had seen in Him, even as He faced the unrighteous sentence that was being carried out against Him.

Finally, mercifully, His journey ended. The wooden instrument was laid down underneath Him as large spikes were hammered into His body. He was then hoisted above the ground. Posterity would record that it was 9:00 a.m. He hung for all the gathered inhabitants to see. For 3 hours people gazed up at Him, some casting the stones of their vile words, as the morning light shined down. The only Man who'd ever lived a fully righteous life. The only Man ever completely deserving of a "reward" in life, receiving the penalty of death instead.

But then physical darkness came.

Many who stood by were confused and afraid. A few seemed excited and expectant. "I have never seen anything like this before," they said. Isn't that the same kind of comment they'd all made to one another during the three years of His impartation into their lives? All the miracles, all the goodness, all the teaching of love. Their hearts had burned with an all- consuming fire any time they were blessed to be in His presence. But what could this sudden darkness mean?

Those who'd sentenced Him seemed nervous and less sure about the course they'd taken.

The mob who'd followed as a pack of wolves to a fresh meal now grew quiet. What had they done to this good Man?

Those who looked on could see that He was carrying something that no mortal man had carried before. It was a contradiction. He was absolute purity, absolute goodness. He was love in the flesh. Kindness and humility poured forth from each look He gave and every event the people had witnessed.

And yet, there was something almost indescribably horrible upon Him too. He bore the look of a Man who carried the weight of the world on His bloody shoulders. Some would say it was as if every base thought, every sickening action of man, every ugly intention and angry word that had occurred under the sun for all eternity seemed to be flung upon Him as he hung there, as more hours passed in the darkness.

Purity and filth seemed to be combined in and on one man. Blinding light and impenetrable darkness joined at one moment in time. He was both beautiful and hideous to behold. They could not look because of the revulsion they felt and yet they could not tear their eyes away because of the wonder of glory they beheld. It made no sense whatsoever but would soon make all the sense in the world.

The judges, the jury, the executioners stood in awed silence. The worshippers, the followers, His disciples, His mother, all gathered around with sorrow that could fill a lifetime of experiences.

Earlier, He had given voice to the anguish in His soul and had spoken into the heavens, "My God, my God, why have You forsaken Me?" But no relief came to the One who had granted relief to the masses. He was alone in His torment. And He tarried, hanging on the thread between life and death, as the darkness grew deeper.

Where had the darkness come from? The sun had been in the sky. There had been no clouds. There was no eclipse of the sun. But suddenly the sun could not give its light, as if an enormous unseen hand was blocking it from their sight. It was a moment unlike any before it in the history of man.

The heaviness—indeed, the gloom that all felt was just like the darkness that now descended on the earth. It was unnatural. No, it was supernatural. Fear now exploded in the hearts of all. Who was this One? And on His anguish continued, as He carried something that none could understand.

When suddenly, from somewhere in the depths of the man a cry came forth. But it wasn't the cry of a tortured human. It came forth with such force. It came with such finality, as if the heavens were declaring it. Indeed, it seemed to those who heard it that possibly God Himself had rent the heavens and a boom had descended upon the hearers as the words were spoken.

But there was more in His cry, and all in the vicinity could sense it. It was like the pronouncement of a great judgment had occurred. It resonated within their hearts and shook their souls to the core. None standing there would leave unchanged. Even the soldier in charge of overseeing the verdict noted with whispered awe, "Surely, this was the Son of God."

His words broke upon the darkness, one . . . last . . . time, summoned like the call of a lion roaring in domination.

In spite of the beating He had taken, a pounding that often resulted in death all by itself, wielded as it was by those expert soldiers who were "gifted" with their whips that were laced with pieces of glass and metal, as each lash wrapped around the torso and ripped pieces of flesh away from the body . . .

In spite of all this, coming up from a hidden reservoir of power within Him . . . coming down like the sound of a trumpet echoing off the mountains, words that would echo throughout the end of time. Were they words of defeat of a man breathing His last tortured breath? No, all would agree later. It was not defeat. *They were words of . . . victory!*

They were words of joy, of exultation! They came with authority, shocking the heavens and shaking the earth, breaking powers and ending dominions. He lifted His head one last time, and the Lion of the Tribe of Judah roared to all those who for eternity could now be His own. *"It is finished!"*

## 25.2

I could not think of a better way to end my long-distance running endeavor than with a run in the biggest and best of them all, the New York City Marathon, which draws over fifty thousand runners each year from all over the world.

But alas, 2020 will always be remembered as the year that COVID-19 changed our world, reportedly contributing to hundreds of thousands of deaths and bringing a fundamental change in how the people of the world went about their daily lives.

As a relatively unimportant consequence, races across the world began being cancelled.

New York City, which was an initial "hot spot" of virus activity and death, quickly followed suit. The mayor determined that there was no way to safely bring 50,000 people into the city for an event that usually had one million spectators in attendance.

Even as society at large adopted never before used terms such as *social distancing*, the running community became familiar with the term *virtual marathon*.

The Cambridge dictionary defines *virtual* succinctly as '*almost, but not exactly or in every way.*' I guess this definition works, although it doesn't seem to capture the difference between running a marathon in front of a million spectators versus running by yourself on dirt roads or empty city streets. I was disappointed.

What to do? I'd been planning for this since September of 2019. I had been logging every run, noting what I wore in every element. I had tracked shoe mileage on four pairs of shoes. I'd purchased two pairs that were a commemorative version put out by New Balance, specifically for the NYC Marathon.

As COVID effects began in March of 2020, I was thinking at that early stage that surely this virus would pass just like every yearly scare or flu warning. I began increasing my weekend mileage to 7, 8, and then 9 miles by May. I wanted to enter the 20-week training period with a head start so I could go out with my best marathon ever.

When the June 24 announcement came that the NYC Marathon was cancelled, I was deflated. It was hard to keep motivation high enough to continue to increase my weekend mileage. I was no longer sure the cost was worth the reward.

I guess it was the completion of this book that brought me through. I'd been on this writing journey for over two years.

By early 2020, I was fully engaged in completing the book and had just a few more "miles" to go before getting myself squared away into the final section, which would end with the writing of the story of this last marathon adventure.

Within a few weeks, I settled into a new plan. I decided that I'd run my marathon around the 6-mile section of dirt roads by my house. I thought I might even invite a few people along for fun. On I trained, but admittedly with less enthusiasm. It just wouldn't be NYC.

As summer moved into fall of 2020, as the virus surged and waned, as people began to decide not to capitulate to the virus and instead, to try to keep living their lives (albeit with some adjustments and safeguards), the Bass Pro Marathon in Springfield, Missouri, announced that they *would* do their yearly in-person event. It was scheduled for the very same day that NYC would have been run, November 1, 2020.

I signed up, as did my brother-in-law, who had run this same marathon with me in the fall of 2018 (mile 14, the title chapter, Go See the Beautiful).

So we began to plan with hope that this race would not be cancelled. We began doing our long weekend runs together and once more discussed every topic in our very interesting world. I soaked it all in, enjoying the camaraderie with my friend and brother-in-law, as the months quickly went by. And before I knew it, the day was here.

## 25.3

We awoke on race day to clear skies and a day that would be full of sunshine. But there was also a stiff breeze of close to 15 mph. Temperatures would hover in the low 40s, meaning windchills into the 30s.

When the gun went off, I'd be in my favorite running shorts, a running T-shirt, arm bands that could come off if I got hot, running gloves, and a warm sweatband around my ears. My thick Feetures socks were on underneath my favorite shoes, the NYC New Balance 860s, which had only 133 miles on them at the start of the race.

Some things were the same. Still excited runners stretching, bouncing around, making one last trip to the porta pot.

And some things were different. To comply with COVID safety guidelines, almost every runner had a face covering as they awaited the start. Marathoners were split from half-marathoners. The only places where two people stood side by side were if you were with the person you came with.

As the started gun sounded, the first wave began. Our corral was the D corral. As the A corral cleared the starting gate, the B group walked in and began. Quickly, methodically, it rolled, with D corral arriving last. A push of my watch, a cross of the starting mat, and my last marathon race began.

## 25.4

We had initially planned to stay with the 4-hour 45-minute pacing group so we'd have a time at just under 11 minutes per mile if we were able to stay with them for the entire marathon. But it seemed from the outset that they were way ahead of pace. Possibly they planned to bank time early and slow down late, but our first mile was at 10:19 pace, mile 2 at 10:34, mile 3 back to 10:22, and mile 4 at 10:31. Surely this was too fast for our goals.

Christopher and I commented on it together, noting that we'd pay for it later if we didn't slow down. Yet we rolled along in the cool morning air, feeling good at this point, as the "work" aspect of it had not yet set in.

We slowed to 10:39 in mile 5. Better. But mile 6 was back to a 10:25 pace. By mile 7, I believe our bodies began confirming what our minds had been saying when we finally let the 4-hour 45-minute pace group disappear from sight. Miles 7-11 were more appropriately (for us) paced between 10:44 per mile to 10:57 per mile.

At miles 8 and 9, the first memorable things of this event occurred. Memories are almost always about the people. This time, a thing I'd never heard in all of my races was suddenly shouted from some yards behind me. *"I can't! I can't!"*

Someone was screaming it at the top of his lungs. A young man was letting loose with a declaration that surely a huge amount of marathon and half-marathon runners think but never want to say, much less declare for all around to hear.

Over the last few miles several of the faster-paced half-marathon runners had begun passing the marathoners. They'd started 15 minutes behind us, but with a quicker pace for their shorter race distance, many were now passing us.

We had seen several half-marathon elite athletes come flying by. Gradually more and more of the half-marathon crowd passed us. The "I can't" individual was running beside a 2-hour half-marathon pacer.

I heard the pacer calmly encouraging the runner beside him. "You can! Keep on. You got so close last year. You can do it."

These encouragements were followed immediately by even louder screams of, "*I can't do it! My legs can't breathe!*"

Very soon they passed us. The pacer had to keep his pace. The young man beside him was laboring mightily to stay beside him. His breaths were coming as if great torrents of anguish were flooding his body. It was almost like the howls of exertion that are heard when a weightlifter hoists an enormous encumbrance over his shoulders. Only this sound was coming out of the runner with almost every breath. It was something to hear and behold.

As they passed a few yards in front, his shouting continued. I saw more runners attempting to encourage him but each time the encouragement was met with the same defeated announcement, even as he ran on beside the pacer.

I noticed that his left leg appeared to be wobbling with each step forward. They were not straight steps. His leg was being thrown outward, as if he was willing it forward, insisting that it continue to do what it could not physically do . . . and the continued cries of, "I can't" filled the air.

Suddenly he slowed. I thought for a moment he might fall over, so awkwardly was the left leg being tossed around. Christopher and I jogged by, quiet words of encouragement being added to those we'd heard others give.

Runners, if they are anything, are encouraging. You can call them insane for tormenting their bodies like this. You can say their priorities must be out of whack to commit this much time to a personal goal. You can claim all manner of things. But if you do not include *encouraging* as one of the adjectives, then you don't know runners, at least the ones I've been around.

Certainly, their personal lives may be a wreck, just like people from all walks of life. But get them out on a racecourse, and these are some of the most determined, optimistic, "You can do it" people you'll ever find.

Yet, in the midst of all this encouragement were the cries of defeat. I recalled my own flameout from a half marathon in Tulsa (Mile 4) when I'd attempted my own two-hour half marathon, had kept the pace for about the same amount of time as this young man, and then had hit a wall that my will could not scale.

As we began to separate from the young man leaving him behind us, we continued to hear his cries of despair, only 4 miles away from his half-marathon finish line. And then it turned to a final declaration that stuck in my brain. He began screaming aloud, *"We cannot control our bodies!"* He said it over and over again.

Wow! What a thought. What a declaration. It was shouted into the middle of a throng of humanity that had been training for months, or years, with that very purpose, to take control over their bodies with a goal to finish a race and finish it strong

Juxtaposed with the alarming calls of defeat was a sweet moment when I saw another young man veer off the racecourse and head to a small crowd of bystanders. I noticed a small child sitting on the ground.

The runner stopped in front of them, grabbed the little boy's face, planted a kiss on his forehead, and was off again, with the encouragement of a small child's loving calls of "Run, Daddy, run!"

I had to smile as I remembered the days, many years ago, of having my own small children whose voices filled my home with love and enthusiasm when I approached. There is nothing quite like it.

Within moments of each other, I'd heard the agony of defeat being voiced and the encouragement of pure love being broadcast.

# 25.5

At mile 10, I began having some concern. We had finally slowed to our more reasonable pace near 11 minutes per mile but the concern was how I felt at this point.

The theory in most marathon training plans is that you run your longest training run three weeks before the marathon. Then you begin to "taper" during the remaining two weeks. We ran 20 miles one Saturday, then 12 miles the next, and ended with an 8-mile run on the weekend before November 1. Our legs, therefore, should have been fresh for the 26.2 event. Our bodies should be rested and healed. Our muscles should be at their strongest point.

But it wasn't working out that way on this day. During our 12-mile run only two weeks prior, we'd kept a 10:06 pace for the entire run. It felt good. We were tired and realized it was too fast a pace to be carried for 26 miles, but it had felt like a good run.

Here, I was at mile 10, feeling much more spent that I'd felt two weeks ago. What about the taper effect!? And even if we'd been pacing between 10:20 and 11:00 for the first 10 miles, that is still much slower than our 10:06 pace for twelve miles two weeks ago.

I voiced my concern to Christopher, and he admitted he felt the same. Possibly the rolling hills had taken more out of us than we had anticipated. Possibly it was the wind. I am not sure. But the feeling increased as we went.

At mile 12, we began slowing appreciably. Whereas mile 11 was our last sub-11 mile, at 10:57, mile 12 jumped to 12:12. A bad sign indeed.

It began with a near fainting event by Christopher. A much stronger runner than I am, he'd been leading the way as my agony was growing. I was several steps behind him when I saw him almost fall. A car just to our right had been waiting for runners to pass so it could enter the roadway. (This was not a closed course, although Springfield police managed primary intersections. Side streets were open to traffic.)

The vehicle beside us ran over something in the roadway that let out a loud "pop" and Christopher jerked his head in reaction, then almost collapsed.

I heard him say "Whoa!" as he stumbled to a stop. I came up beside him and he said he'd almost blacked out. He couldn't figure out what it was unless it was how he'd jerked his head. We decided to walk for a bit to make sure he was okay.

Within a quarter mile or so, he was ready to begin the jog. But we both realized we were not in the good shape we had expected we'd be in at mile 12. There was agreement, spoken and unspoken, that we'd take it easier and soldier on.

Miles 13 and 14 were paced near 12 minutes per mile. I heard his watch give us the overall pace at the end of 14 miles as just under 11 minutes per mile for the entire course up to this point. I knew my hope for a best-ever marathon was slipping away. I think my commitment to mid-week training levels had been insufficient. The loss of the NYC Marathon opportunity had certainly affected my training regimen. At this moment, I didn't care. I was feeling lousy at mile 14. All I wanted to do was somehow finish, as misery began to set in for the next 12.2 miles.

Within minutes, Christopher informed me that his foot was injured. He'd been monitoring this foot during the last weeks, rolling it out, doing whatever he could. But prior to this day, nothing had felt like this. Rather than just pain, it was burning. He downed some pain meds he'd brought along for the run and decided to see if he could "power through" until the meds brought some relief.

Just before mile 16, he decided he couldn't go on without risking an injury that could include weeks/months of inability to run. I agreed that he shouldn't risk it, as bitter as it was for him to swallow this disappointment after all the months of preparation.

I thanked him for the months of running together and the good memories we'd made, told him I'd see him soon. He apologized. There was no need. I also knew he wouldn't want me to stop. I had to go on and try to finish, in honor of all we'd done over the last four months.

I picked up my pace and went on. After our last two miles together, which had included some walking and had paced at around 14 minutes each mile, I put in a 12-minute mile 17, thinking I'd make up some ground that we'd lost. But I discovered after mile 17 that I was done as it pertained to goals and time achievements. Only one goal, one achievement mattered to me for the next, torturous nine miles: Finish the race. Get it done. Do not quit on your last marathon, no matter how hard it might become.

## 25.7

There is not much to tell of miles 18 through 26. They were miserable. They went by in some kind of fog of anguish. I remember praying for people. I remember straightaway areas where I'd close my eyes for possibly 5 or 10 seconds as I barely loped forward in a lethargic jog.

I remember walking up to intersections being monitored by police and summoning energy to get quickly through the passageway. I didn't wonder what the people in the cars thought. I didn't care.

I became almost oblivious to anything but the road ahead of me and the seeming stoppage of time. I contemplated time and how quickly days pass when we are on vacation or with special people at special events. But then how an hour can seem like an eternity when misery is involved in every second of each minute of that hour.

And then she came driving by.

The open course brought a blessing to me in the form of my wife, pulling beside me in the car, calling out a word of encouragement. She asked if I needed anything, water perhaps. I came over to the car and filled one of my water bottles from the last bit of hers. I think she asked how I was doing. I think my response was, "I'm wasted." It was just past mile 21.

She could not remain beside me in the middle of the street. I had been walking when she came. I began walking again as she said last encouraging words and "I'll see you at the finish line." She saw me, encouraged me, and knew I'd finish in spite of the agony I was in.

I've never been a support person or a bystander for a big race. I think I'd like to do that in the future, to see the determination in the faces of people who are doing what their bodies are demanding that they not do. But I have watched runners as they passed me on the last miles of their own race.

Over the endless eternity of my last two miles, I was passed by an old guy who was jogging at a pace that almost any normal person could walk. I was struck to find that as I walked more than I jogged, his determined miniature jog, which he never stopped doing the entire time he was in my sight, actually *was* faster than my pace. Slow and steady, steady and slow.

I recall an elderly couple who came by, using timed watches that dictated when to jog (about 30 seconds) and when to stop (about 30 seconds more). The lady, possibly 65 or 70, seemed as miserable as I was but somehow, she passed me and by the time mile 26 came into my view, she was gone from it.

I watched 5-hour, 5:15, and 5:30 pacers all pass me, the last of whom came near the end of the race and must have been slightly ahead of their 5:30 pace.

Suddenly, the "I can't do it!" declaration came back to mind. Normally, I would pick up the pace and try to keep up with pacers. On this day, I tried for about a minute and quickly quit the jog each time. I was that spent, that washed out. When the 5:30 pace group went by, I didn't even care. Finish. That's all I cared about.

There is one last thing in my last marathon that I should mention. It was a miniature miracle in the midst of enormous misery. Aren't those the best?

My GPS watch is a Garmin. My wife bought it for me years ago. It is not top of the line, but it has faithfully tracked my runs. One problem: It will not last for a marathon distance. I've had it fully charged for our long runs and it will give me two warnings and quit on me with a completely spent battery. This usually occurs at about the 4-hour mark of usage.

But my NYC virtual marathon had to be digitally proven by one of these devices. I'd linked it to a Strava account, which is the official site to link with the NYC virtual race. I was almost certain it wouldn't last but decided not to spend the hundreds of dollars on a new watch just to prove to NYC and Strava that I'd done their virtual race. I really wanted it to work but it wasn't worth that much money.

So on this day, where I'd hoped to complete the marathon in 4 hours 45 minutes, I had prayed that maybe the Lord would do me this silly favor of letting my watch stay powered 45 minutes longer than it normally does.

At about hour 4, I got my first warning. I knew it usually lasted 30 minutes after that first warning, so it was already showing signs of lasting longer than usual. I also knew by hour 4 that I'd likely not finish in less than 5 hours.

However, my watch stayed on. If there was anything that pushed me to begin jogging again, it was my watch. In my haze of anguish, I recall thinking about it time and time again (no pun intended) over the last few miles. "Wow . . . 4 hours 45 minutes and it is still on. Lord, will you keep it on for me?"

But how much longer can it go? At five hours it was still on, still showing the same level of zero battery power that it had shown for the last hour. I couldn't believe it. And yet, I was still a little over two miles away.

My last 6 miles had all been in the 14-minute range and I couldn't imagine speeding up, but I tried. I had 14:05 at mile 24, 14:50 at mile 25. Still my watch was on, as it crossed 5 hours and 15 minutes. My last mile. Could I summon effort, and would my watch make it? Or would I get 2 tenths of a mile out only to see it finally crash just minutes before I was done?

Pain, time, agony, watch, go, can't, must. My mind was a jumble. How can 10 minutes be such an eternity?

My 26th mile was at a 13:59 pace, my first sub-14 mile since mile 19.

Then I began to hear the loudspeaker as people were crossing the finish line. I passed the 26-mile point. Two-tenths to go! It might make it. I pressed my legs forward.

I saw the finish line. My watch had lasted an hour and a half after the warning of failing battery. It wasn't possible. But it was happening. At mile 26.17 it gave me a 2nd warning. In the past, it would almost immediately die after this warning. It gives you this final moment so you can push "save" before it dies. I pushed my legs forward for the final three hundreds (.03) of a mile.

I saw 26.2! (Note: The finish line was still about 2 tenths of a mile away. This is normal because a runner rarely runs an exactly straight race as he veers from side to side along 26 miles of roadway.)

Even though the finish line was in sight, I didn't dare let my watch try to stay on another two or three minutes while I covered the remaining distance. I pushed "save" on my watch; it showed me the words *run saved* and immediately powered off. I didn't shut down the power. It saved and died. I will call it my mini miracle of my final race. As soon as I crossed 26.2 on its readout, it was done. And so was I, almost.

Finish lines are for sprinting. I'd trained myself to that as well. No matter how hard my midweek runs were, I tried to run hardest at the end. The same was true for most of our long runs. Finish strong! On this day, I could only muster one thing. I could jog. I would not walk across the line.

I saw my wife as I rounded the corner that led off the main street by the Bass Pro Shops and into the driveway where the finish line stood, a mere 15 feet away. She was filming. I lifted my arms. I crossed the mat. My last marathon, my NYC virtual marathon, was done.

# 25.9

I suppose it is fitting that my last marathon and my last chapter be "virtual" in nature, or "almost but not exactly or in every way."

Because this wonderful and amazing life is the very essence of virtual when compared to the life that is to come, you could almost say it is a practice run for the real or main event.

And yet, so many do not believe that anything comes after our bodies are planted six feet underground. To them, this life *is* life, and it is all there is.

I recall again the words of the young man who was attempting to run a 2-hour half marathon, whose body would not complete what his mind had called for. "I can't" and "We can't control our bodies!"

There can be similar hopeless feelings among those who are approaching the end of their lives. They have lost the ability to control.

No matter how hard we try, and we *do* try really hard at times, we cannot put off the inevitable. "*It is appointed unto man once to die.*" This is a shattering truth if there ever was one. No living and breathing person can escape this sentence. It will come.

In our "virtual" existence, we do our best to delay the impending event even as it gains more traction in our day-to-day lives. I'll eat right. I'll live right. But deep down, we know that we are only one breath away from one that could be our last. But then we'll take a right turn into Scarlett O'Hara philosophy and "think about that another day." Until the funeral of a loved one comes. Then it hits us right in the face. *The finish line will come.*

I have just this question: Will we cross it with hope or without it?

# 26.0

Almost three years of my life have gone into writing this book. The idea that was birthed after a whim to run a marathon in April of 2018 has now come to a conclusion. I must make a confession.

I set out to provide lessons from running that could apply to any life. How should a family work and be healthy? How should that key building block of society function? I proposed ideas for how people should treat each other. I looked at ways that life challenges every one of us and how we can choose to respond to the hardships we all endure. I truly hope the contemplations of running and life were helpful to some in a small way. But even so, it was only a shadow of the substance I was really shooting for.

That substance came more into focus, I hope, during this last section of the book, which began to look more directly toward the reality of kingdoms of darkness and light . . . and the King of light.

Because I believe the One who spoke into the darkness, "It is finished," has Himself finished *the only race that ever mattered*. He alone ran a perfect race, fully and completely controlling His body. And then, the King of justice took upon Himself all of our unjust acts, freely letting His blood be spilled as payment for the sins of all mankind.

But that same man, Jesus, was seen alive again, 3 days after being buried. He then appeared to more than 500 people. History recounts that many of those witnesses would later be killed in brutal ways for one reason—because they would not deny their claims of Jesus being alive after having been crucified. They could not do so because they'd seen it with their own eyes. He had died. And He is now alive again.

Because of these events, the world has been turned upside down. Still, 2,000 years later, the truth of Jesus is *the* divisive matter of our times. But the truth is still true. Death is not the end. It is the beginning for those who choose life, who choose to believe in the sacrifice of the Son of God.

So what comes next? Singing on clouds for eternity? I don't think so.

The Creator who formed mountains and trees and oceans and all living creatures, great and small, the One who spoke a sun and moon and galaxies into existence, is a creative God, a glorious God.

There are hints in the Bible about what real life will be like. There is mention of a new heaven and a new earth, of cities and healing trees of life. There is mention of work and action, of coming and going, of rulership and service. There is reference to a kingdom wherein we will reign as brothers to the King!

There is the promise of being able to be with the One who, in the beginning, came down into a garden and walked with a man and a woman in the cool of the day; a Father delighting in His children.

Why would all of this be? It is because of sacrificial love like we have never known.

*"By this the love of God was revealed in us, that God has sent His only Son into the world so that we may live through Him. In this is love, not that we loved God, but that He loved us and sent His Son to be the atonement for our sins."*

Of all the wonders our eyes can see, of all the thrills our bodies can experience, there is nothing so wonderful as encountering the amazing love of the One who made us.

For God so loved . . . that is the reality. It is not virtual. At least, it doesn't have to be. He sent His Son for us. Jesus, a friend of sinners.

And He calls, "*Let anyone who is thirsty, come. Drink of the water of life without cost.*"

Let anyone who will, walk into the light and . . . come to The Beautiful.

*"I have fought the good fight, I have finished the race, I have kept the faith."*

## MILE 26.1

# *Finishing Strong*

T he paths and the crossroads of this life are as diverse as the humanity who travel them.

But there is a finish line for all of us.

The early miles of the long race are filled with vigor, expectation, and a temptation to run faster than you should or make decisions without the benefit of wisdom or careful consideration. We are young. Promise is all around. It is our time, our day. By golly, we'll conquer any challenge.

But then reality sets in. At about mile 7 or 8 of the race, some of the energetic fervor has waned and a sobering realization sets in—this is going to be work. It's going to be hard. Why, I'm not even sure I want to do this. (Some these days call it "adulting" and I've heard many young people who are newly on their own, facing the bills and the responsibilities their parents used to shoulder for them, suddenly stop and admit that this adult thing is tough.)

And here is where the training of parents comes into play. Have they prepared the young one for the challenges ahead? Have they laid the groundwork? Have they shown by example how a person handles disappointment, turmoil, daily trials, financial struggles, emotional difficulties, and unexpected or shocking losses? Have they taught them to face the obstacles head on rather than running away or simply sitting down in the middle of the road to quit? If so, when reality does set in, that young one is much more prepared to look at mile 7 or mile 8, to realize it is hard, and to move their determined stride forward.

They are ready to build gradually rather than sprint at every corner. They will save for that used car rather than acquire years of debt for the fancy new ride that "we all deserve" according to the "have it all now" wisdom of this age. They will take the hit of a stunning trauma, and rather than folding up in a ball and checking out, they'll seek help, they'll find new strength, and they'll weather on through the storm even if they can't see the next step in front of them. Mile 7 and mile 8 are decision miles. This run hurts, it is unbelievably hard, and I will… run on, or… I will give up right here and quit.

Miles 9 through 19 are the daily grind of life lived in most homes from age twenty-something through age 60 or 70 something. There is not usually much that is flashy in those miles. We are not yet near our victorious finish line goal. We are simply trudging on, weathering the elements (cold, wind, rain, heat), enduring the hardships (blisters, cramps, uneasy stomach, aching knees and feet), doing our best to keep our minds right, focused on the prize:

Here, life is lived in every facet mankind can imagine. Momentary victories, surprising defeats. Houses bought, roofs leaking, children raised, unexpected injury or illness occasionally brought to bear. Here a husband and wife commit together to weather every storm, to appreciate every joy and, come what may, to carry on. They will be an example of strength to those children who look on, integrity when a brief little lie is easier, and faith that there is something so great ahead that they will not—ever—give up. Or not.

Through miles 9 to 19, some may cash it in and admit defeat. Some may decide there really should be more out of life than what they're getting and, along about mile 15 or so, they decide to try something (or someone) new. They'll see if they can find that thing that will surely make this race easier and better, somehow more "fulfilling for their needs" and not so stale, and same ole, same ole. And there the crash comes as the liar meets the idiot, shakes his hand, and leads him down a path where his liver will be pierced, bringing pain and heartache he/she could never have dreamed of. It is where those who have loved are shattered and the loss becomes worse than death itself.

Oh, I agree. These mile periods I'm mentioning can be quite different. The quitters can decide to quit at mile 7, after all. They may stop and start their race with so much regularity that they are like a little child in a bumper car ring, head popping and whipping this way and that, life a constant turmoil and a resting place for "drama."

The things that tempt you are common to man. Those things tempt us all. The questions are these: What has the training been? Where do the vision and hope lie? And are you willing to push through all the adversity, running straight on with each new day? Or are you the type who will back away and look for an easy way out? Miles 9 to 19 generally bring each one to moments of reckoning; to crossroads of life where the things that happen after *this* day will never be the same, for the good (though very hard) or for the bad (though very enticing).

Miles 20-25, I love you! But my gosh! Every muscle in this body is on fire with pain in places I never knew existed. The start of each new day comes with a groan. The press forward to claim each of the final miles is difficult upon difficult—and yet, I'm trained to it so on

I go. And so, in a deeper sense, there is joy unspeakable and full of glory. It is inside my being, not outside. It is not my aching legs that are joyful. They are quite upset at me right now. No, it is not my feet singing praises. Why, even my arms are sore from the constant to and fro motion and I do believe that most of my body parts are thinking they've never felt this kind of abuse.

So no, my physical body is not happy with me *at all!* But my inner man is rejoicing. Ha ha! I *am* going to finish this race after all! Not only that, I'm going to finish it strong!

And mile 26 comes. A body part now joins with the excitement of the inner man. My face . . . it is smiling as I run. And like a beloved old Collie who was with me as a boy, who one day suddenly had energy she'd not had in years and for a day, she frolicked! (Yes, within a day or so, she was gone. It was one last bit of enjoyment with her "people" as if she knew the time had come.) But like that old dog did, my body (if the training was right) suddenly finds a hidden reservoir of energy. I see the finish line in the distance, still a half mile away, perhaps, but there it is. There is knowledge of a crowd of onlookers who will be cheering from the sidelines and balconies, and family members looking on with a sense of awe, pride, and joy.

More body parts join in the game. My mind flashes back to the years of training, to the cold mornings out from under warm covers, to the injuries, the rehabilitation, the unexpected help, to runs too countless to remember. Face smiling, mind recalling, possibly tears beginning to slip from eyes that have seen so many things during this long race.

And the finish line approaches. The legs begin to pump as if it were mile 1—let's *go!* Suddenly, the arms demand respect for all they've done, and they shoot into the air in triumph. The feet are churning forward . . . and the heart and lungs chime in. Pumping, whooshing, exulting, when suddenly out of the depths of that heart and those lungs, the mouth lets forth with "YES, YES!" as the finish line is crossed and every part of the body, soul, and spirit within rejoice. It is done!

A roar is all around. Someone is announcing my name. "Russell Johnson has just crossed the finish line!" "Well done! Enter into the joy . . . !"

I wonder. Will my grandmother be there? She who passed the baton to my father, who passed it to me? Will my grandmother's mother be there? I vaguely recall her as a little boy, her sweet smile and her pious appearance. She passed that baton to my grandmother. Will my father be standing there with tears pouring down his cheeks? Tears of joy. And my mother! She who left this earth way too soon because of that awful disease that sapped the life from every muscle in her body at such a young age. There is nobody there I wish to see more; to be able to hear the sound of her voice. Will she be there? If so, she'll be doing that silly jig she dances when I wrote a song one day... showing me life in her once lifeless legs showing me the life in her once lifeless legs, showing me that she no longer needs my hand to help her around the field.

Will I hear a roar, or rather, will it be a crescendo of joy unlike anything heard this side of heaven? The professional sporting events I've witnessed in this life that shook the concrete pillars of stadiums as 60,000 people screamed for their team—will those screams seem like a whisper compared to what we will hear at that finish line?

And then One will come with a shout that rends the heavens . . . with a smile that heals all wounds . . . with eyes of such love that every pain endured during the great race just finished will quietly melt away. And there will be no more pain, nor sighing, nor tears. There will be only words of love: "Well done!"

*"For the vision is yet for the appointed time; It hastens toward the goal and it will not fail. Though it tarries, wait for it; For it will certainly come; It will not delay."*

# *A Vision Fulfilled*

(Written about 30 years ago)

*In the middle of the night, as I responded to my daughter's call, something struck me and moved me in my inward being. It wasn't as if it hadn't happened before (because it has countless times), and it wasn't as if I hadn't considered it before (because I'm sure it's crossed my mind). It was very simple, actually, two simple little powerful words. But of all the words, could any have more meaning? Could any have such effect? Could any cause such comfort and rest as these two?*

*I don't know. But my whole life is maintained by those words. Everything I am relies on them and I believe that all the world should know them in their hearts.*

*To a child, they are security. Those words are peace and safety. They mean, "There is no cause for fear."*

*If my little one falls, she wants to hear it. If she's sick, she desires it. If she's lonely or restless; if she hurts inside; or if she just can't get her toy to work right, she searches for those words. If she's hungry, if her shoe won't go on, and anytime she cries, her heart desperately needs those words.*

And as happened on this night, when it is night, the house is dark, and her dream just isn't quite right; or her covers came off; or something has made her afraid, there is nothing so sweet as for my little child to know that those two words are about to break the air . . . "Daddy's here. Daddy's here."

Ah, that means it's okay. That means I can rest. That is all I needed to hear.

And it struck me tonight just how important those words are. It seems to me that the hidden inner cry of all creation is a yearning for its Creator. And we, the children of the earth, search in many areas, up many blind alleys, groping for eternity; reaching out as a blind man into every high imaginable; to drugs, alcohol, wealth, and power, to higher thinking, and to supernatural experiences with gods made up in our minds.

If all of creation could only come to the one true Creator and feel His undying love and hear His words coming softly to them when they first believe. "Daddy's here."

Something in me from the depths of my being calls out "Abba, Father, Daddy." And my empty heart has heard, "Son, I have loved you with an everlasting love. Behold, you are Mine."

Thus, as with my own small child, I am secure. When my day's been crazy, the world's gone crazy, or when I burned the last pizza of the night, I still can rest. When I feel for my loved ones and their pain becomes mine; or when I am fighting with doubts or fighting with fear; when I question, "Do I really know what's going on around here?"

When turmoil builds up, when pressure gets high, when pain is almost too much to bear; I have a place I can go, a place I can hide.

And as I call from inside, I reach up toward the sky. My lips form the words and I whisper the sound, "My Lord, Father, Daddy, are You there?"

*And I hear, "Daddy's here, Daddy's here."*

\* \* \*

My daughters had a daddy who was there. They also had a wonderful mother. But not every child has the blessing of a home filled with the love and guidance of a mother and a father.

As I come to the end of my narrative, I consider the words a co-worker wrote to me recently as she began her day. She told me about seeing two small children wandering around on the street near her house but not appearing as children normally do when they are heading to school. These seemed lost. It was cold out. She stopped to see if they were okay. Indeed, they were lost.

One child was about ten years old and the younger one was three. They were welcomed, shivering, into my co-worker's car. She began to drive the neighborhood, hoping they might recognize their house. During the ten minutes it took to find it, she was asked by the older child not to call her parents, who were apparently "going through a hard time right now." She said she didn't live with them anymore and was staying with the parents of the 3-year-old.

After leaving them at their house, my co-worker expressed her desire to go home and hug her own small child extra tightly that night. I agreed with how heartbreaking this was but suggested she realize that she had just imparted care and compassion to those young children, possibly the bright spot in their day or their year.

I wonder, what will their life's race look like? Scan the globe and consider, what kind of race will the millions of injured young lives be like? The next time one of them angers you, think first about what they may have endured during ages 1 through 10 that brought them to the place where they now stand . . . possibly with an outer crust of anger and rebellion that hides an inner soul in great turmoil.

The world is so broken. And there are innumerable twisted hearts and lives in the wake of its destruction.

But there is an answer for every hurting soul. It is found in the dispensing of the pure love of God, which should be exhibited through the actions of genuine sons and daughters of God.

For He is the one with both the power to declare and ability to accomplish: "*Behold, I am going to do something new, now it will spring up; Will you not be aware of it? I will even make a roadway in the wilderness, rivers in the desert.*"

He it is who says, "*I will give them beauty for ashes, the oil of gladness instead of mourning, the cloak of praise instead of a disheartened spirit, so they will be called oaks of righteousness, the planting of the Lord.*"

I am reminded of the picture I included at mile 17. It was of a tub on the ground in the middle of tornadic devastation, where nothing else was left standing. I recall the story of the husband lying over the family, protecting them from the storm.

That powerful image brought to my mind the occurrence of three crosses upon a hilltop, where a man—*the* man—allowed His body to be stretched out upon a cross and His blood to be shed. In so doing, He created a pathway to life and the opportunity for every man, woman, and child to enter a "tub," an ark, a place of safety, no matter how great the storm and no matter how "lost" we have been. He is the shelter in the storm. He is the healer of the wounded soul. He is the hope of the world.

\* \* \*

A couple thousand years ago a man was on trial, having been unjustly and falsely accused by his countrymen, and he was on his way to Rome to stand before the powers of that time to have his case heard. But on the way, a local authority decided he wanted to hear from the accused.

The man, named Paul, spoke in his defense:

"I am standing trial for the hope of the promise made by God to our fathers; the promise to which our twelve tribes hope to attain, as they earnestly serve God night and day. And for this hope, O King, I am being accused by Jews." And then he asked this question: "*Why is it considered incredible among you people if God does raise the dead?*"

Why indeed? Why is the supernatural a thing for horror movies? When in fact, *the* supernatural is a God who is able to speak and create life. And a God who has power over life and death. Why is it so hard to believe?

The truth is that there is hope for life eternal for those who would receive this "hope of the promise of God" that Paul spoke about at his trial over 2000 years ago. It is a promise that is available to every person born, no matter your race, social status, economic ability, or previous belief system; and no matter the hurts you have endured.

Jesus said, "*I am the resurrection and the life; the one who believes in Me will live, even if he dies, and everyone who lives and believes in Me will never die.*"

And then He asked the question of the ages, the question that is now asked of you, the reader: "***Do you believe this?***"

So simple. And yet so hard for the masses to believe, in all their great knowledge . . . a knowledge that has no power to save or truly help anyone.

\* \* \*

I've run 4 big races in my natural life, four marathon tests of endurance, pouring out every ounce of my energy, my will, my desire. I've had four finisher medals placed around my neck.

I've run 4 big races in my spiritual life, four areas that required 100 percent commitment, every ounce of energy, will, and desire; four areas of great joy and unspeakable reward.

1. I committed to a race with Jesus—giving my life to Him, believing that only by His blood is my sin covered and only by the power of His resurrected life is eternal life given to me. And in this commitment, I committed to His people, His church. He has been the light of my life and the lamp to my path.

2. I committed to run a race with one woman for the entirety of my life on this earth. Through valleys and over mountains, we have run. It has been hard at times and pure joy at times, but it has always been the two of us together, no matter what. Thirty-seven years later, she is still the delight of my every day.

3. I committed to my girls, my three lovely gifts from God. To pour into them, with every ounce of my being, the love that God put in my heart for them. To direct them, to teach them, and now to support them and be an example to them. This commitment now extends to their husbands and the 9 grandchildren who have come from their union . . . and to the countless future great grandchildren, some of whom my eyes may be blessed to see and others who will go on after this body of mine goes to the grave. These are the joy and greatest reward of life for my wife and me.

4. I committed to this world that God so loves, that my life might somehow be a ministry to some—to any who will hear—to any who will receive words of life passed from the life giver, through my life or my words, to them. This is still a driving force that requires my time, energy, and sacrifice so that my race can be completed with a holy purpose instead of it being run for the passing pleasure of a man in this short life.

In each of the four physical marathons, I refused to quit. For every spiritual marathon, I will not quit.

A very real finish line will one day be crossed. It is the finish line of all finish lines. Our time will be through. And what will we have done with it? What will remain?

My prayer is that it may be to the glory of the One who made me, who made my feet to run in the race of the ages.

My prayer for you is that it may be so for you, too. That you may find in your finish line the beauty of heaven that awaits all who have believed in His name. And that your loved ones will stand beside your grave and look up into the sky and speak parting words to you with smiling and tear-stained cheeks . . . "Go Papa, go Daddy, go Nana, go Mama, go brother, go sister, go daughter or son, go my dearest bride or groom—go on!"

And may their voices pause as their minds get a glimpse of the truth and a thrill of goosebumps shakes them to the core. May their whisper break the silence as with awe they declare unto you their final words.

"Go, my beloved!
Race like the wind!
Go see the beautiful!
I will see you again!"

# The Cool-down

My wife of all these decades has been my constant encourager. She pushed me to write when I thought nobody but our kids and our parents would ever read what I was laboring over, and when I believed the task was not worth the effort or was beyond my ability to accomplish.

Our parents provided kind words as they viewed first drafts. Sometimes I learned from them that one chapter had made them cry, or another chapter was the best allegorical example they'd read on a given issue. Parents can be forgiven for propping their kids up with praise.

Each of my girls added uplifting comments at just the right time. As I was working on publishing the finished product, thinking it unlikely that the masses would ever find a book in the sea of online offerings, one of my girls told me it was the best book she had ever read. Wow! I have a tiny suspicion that she may be slightly biased. Again, forgivable for daughters to feel this way about their daddies.

Nola Linn provided a school-teacher's initial edit for my book, getting it in shape so that I would not be embarrassed to turn it over to a professional editing company. Nola also built me up with reassurance, saying, "This book needs to get in the hands of lots of people, as soon as possible."

Barbara Kimble came highly recommended for professional editing. Barbara noticed inconsistencies that surprised me, directed me in areas that needed clarification, and encouraged me through the process. Nola and Barbara made the final product better and more readable. Any errors in the final manuscript can be attributed to me as I continued to tinker right up to the time of sending it to the publisher.

And then there was my older brother. With almost every mile of my book, he provided valuable feedback that I needed to hear. He has my great respect and admiration. In some ways, his words were the ones I wanted to hear most because we do not view everything with the same lens. So with each chapter I wrote, I wondered how he would receive it. His responses gave me hope that others who view things differently than I do can also take a look and might receive strength and encouragement.

I am most thankful, though, for the giver of words, for the Lord Jesus, who is Himself *the Word* of life. It is my prayer that this book might accomplish one primary purpose: to glorify the Creator and giver of all good things, and to make His great name known in all the earth.

Unto Him who is able to do exceedingly abundantly beyond what we ask or think, be the glory, forever and ever. Amen.